FRONTIER CROSSROADS

Number Seven:
Canseco-Keck History Series
Jerry Thompson, General Editor

FRONTIER CROSSROADS
Fort Davis and the West

Robert Wooster

Copyright © 2006 by Robert Wooster
Manufactured in the United States of America
All rights reserved
First edition

The paper used in this book meets the minimum requirements
of the American National Standard for Permanence
of Paper for Printed Library Materials, Z39.48-1984.
Binding materials have been chosen for durability.
∞

Library of Congress Cataloging-in-Publication Data

Wooster, Robert, 1956–
  Frontier crossroads : Fort Davis and the West / Robert Wooster.
    p. cm. — (Canseco-Keck history series ; no. 7)
  Includes bibliographical references and index.
  ISBN 1-58544-475-8 (cloth : alk. paper)
    1. Fort Davis (Tex. : Fort)—History. 2. Frontier and pioneer life—Texas—Fort Davis
(Fort) 3. Community life—Texas—Fort Davis (Fort) 4. United States. Army—Military
life—History—19th century. 5. Texas—Social life and customs—19th century.
6. Frontier and pioneer life—Texas. 7. Texas—Race relations.   I.Title. II. Series.
F394.F63W654 2006 976.4'934—dc22
                              2005016482

976.4934
W917f

CONTENTS

$24.95   Ingram   lolob

NOV 2 9 2006
GERMANTOWN COMMUNITY LIBRARY
GERMANTOWN, WI 53022
WITHDRAW

ILLUSTRATIONS

PREFACE

stablished in 1854 near Limpia Creek and Wild Rose Pass in the heart of the Trans-Pecos, Fort Davis is one of Texas' most historic and enchanting places. Julius Froebel, a German traveler during the 1850s, proclaimed that "nature appears here, more than anywhere else I have seen, like a landscape-painter, composing a picture with the most simple yet refined taste." Another observer found Fort Davis to be blessed with "the most wonderful scenery in Texas." Moreover, the temperature extremes that characterize West Texas are less evident in the area immediately surrounding the post. "The climate of this part of Texas is probably the finest in the world," one thankful inhabitant concluded after a mild winter. Brig. Gen. David S. Stanley, commanding the Department of Texas, summed it up best: "The salubrity of the climate, the low price of wood, hay, and grass make it the best site for a military post in the wide territory of the Rio Grande and the Rio Pecos."[1]

Located astride communication lines linking San Antonio, El Paso, Presidio, and Chihuahua City, Fort Davis commanded a strategic position at a military, cultural, and economic crossroads. In 1883, commanding general William T. Sherman deemed it a "first class" post, and patrols from Fort Davis and its many subposts long combed the Trans-Pecos.[2] It thus served as a place of encounter, conquest, and community. Jumanos, the region's early American Indian inhabitants—hardly "native" to the region themselves—found their claims challenged by Apache and Comanche intruders. In turn, Spanish, Mexican, and U.S. governments sought to oust the Apaches and Comanches in favor of their own settlers. In common with most military posts, the fort here spawned a thriving local community. That of Fort Davis proved to be a particularly intriguing blend of Hispanic, black, Anglo, and European immigrants; as such, its history provides an excellent means of examining, at a local level, a society that publicly proclaimed the virtues of democratic egalitarianism. Finally, Fort Davis was also an economic nexus; as was so often the case throughout the American West, the men and women who came to the region often found their fortunes to be closely linked to the interest of a faraway government. Not surprisingly, private entrepreneurs alternately profited from and criticized the ebbs and flows of public subsidies.

Enriching the post's history were the members of its military garrisons, whose backgrounds and experiences represented a rich mosaic of nineteenth-century American life. Lt. Arthur T. Lee, reputed to have studied art under the noted portraitist Thomas Sully, left dozens of prized watercolors depicting his Texas service. William "Pecos Bill" Shafter and Benjamin Grierson, two of the old army's most fascinating personalities, numbered among its post commanders. Moreover, Fort Davis was closely associated with the black regulars who composed a significant portion of the U.S. Army after the Civil War. All four of the post-1867 army's black regiments served there; Lt. Henry Flipper, the first black graduate of West Point, was court-martialed for having allegedly engaged in "conduct unbecoming an officer and a gentleman" while stationed at Davis.

A few words about terminology. Scholars have long struggled with concepts of what American frontiers really were. Bemused general readers probably find the antics of their more academic brethren a bit puzzling, but the debate is more than simply a case of gratuitous semantic hairsplitting. Words have meaning, and meaning has power. During the late nineteenth century, Frederick Jackson Turner proposed that the frontier experience, which fostered freedom and democracy, had produced a unique American heritage. Turner's allies, most notably Ray Allen Billington, honed and refined his dramatic thesis in the mid-twentieth century, explaining that the frontier was both "place" and "process," a region where "a low man-land ratio" and abundant natural resources "provided an unusual opportunity for individual self-advancement." Despite Billington's useful qualifications, many came to doubt the legitimacy of Turner's bold assertions. "Frontier," warned Francis Jennings, one of Turner's fiercest critics, was a culturally biased term that implicitly pitted "civilization" against "savages." Moreover, though often assumed to lie on the outer peripheries of Western European interests, frontier regions hardly seemed peripheral to the peoples who lived, loved, fought, and bartered there. Seeking to avoid the term altogether, Richard White instead described a geographic "middle ground" between cultures where "new systems of meaning and change" were developed. Mary Louise Pratt has settled upon "contact zones" as a neutral alternative.[3]

The critics have posed a useful scholarly corrective to Turner's omissions and excesses. By focusing almost exclusively on males of Western European background, his works ignored the experiences of women and racial and ethnic minorities. The more inclusive studies of the post-Turnerians have described a richer, more diverse, more realistically complex history of our shared past. Still, I dare to say that most westerners—including the residents of modern-day Fort Davis—see their region as having been a "frontier" and would be somewhat puzzled at the more academic "middle ground" or "contact zone." Gregory H. Nobles's description of his own efforts to wrestle with designations such as "Indian" and "frontier" seems especially apt: "A phrase like 'indigenous peoples in the inter-group contact situation' may be less culturally encumbered than 'Indians on the frontier,' but the latter reads better." As such, I have stuck with the term "frontier," not as a challenge to revisionists, but to reflect the use of the term by Fort Davis residents, then and now. Hopefully, I have done so in a sensitive manner that captures the opportunities as well as the challenges of this crossroads experience.[4]

As was the case for so much of the American West, military events hold the key to understanding the history of Fort Davis. In the end, armed might determined the ownership of the Trans-Pecos. Apaches and Comanches gained influence here because of their prowess in battle; Spain and Mexico were unable to fully establish their presence because they could not crush Indian resistance. Conversely, the United States claimed West Texas by virtue of its superior army. And the influence of the military forces that occupied the region quickly extended far beyond the battlefield. For nearly half a century, the U.S. Army served as the primary engine for local economic development, attracting outsiders seeking jobs, fresh starts, and fortunes to the Davis Mountains. Soldiers escorted the travelers, improved the roads, laid the telegraph wires, and protected the railroads that linked the region to the outside world. In the process, they built a community that reflected the values and practices of the societies from which they had come. Some contemporary historians—especially those espousing what has often been labeled the "new" western history—have shied away from military affairs. The story of this little corner of the West suggests that such an approach yields a very incomplete history indeed.

R esearch for this book originated during the late 1980s, when the National Park Service contracted me to write a comprehensive history of Fort Davis. Aimed largely at meeting the needs of Park Service personnel and specialists, the resulting document, *History of Fort Davis, Texas*, was published by the National Park Service in 1990. The Texas State Historical Association published a much-abbreviated version of that work, *Fort Davis:*

Outpost on the Texas Frontier, four years later. I am grateful to both groups for allowing me to go ahead with the present book.

Jerry Thompson, Professor of History at Texas A&M University–International and editor of the Canseco-Keck Series at Texas A&M University Press, along with Mary Lenn Dixon, editor-in-chief of the press, came up with the idea for completely revising my original work in a form more suitable for general readers. They also arranged a grant that allowed me to update my older research and take the time to completely rethink and revise the text. Mary Williams, who as long-time historian at Fort Davis National Historic Site knows more about the old post than anyone else, has always given freely of her time and knowledge. Pat Thomas helped edit the original Park Service manuscript and meticulously worked with manuscript census photocopies. Sonya Witherspoon found a way to translate materials from outdated word-processing programs on 5¼-inch floppy disks into formats friendly to contemporary computers, thus making it much easier to manipulate old text. Verity McInnis entered editorial changes and helped make the Grierson family, stars of any decent work on Fort Davis, become much more lifelike, at least in my own mind. Jerry Thompson and Lt. Col. Thomas "Ty" Smith closely read the resulting manuscript, pointing out additional sources and saving me from a score of embarrassing errors. Of course, any mistakes that remain are my responsibility.

For more than a decade at Texas A&M University–Corpus Christi, I have had the distinct good fortune of having Paul Hain as my academic dean. His support for my academic endeavors and defense of academic freedom have helped me, and the College of Arts and Humanities, through times good and bad. Thanks to an extremely generous donation by Margaret Turnbull, the Frantz History Endowment Fund and Frantz Professorship Endowment have funded course release, travel, and research assistants. Anthony Quiroz, one of my colleagues on the history faculty, provided sage advice on sources and approaches. Another historian, David Blanke, offered wise counsel and insightful comments on my introduction. His support and suggestions greatly improved the finished product. Stephanie Fritsche prepared the maps on pages 21 and 93, and I wish to extend my gratitude for this service

But I owe my biggest thanks to three very special people. I have been, and continue to be, the most fortunate of sons. My mother, Edna Wooster, has tolerated the long academic conversations of her husband, son, and daughter-in-law with unfailingly good cheer. My father, Ralph A. Wooster, has served as the ideal role model and academic mentor. And my wife, Catherine I. Cox, has generously taken time from her own studies of Shakespeare, Milton, and the plague in England to secure the illustrations for this project. It is to each of them that I dedicate this book.

FRONTIER CROSSROADS

CHAPTER ONE

CROSSROADS OF EMPIRE

On October 20, 1682, seven American Indians appeared at El Paso del Norte (present-day Juárez, Mexico), where Franciscan friars, representing the Spanish empire as well as the Catholic Church, had established a mission two decades earlier. The tiny station had recently taken on increased importance, as a massive Pueblo Indian revolt two years earlier had forced many of the residents of Spanish New Mexico to find succor farther south. Leading the Indian delegation was the magnetic Juan Sabeata, blessed with a flair for diplomacy. As a Jumano Indian, Sabeata belonged to one of the most important—and enigmatic—peoples of the American Southwest. Jumano traders had long disseminated material goods, cultural mores, and information across the vast southwestern plains. But the first waves of a larger and more militaristic people, the Apaches, had recently begun to challenge the lucrative Jumano connections, and for defense the Jumanos needed help.[1]

Sabeata's application to Spanish officials was extraordinarily perceptive. He wanted the Europeans to help his people fend off the Apaches but was careful to couch his request in terms that his potential allies might find appealing. Having grasped the interconnected triad of Spanish interests in the New World—spreading Christianity, increasing wealth, and keeping other Europeans out—Sabeata touched all bases. His Jumano kin, based at the junction of the Rios Concho and Grande (La Junta), desired a mission. "There must be more than 10,000 souls who are asking for baptism," he explained. Not only that, the Jumanos enjoyed alliances with thirty-six other nations that extended far into the eastern plains, including "the great kingdom of the Texas [Tejas]" and "the great kingdom of Quivira," the legendary Plains site reputed to be rich in gold and silver. As if to ensure that Spain would accept his invitation, he allowed, almost as an afterthought, that other Europeans were entering the region from the east "by water in wooden houses."[2]

Sabeata's proposal must have been irresistibly tempting to his hosts. Formal relations with the Jumanos promised not only the temporal rewards of spreading God's word but also the worldly benefits flowing from expanded mercantile opportunities with the friendly Tejas Indians and exploitation of what was believed to be the fabulously wealthy "Gran Quivira." Since rumors of European intruders were a matter of Spanish national security, Capt. Juan Dominguez de Mendoza and twenty soldiers were assigned the job of following up on the Sabeata visit. Three barefoot Franciscan friars, eager to establish a Catholic mission at La Junta, a strategic communications center at the intersection of trails and rivers linking the Great Plains, New Mexico, and Mexico, set forth shortly thereafter. Thus lay the roots of the first long-term Spanish presence within easy striking range of the Davis Mountains, scene of what eventually became one of the most intriguing crossroads of the American West.[3]

T he Davis Mountains, whose crisp, clean air; temperate environment; and heights just high enough to be fairly called mountains yet low enough to be scaled by all but the faintest of heart, have long attracted human inhabitants. Sixty-three prehistoric sites have been identified in Jeff Davis County alone. Several spectacular pictograph displays are found near Mount Livermore, 15 miles west of present-day Fort Davis. Another site to the northwest, dated shortly after 600 A.D., depicts men using bows and arrows to kill game. Evidence of Paleo-Indian activity near Van Horn, in the Guadalupe Mountains, and near Langtry (approximately 50, 75, and 125 miles from Fort Davis, respectively) has also been unearthed.[4]

Unfortunately, these sites offer only tantalizing hints about the lives of peoples who would be overwhelmed by the expansion of the Jumanos. Multi-ethnic in origin, the Jumanos had pushed southward from New Mexico down the Rio Grande in the eleventh century. They probably spoke a Tanoan language, one of a family of dialects used widely in what is now the central and southwestern United States. Numbering between twenty thousand and thirty thousand persons at the apex of their power, the Jumanos had by the 1580s established five large villages around La Junta. Dominating the trade network that originally featured exchanges of turquoise, pottery, bows and arrows, food, and animal skins, they later incorporated horses and mules into their market economy. Farther into the plains, their cousins relied heavily on the buffalo and lived in movable grass huts. At La Junta proper, however, Jumanos mixed the buffalo cultures of the plains with the agriculture made possible by irrigation from the Rio Grande. Heavily tattooed, they lived in flat-roofed, communal houses constructed of adobe and wood. The first Spanish visitor to the area, Álvar Núñez Cabeza de Vaca, that most intrepid of wanderers, described the inhabitants of La Junta as "the finest persons of any people we saw, of the greatest activity and strength, who best understood us and intelligently answered our questions."[5]

But revolutionary changes lay ahead for the Jumanos. Repeated seventeenth-century droughts crippled agricultural enterprises. Even more ominously, the Spaniards, drawn by the region's mineral wealth and pastoral potentials as well as a zeal to Christianize its inhabitants, had pushed into northern Chihuahua. With Spanish civilization the newcomers also brought slave hunters, who found the La Junta area ripe for their trade in human cargo. Although the Spanish government officially abolished the slave trade in 1585, the measure was routinely flaunted, leaving a bitter legacy among the tribes. To make matters even worse, Old World diseases overwhelmed the Jumanos' biological defenses. In the wake of sharp population declines, fragmented remnants of former bands reinvented themselves in an effort to survive the triple threats of climate change, conquest, and disease.[6]

Attacks from Apaches—usually Mescaleros—further weakened the Jumanos. By the seventeenth and eighteenth centuries, Mescalero Apaches had found a convenient void in the region surrounding latter-day Fort Davis. Using the mountains and arid plains of the Trans-Pecos to their fullest advantage, they launched devastating raids against the remnants of the once-flourishing Jumano villages, as well as exposed Spanish settlements in Chihuahua and New Mexico. Striking weaker opponents, Apaches refused to fight except when confident of victory and eluded all but the most determined pursuers. They followed a seasonal migration, moving in search of buffalo herds and the mescal plant after which they were named. Mescaleros also gathered wild desert plants—sunflower seeds, yucca, cactus fruits, mesquite beans, acorns, juniper berries, and screw beans, among others—to diversify their diet. Clad in buckskin shirts and breechclouts, they lived in tepees of buffalo skins or brush and took pride in their long, straight black hair. The intense demands of environment and culture kept them in superb physical condition; one Spanish diarist concluded that "they have better figures, are better warriors, and are more feared" than those peoples at La Junta. Indeed, the Mescaleros would come to dominate the Trans-Pecos and eastern New Mexico.[7]

Gender often defined Mescalero living patterns. Women gathered and stored wild plants and foodstuffs, made clothing, collected fuel, prepared meals, cared for children, and maintained the home. Men hunted and defended the band and, after the Spanish introduced horses to the south-western plains, their herd. Apache males also made and maintained weapons, riding gear, and ceremonial attire. With mobility at a premium, artifacts tended to be small and portable. Water jars, baskets, grinding instruments, and grooming devices dominated the list of family possessions. Bows and arrows, spears, axes, knives, and war clubs formed the basic weapons of war until supplemented by European muskets and rifles. Typically, several ex-tended families formed the core of a local band. When a man married, cus-tom required him to leave his blood family and live with his wife and parents-in-law. A male, whose position was neither hereditary, permanent, nor authoritarian, led the group. Dependent upon his personal eloquence, bravery, diplomacy, and generosity, an effective chief organized workable coalitions for military and ceremonial occasions.[8]

But Mescalero power would not go unchallenged. Diseases took a grave toll, as did the wars, slave raids, and occupation of Chihuahua by the Spaniards. The Apaches also suffered from the attacks of Comanches, an even more militaristic group of tribes whose recent acquisition of horses had transformed the erstwhile gatherers of the Rocky Mountains into the most feared mounted warriors of the southern plains. The very word adopted by Europeans to describe Comanches reflected the feelings of outsiders about these militaristic peoples: the original Ute word was *Komantcia*, or "enemy." Comanches, on the other hand, saw things quite differently; their own term for themselves meant "human beings," implying a perceived superior-ity over outsiders. By the mid-nineteenth century, Comanche attacks, Span-ish slavers, and disease had reduced the Mescalero population to fewer than three thousand.[9]

Spain, early modern Europe's most powerful empire, was also drawn to the crossroads region that later became Fort Davis. Indian attacks into Chi-huahua, suspicions about the possible presence of European rivals, rumors of mineral wealth, and hopes of religious expansion stimulated Spanish in-vestigation of the northern frontiers of its New World empire. Antonio de Espejo, a prominent cattleman interested in promoting settlement, had sponsored a large entrada through La Junta, the Davis Mountains, and the Pecos River basin in 1582. Crossing the Rio Grande farther north at Juárez, Juan de Oñate began the more lasting settlement of New Mexico sixteen years later. Emerging colonization efforts there had temporarily displaced La Junta as the strategic apex of New Spain's far northern frontiers, but the region remained a potentially lucrative target for future expansion.[10]

A century later, Juan Sabeata's request for assistance, combined with the long-term impact of the Pueblo revolt of 1680, led Spain to establish several

San Juan, a Mescalero Apache, was among many Indians who posed for photographs during the late nineteenth century. Courtesy National Archives.

missions at La Junta in 1683–84. But costly foreign wars, recurring Indian revolts, and the growing burdens of administering its sprawling empire forced Spain to reduce expenses wherever possible, and the potential benefits resulting from Sabeata's optimistic proposals would never be fulfilled. Amid this climate of retrenchment, the missions at La Junta were soon abandoned. Subsequent Spanish forays into the region were sporadic until 1747, when three military expeditions provided sufficient impetus to reopen several missions, the largest of which numbered 172 souls. In 1759, the Spanish began work on the first presidio at the junction, El Presidio del Norte de la Junta, in response to several rebellions by local Indians. Although the garrison fended off an assault later that year, the presidio failed to overawe the Indians of the Trans-Pecos and was abandoned in 1767.[11]

Despite such failures, the site's strategic importance remained obvious. Spanish interest in La Junta was briefly rekindled during the late 1760s when, as part of colonial reforms during the reign of King Carlos III (1759–88), Field Marshal Cayetano María Pignatelli Rubí Corbera y Saint Climent (the Marqués de Rubí) recommended the reoccupation of the La Junta presidio. De Rubí hoped to exterminate the Apache threat by combining offensives launched from frontier posts such as La Junta with an alliance with the Comanches. But other imperial obligations limited Spain's available manpower and resources, and coordinating military campaigns in the sparsely populated Big Bend of the Rio Grande proved extraordinarily difficult. As such, Presidio del Norte held only 106 men during the late 1770s and early 1780s. Attempts to cement a Spanish-Comanche alliance against the Apaches remained illusive, and hostile Indian raiders continued to launch thrusts deep into Mexico. A revolution in Mexico sparked by Father Hidalgo's *Grito de Dolores* further diverted the attention of colonial administrators away from affairs at La Junta. In 1819, desperate imperial officials entertained plans to include troops based at Presidio del Norte in a punitive campaign against the Comanches and the Apaches. Again, however, Spain could spare neither the soldiers nor the colonists to occupy and safeguard the Trans-Pecos.[12]

The continued difficulties at La Junta symbolized the larger problems plaguing Spain's northern New World provinces. Beset by imperial pressures, Spain could never devote enough resources to solidify its hold over the Trans-Pecos. La Junta had served as a useful buffer against Indian raids on more valuable Chihuahua, but settlers were rarely encouraged to move farther north, since such expansion would only further disperse Spain's already scarce resources along its tenuous northern colonial frontiers. Religious conversion had not been without influence among the Indians, some of whom had accepted Catholicism. But the uncertain life found at the isolated missions, punitive Spanish assaults, and illegal slaving expeditions for the mines in Mexico offered most Indians little incentive for friendship. Moreover, Spain's inability to stop Apache raids weakened its image in the eyes of prospective converts.[13]

Challenges to New Spain culminated in 1821, when a conservative/moderate coalition forced the crown to concede Mexican independence. Frequent changes of government made it difficult for the struggling young nation to focus on its uncertain northern borders; when it did, policies crafted in Mexico City often conflicted with the needs of its frontier populace. A penal colony at present-day Ruidosa, some twenty-five miles upstream, replaced the crumbling presidio and missions at La Junta. But the Condemned Regiment garrisoned there, consisting of criminals assigned to protect the frontier in lieu of serving out their prison sentences, inspired little confidence. Despite generous promises of support, few of the authorized pesos, supplies, or soldiers found their way to the borderlands. Military leaders, ever alert to the changing political winds of the troubled era, siphoned off huge sums for their personal estates and stationed their most reliable troops near Mexico City or Veracruz. The resulting defenses were wholly inadequate; one report estimated that Indian raids along the northern frontiers between 1820 and 1835 killed five thousand people, drove off four thousand others, and destroyed one hundred settlements.[14]

A few adventurers nonetheless saw in the Trans-Pecos great opportunity. Enterprising capitalists envisioned huge profits if viable trade routes could be established between Missouri and Chihuahua City through La Junta, and the region held out enormous potential for mining and ranching. In 1832, Lt. Col. José Ronquillo, commander of regional frontier forces, successfully petitioned for a massive 2,345-square-mile grant on the north side opposite Presidio del Norte. The gigantic grant started on the east bank of Cibolo Creek and ran up the Rio Grande for some 35 miles to present-day Ruidosa. It then extended northeast, past the future site of Fort Davis, to Alamo de San Juan. To the southeast, the grant included land stretching into modern Brewster County, then back to the Rio Grande through the Puerto del Portillo Mountains. Ronquillo built a stone house on Cibolo Creek, cultivated a patch of land, installed a modest cattle herd, and opened a small silver mine. Upon his transfer, however, he sold his grant, which was eventually purchased by Juana Pedraza.[15]

Still, the non-Indian population remained small, and Texas' war for independence in 1836 rendered Mexico's occupation of the Trans-Pecos even more problematic. Hundreds of miles from the fighting at the Alamo, Goliad, or San Jacinto, the region remained low on the central government's priority list. The newly independent Republic of Texas and the United States posed

further threats to Mexican sovereignty. As these northern republics drove
eastern Indians onto the plains, Comanches in turn sought out easier sources
of food and plunder to the south. To make matters worse, ever-increasing
numbers of American merchants entered into the lucrative Indian trade, ex-
changing munitions and alcohol for stolen booty and further diminishing
Mexican influence in the process. War against France in 1838 only exacerbated Mexico's defensive weaknesses.[16]

Its frontiers aflame, the state of Chihuahua revived the colonial system
of offering cash bounties for Indian scalps. Critics countered by claiming
that bounty hunters, who seemed all too eager to submit the scalps of friendly
Indians and Mexican citizens along with those of peoples deemed hostile,
simply fomented additional unrest. Desperately attempting to purchase a
settlement, in 1842 Gov. García Conde offered Indians an annual tribute of
five thousand dollars, supplementary rations, and the right to sell their stolen
loot in return for peace in Chihuahua. Unfortunately for Conde, the latter
provision only encouraged Comanche raids into neighboring states, leading
to his removal from office in 1845. With some reluctance, the state again
turned to a bounty hunter, in this case James "Don Santiago" Kirker, whose
company of Delawares, Shawnees, and Americans turned in 487 scalps by the
end of 1846. Even so, Chihuahuan legislators continued to acknowledge the
omnipresent Indian influence. "We travel the roads at their whim," complained the beleaguered solons; "we cultivate the land where they wish and
in the amount they wish; we use sparingly things they have left to us until the
moment that it strikes their appetite to take them for themselves."[17]

The Mexican War saw the transfer of the Trans-Pecos from the uncer-
tainty of Mexican rule to the buoyant assertiveness of that of the United
States. As American troops occupied Monterrey, Mexico City, Santa Fe, and
California, Col. Alexander W. Doniphan's 850-man First Regiment of Missouri Volunteers captured El Paso and Chihuahua City. In the resulting
Treaty of Guadalupe-Hidalgo, Mexico recognized Texas independence, accepted the Rio Grande as the Lone Star State's southern boundary, and ceded
the Southwest to the United States. In return, Washington paid $15 million
and assumed Mexican debts estimated at an additional $3.25 million. It also
promised to prevent Indian raids from its newly won lands into Mexico.

The U.S. victory brought a vigorous new contestant to the imperial
struggle for the Trans-Pecos. Like the Jumanos before them, Apaches and
Comanches would continue to contest the Fort Davis region for another
three decades, but they had neither the numbers nor the technologies to
check the determined inroads of these latest invaders. And like Spain before
it, Mexico had never mastered the region's vast size, arid lands, and relative

inaccessibility. Plagued by domestic strife, Mexico's frontier settlers had viewed their central administration with ambivalence. Local governments seemed paralyzed; the mission system collapsed as secularization and the scarcity of priests tested even the most faithful. Nor was Mexico able to convince sufficient numbers of loyal colonists to move north of the Rio Grande. Furthermore, shortages of soldiers and money prevented Mexico City from establishing a fair or consistent policy toward the Indians who had come to the region.[18]

By contrast, the U.S. system seemed ideally suited for expansion into western Texas. Nineteenth-century American society encouraged individual initiative and enterprise among white males. Although often affected by the inconsistent winds of politics, U.S. policymakers offered newly organized areas the prospect of full equality with the older states. Abundant resources and irrepressible confidence gave the youthful nation a fearsome vitality. French Louisiana and Spanish Florida had been sold rather than risked to American expansionism. In the north, Russia had also retreated before the Yankees; even mighty Britain declined to openly challenge the United States on the North American continent after the War of 1812. To be sure, like Spain, Mexico, and the Republic of Texas before it, the United States found the occupation of the rugged Trans-Pecos a tenuous proposition. Yet commercial interests—the discovery of gold in California, the trade with Chihuahua City, the projected transcontinental railroad—combined with the self-assured mobility of many Americans to give the nation enormous advantages in the long-standing contest for empire.

With the Stars and Stripes now flying over the Fort Davis area, American opportunists swept in, hoping to capitalize on the new political situation. John W. Spencer established a ranch on the northern side of the river above present-day Presidio. Ben Leaton, one of the region's most powerful and notorious entrepreneurs, married Juana Pedraza, the widowed claimant of the huge Ronquillos grant, and built a sturdy pueblo stockade, Fort Leaton, on the Santa Fe–Chihuahua City trail. Always with an eye to the main chance, Leaton operated as an unofficial customs agent, trader, and rancher, swapping arms and alcohol to Indians in exchange for stolen merchandise. Even the Indians who dealt with Leaton were not safe, for he was not averse to selling their scalps to Mexican officials in Chihuahua when the price was right.[19]

Leaton's dreams of empire would be ended when a former associate, John Burgess, killed him in 1853. But the death of one man would not dam America's expansionist tide. Spurred on by the discovery of gold in California in 1848, Texas Ranger Jack Hays and his escort passed the future site of Forts Davis during a foray into the Big Bend, reporting favorably on the terrain and availability of water. A year later, Lieutenants W. H. C. Whiting and William F. Smith followed up the Hays trail, encountering "a beautiful little brook" that they named Limpia Creek. They dubbed the resulting defile Wild Rose Pass in honor of the spectacular flowers then in bloom. Just beyond the pass, the Whiting-Smith team located a grove of cottonwood trees on the edge of an open plain. They called the place "Painted Comanche Camp" for the pictographs that decorated the trees. Another team, headed by Robert S. Neighbors, federal Indian agent for Texas, and John S. "Rip" Ford, Texas Ranger, was blazing another western trail. The Neighbors-Ford party took a more northerly track through the Guadalupe Mountains to El Paso. Near present-day Balmorhea, they found what they believed to be an old Spanish military station, probably a forgotten outpost or aborted mission effort.[20]

But conditions on the trails remained problematic. One group of gold seekers, for example, tried to follow the old Hays trail to Presidio del Norte. "We traveled two hundred and forty miles without seeing any timber and at two different times we drove two days and nights without water over mountains and ravines on the route that Jack Hays said he found water so plenty," wrote one member of the party, "and if he [Hays] had been in sight he would not have lived one minute." Additional reconnaissance was obviously necessary to ensure safer western crossings. Lt. Francis T. Bryan took charge of scouting a northern passage through the Trans-Pecos; Bvt. Lt. Col. Joseph E. Johnston headed efforts along the lower Whiting-Smith road. Already a hero of the Mexican War and destined to become one of the Confederacy's most important military leaders, Johnston demonstrated that the Whiting-Smith route was slightly shorter and offered more dependable sources of water and wood than the northern trail. Seeking out additional information about western Texas, Capt. Samuel G. French led another team out from San Antonio. A veteran of the Whiting-Smith expedition, French again commented favorably on the region near Wild Rose Pass, which was "most beautiful to the eye." Abundant fuel and grass were available nearby at the Painted Camp. Remains of a few Indian campgrounds lay just up the Limpia, and water seemed plentiful.[21]

As the army's repeated explorations had suggested, immigrants to California, the mail route west of San Antonio, and the Chihuahua trade required military protection. To help shield the intruders from Mescalero and Mimbres Apache attacks to the west, the army had established Forts Conrad and Fillmore along the Rio Grande in New Mexico. But Captain French's disappointing follow-up report in 1851 temporarily dampened efforts to find a site for a post in the Trans-Pecos. On this return visit, Smith found that

A member of Maj. William H. Emory's Boundary Survey left this image of Limpia Creek and Wild Rose Pass during the early 1850s. Courtesy Fort Davis National Historic Site.

a recent fire had left only ashes where green grasses had once thrived. Limpia Creek was now but a thin trickle near its source at the Painted Camp. Only by two days of forced marches, covering ninety-six miles through blistering heat to the Rio Grande, did French save his thirsty command. The condition of the Indians west of the Pecos, he reported, was "truly lamentable." "Denied the possession of lands and a home . . . leading an existence more filthy than swine," it was no wonder, he concluded, that they attacked travelers.[22]

But something had to be done, for it was more than five hundred lonely miles between the tiny settlement at San Elizario (near present-day El Paso) and Fort Clark (near present-day Brackettville), established in 1852. Following an extensive inspection tour later that year, Col. Joseph K. F. Mansfield called for the military reoccupation of El Paso (abandoned in 1851) as well as for construction of three new posts on the road to San Antonio: near the point where the route left the Rio Grande below El Paso; on the headwaters of the Limpia Creek; and just east of the Pecos crossing on Live Oak Creek. Overextended, understaffed, and with little strategic direction, the army could not immediately respond to Mansfield's recommendations. Unenviable, then, was the situation inherited by the new commander of the military Department of Texas, Bvt. Maj. Gen. Persifor F. Smith, who had been instructed to "revise the whole system of defense," establish new posts where needed, protect settlers, carry out treaty obligations with Mexico, and pursue hostile Indians while at the same time reducing expenses![23]

The conscientious Smith, who had fought in the Second Seminole War in Florida, distinguished himself during the war against Mexico, and commanded the raucous Department of the Pacific during the California gold rush, did not shy away from his difficult task. He constructed a line of posts just ahead of settlement in Texas—from Fort Belknap (established 1851) to the north, Smith's defensive network included Forts Phantom Hill (1851), Chadbourne (1852), McKavett (1852), Terrett (1852), and Clark (1852). An older line of forts, including Worth (1849), Graham (1849), Gates (1849), Croghan (1849), Mason (1851), and Martin Scott (1848), provided interior defense. To guard the Rio Grande valley, Forts Bliss (1849), Inge (1849), Duncan (1849), Ewell (1852), Merrill (1850), McIntosh (1849), Ringgold Barracks (1848), and Brown (1846) formed what on paper appeared to be a formidable double line of garrisons. The theory seemed elegant enough. In the event of Indian incursions, infantry stationed at the outer posts would alert cavalry manning the interior line, where they had been stationed to reduce the costs of feeding their horses. The troopers would pursue the intruders as the foot soldiers cut off their retreat. In practice, however, the infantry had little means of summoning the cavalry in time for effective action. Furthermore, the 150 miles that typically separated the posts made it impossible to monitor every incursion. Finally, this system left the road to El Paso unguarded west of Fort Clark.[24]

To fill the latter gap, Quartermaster General Thomas S. Jesup recommended the junction of the Rios Concho and Grande at Presidio as "the true strategic point." Department commander Smith, however, disagreed, countering that the barren terrain on the river's north banks there rendered any permanent military post untenable. Instead, Smith fixed his interest on the site located by Smith and Whiting, examined twice by French, and recommended by Mansfield—Painted Comanche Camp, near Limpia Creek and Wild Rose Pass. Four companies of Smith's Eighth Infantry Regiment had successfully camped there while en route to El Paso the previous December. To ensure that he made an informed decision, Smith promised to lead a column into West Texas himself. His work would permanently alter the landscape of the Davis Mountains.[25]

CHAPTER TWO

AGENT OF EMPIRE
The U.S. Army

Having determined that a garrison in the Trans-Pecos was necessary for frontier defense, Bvt. Maj. Gen. Persifor F. Smith and his escort reached Painted Comanche Camp in early October 1854. He was impressed by the site's strategic locale, about 475 miles west of San Antonio and near trails to Presidio del Norte and El Paso. Grazing, water, fuel, and building materials could be found nearby, and Indian attacks were frequent, a mailbag carrying several of Smith's communications having been lost in one such incident. Smith named the new position Fort Davis, in honor of Secretary of War Jefferson Davis. Hoping to protect his regulars from cold winter northers, Smith tucked the fort into a canyon flanked on two sides by steep rock walls. The initial garrison comprised six companies and the headquarters, staff, and band of the Eighth Infantry Regiment. But only twelve of the twenty-three commissioned personnel assigned to the units stationed there were actually present, the others being away on courts-martial, recruiting details, and temporary staff detachments. Two hundred twenty enlisted men rounded out the garrison.[1]

Like a hundred other western posts, Fort Davis was part of a process of conquest in which American soldiers and settlers pushed inexorably forward, linking the Pacific Ocean with the east. Most of these men and women were certain that a Christian God supported their quest to civilize the barren lands. "We are the most favored people on the face of the earth," Pres. James K. Polk had proclaimed in his 1848 annual message. Settling this wilderness, they must brush aside what they perceived to be the uncivilized occupants of times past. But in reality they were not occupying an empty landscape. Indians, conquistadores, missionaries, rogues, and settlers—all had passed through the vicinity of what Americans once referred to as Painted Comanche Camp.[2]

By annexing Texas, resolving the Oregon dispute, and seizing the Southwest, the United States had staked its claim as a continental power. Completed with dramatic suddenness, the new acquisitions also changed the relationship between the federal government and western Indians. Traditionally, U.S. policy had been predicated on the assumption that a permanent frontier had been reached. Indians were removed to areas west of this imaginary line; military forts, constructed ahead of white settlement, theoretically preserved the peace. Yet reality was far different. The "permanent" line was always shifting west, invariably into lands Indians had once been presumed to occupy "in perpetuity." By shattering the myth of a permanent Indian frontier, the most recent expansion had rendered an unrealistic and ineffectual policy obsolete. Furthermore, a diverse array of cultures and peoples lived in the lands now claimed by the United States. Many of these occupants, including Apaches and Comanches, posed a significant military threat to east-west communication routes.[3]

In 1849, Congress made a somewhat halfhearted effort to address these problems by creating the Department of the Interior. Along with pensions and the federal domain, the new department's responsibilities included Indian affairs, formerly housed in the War Department. Few government officials explicitly advocated the extermination of American Indians; at the opposite extreme, few saw much value in tribal cultures or lifestyles. The consensus instead held that Indians should adopt the ways of Western civilization. With missionaries and teachers in their midst, they would give up their outmoded ways and become respectable Christian farmers. Accordingly, Indians must be separated from the evil influences of the very culture they were supposed to accept—alcohol, disease, and greed. Although rarely acknowledging this essential paradox, policymakers hoped that reservations might at least allay the problem, for a final military solution was neither desirable nor practical. As Secretary of War Charles Conrad (1850–53) reasoned, "It would be far less expensive to feed than to fight them." Arguing that contact between Indians and the general public inevitably led to trouble, Conrad advocated a "rigid adherence to the policy . . . of setting apart a portion of territory for the exclusive occupancy of the Indians."[4]

Texas posed special challenges to the reservation scheme, for unlike other states and territories, it retained ownership of its public lands. In order to establish reservations for the thirty thousand Indians of the Lone Star State, the United States would have to convince Texans to cooperate. In 1854, a reluctant Texas legislature did just that, granting jurisdiction to the United States to establish two reservations (known as the Brazos and Comanche reserves) along the upper Brazos River. If things went well, a Mescalero Apache reservation west of the Pecos River would follow. The Brazos reservation, occupied by semiagricultural tribes such as the Caddo, Waco, Tawakoni, Tonkawa, and Delaware, initially met its designers' objectives. But Texans never accepted the Comanche reservation, and in 1859, following a series of ugly incidents, the residents of both reservations were hustled across the Red River into the Indian territory. Forgotten was the reserve west of the Pecos River or any possibility that the United States would allow the major Trans-Pecos tribes to retain even a portion of their traditional lands.[5]

The job of removing the tribes to reservations fell to the regular army. The coupling was ironic, for neither American society as a whole nor the army itself was entirely comfortable with the latter's de facto mantle as agent of empire. Fears of a standing army ran old and deep among those weaned on often-apocryphal tales of patriotic American minutemen defeating hordes of mercenary British redcoats. The success of volunteers during the recent war against Mexico confirmed popular perceptions that the United States did not need a large regular force. As President Polk put it, "That war demonstrated that . . . a volunteer army of citizen soldiers equal to veteran troops, and in numbers equal to any emergency, can in a short period be brought into the field. . . . They are armed, and have been accustomed from their youth up to handle and use firearms. . . . They are intelligent, and there is an individuality of character which is found in the ranks of no other army."[6]

Bashing the army often made good political sense. Blunt-spoken Sen. Thomas Hart Benton (D-Missouri) proclaimed regulars to be no better than "school-house officers and pot-house soldiers." Rep. Joshua R. Giddings (R-Ohio) summed up the attitudes of many. "I am opposed to any measure which contemplates an increase in the Army," thundered Giddings. "It is a time of peace. . . . We see our officers now in almost every city strutting about the streets in indolence, sustained by the laboring people, fed from the public crib, but doing nothing whatever to support themselves or to increase the wealth of the nation. Sir, I would discharge every officer, and let him support himself."[7]

The army brought much of this criticism upon itself. Many in the nation's military establishment seemed more interested in scoring personal victories than in burnishing the army's tarnished image or in more effectively implementing its functions as agent of empire. Command of the army, for example, was extraordinarily muddled. Constitutionally, the president was commander in chief of the armed forces. By tradition, he delegated oversight responsibilities to his secretary of war. Since 1821, the nation's highest-ranking army officer had served as general in chief. The arrangement almost begged for conflict between career officers who wanted to exert their professional expertise and secretaries of war who sought to assert civilian control over the military. Only the relatively lax administrations of a succession of war secretaries more noted for their political abilities than their military acumen or interests had prevented a showdown.[8]

The uneasy truce was shattered after the Mexican War. Maj. Gen. Winfield Scott, whose pomposity and disputatious behavior were matched only by his military brilliance, had in 1849 transferred his office from Washington to New York to distance himself from his hated rival, Pres. Zachary Taylor. Pres. Franklin Pierce's selection of Jefferson Davis as secretary of war in 1854 further complicated the army–executive branch rivalry. A West Point graduate and Mexican War hero, Davis felt inferior to no one when it came to military issues. Cold, insensitive, and one of a select few whose vanity nearly matched that of General Scott's, the new secretary sought to assert his authority as the president's delegate. Scott resisted, setting off an extraordinary exchange of correspondence that, when published as a Senate document, totaled 254 printed pages of bitter invective.[9]

Such an atmosphere boded ill for efficient administration or systematic planning. The structure of the army's support services revealed similar internal divisions. The heads of the army's nine staff departments—adjutant general, commissary general, inspector general, paymaster general, quartermaster general, surgeon general, chief engineer, colonel of topographical engineers (this department was abolished in 1863), and colonel of ordnance—reported to the secretary of war rather than the general in chief. The small, permanent staff offices in Washington—usually including only the chief, a subordinate officer or two, and a handful of clerks—belied their tremendous influence. Safely ensconced in the capital, the staff chiefs jealously fended off any attempts to restrict their independence by cultivating relationships with a protective Congress. Most war secretaries found it easier to avoid the problem than to tackle the staff fiefdoms; even the strong-willed Davis could not enforce a system of rotation between line and staff officers.[10]

The tiny bureaucracy in Washington enjoyed a long reach by virtue of its field officers. Assistant adjutant generals oversaw the formidable array of military paperwork. Commissary and quartermaster officers managed the purchase and delivery of rations, supplies, and transportation. Inspectors reported on the condition of army posts and units; paymasters delivered much-awaited (and frequently delayed) pay. Ordnance officials supplied the troops with weapons, and surgeons provided medical care. Engineers oversaw construction of military roads, river and harbor improvements, and coastal defense; topographical officers surveyed and mapped vast sections of the American West. Officers stationed with their regular units were intensely jealous of the perks and powers accorded these staff rivals, whose bureaucratic armor seemed impenetrable.[11]

Strategic planning received little attention. During the 1830s and 1840s, the War Department had attempted to build a military road parallel to what was believed to be the "permanent" Indian frontier. With garrisons situated along the road, commissary and quartermaster spending might be reduced and Indians and non-Indians separated, relegating future conflicts to the dustbins of history. But the acquisition of Oregon, Texas, and the Southwest had wrecked these plans; in the absence of any better solution, the army had lapsed into a more haphazard approach. Forts were constructed in locales that seemed in danger of Indian attack or that could provide resources for construction and habitation, but with little regard to their relationship to any larger design. As had been the case in the selection of the site for Fort Davis, convenience trumped more ethereal considerations.[12]

One historian has accurately characterized the army's perception of the wars against the Indians as a "fleeting bother," unworthy of serious intellectual attention. Henry W. Halleck's *Elements of Military Art and Science* (1846), the leading American work of its type, contained little of value to the frontier soldier fighting Indians. The two most up-to-date tactical manuals, Capt. William J. Hardee's *Infantry Tactics* (1855) and Col. Philip St. George Cooke's *Cavalry Tactics* (officially adopted in 1861), dealt with conventional warfare rather than situations encountered when fighting Indians. A West Point education offered little help. More interested in producing engineers who could also be soldiers than soldiers who knew how to fight Indians, Military Academy administrators emphasized mathematics, the sciences, and conventional warfare rather than frontier tactics and strategy. Lt. Edward L. Hartz, stationed at Fort Davis during the 1850s, reflected the general consensus. Commenting on an Oregon border dispute, Hartz noted: "A war with England . . . would open a field fraught with more scope for true military action than we can ever hope for in our police like expeditions after concealed and never-to-be met with Indians."[13]

Energetic young officers seeking to learn something of Indian fighting might have read a few pages of Colonel Cooke's *Scenes and Adventures in the Army: or, Romance of Military Life* (1857) or scanned George Catlin's *Letters and Notes on the Manners, Customs, and Conditions of the North American Indians* (1841) for information on Indian culture. And following a government-sponsored tour of the Crimean War, in 1857 Capt. George B. McClellan suggested that the army develop light cavalry designed to fight Indians. In sharp contrast to most other army intellectuals of the age, McClellan argued that the first consideration of the cavalry should be "the nature of its service against the Indians." Yet the War Department never formally adopted his report. In the absence of official guidance, officers relied on improvisation and whatever insights they happened to pick up on their own.[14]

Finding a way to supply the scattered garrisons at a reasonable expense generated considerably more official attention than did discussions of frontier tactics or strategy. Whereas in 1845 the army's annual transportation costs had been $130,000, by 1851 they exceeded $2 million, inflated largely by the need to station troops in the recently acquired territories. In a desperate effort to stem the tide of red ink, the War Department ordered western commanders to replace more expensive civilian employees with extra-duty military personnel whenever possible. Secretary of War Conrad even directed that all frontier garrisons plant gardens as a means of cutting food costs. Davis, Conrad's successor, searched for more-comprehensive solutions. Recalling visions of the Great American Desert and the permanent Indian frontier, he speculated that "a line . . . has been reached, beyond which civilization has ceased to follow in the train of advancing posts." By concentrating its manpower at selected positions along this line, the army could improve discipline, reduce expenditures, and display strength rather than weakness to the Indians. Robust columns would periodically take the field as forceful displays of the nation's power. To provide the necessary infrastructure, reduce expenses, and enable the army to shift troops about as necessary, Davis championed construction of a transcontinental railroad. A Mississippian, he made no secret of his belief that the railroad should follow a southern route.[15]

But the transcontinental railroad floundered amid the treacherous sectional seas of the 1850s, dooming any immediate hopes of consolidating small frontier posts or achieving significant cost savings. As astute observers recognized, soldiers from even the biggest posts could not be everywhere at once; an army escort could scarcely guard every community and accompany every traveler. With neither resources nor mandate to change, the army continued in its old ways. This meant more small posts to guard the San Antonio–El Paso road. Fort Lancaster was constructed near the junction of the Pecos River in 1855; Camp Hudson, sited about forty miles from present-day Del Rio, came the following year. Forts Quitman (near the Rio Grande, about seventy miles southeast of present-day El Paso) and Stockton (about sixty miles northeast of Davis) were added in 1858 and 1859, respectively, to help secure the Trans-Pecos.

Even as he fought a losing battle for his transcontinental railroad, Secretary Davis also hoped to cut costs through administrative reforms. Previously, the War Department had sectioned off the country into the Eastern,

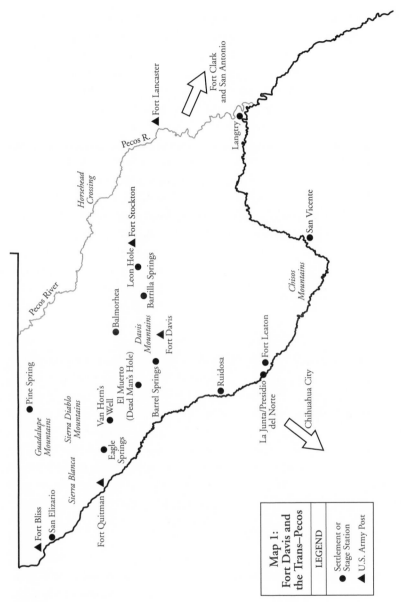

Fort Davis and the Trans-Pecos

Fort Clark
and San Antonio

Fort Lancaster

Pecos R.

Langtry

Horsehead
Crossing

San Vicente

Leon Hole ▲ Fort Stockton

Pecos River

Barrilla Springs

Balmorhea

Chisos
Mountains

Pine Spring

Davis
Mountains

Fort Davis

Guadalupe
Mountains

Van Horn's
Well

El Muerto
(Dead Man's Hole)

Fort Leaton

Ruidosa

Sierra Diablo
Mountains

Barrel Springs

La Junta/Presidio
del Norte

Chihuahua City

Eagle
Springs

Sierra Blanca

Fort Bliss

San Elizario

Fort Quitman

Map 1:
Fort Davis and
the Trans–Pecos

LEGEND

● Settlement or
   Stage Station

▲ U.S. Army Post

GERMANTOWN COMMUNITY LIBRARY
GERMANTOWN, WI 53022

Western, and Pacific divisions, with these units then subdivided into numbered departments. In 1853, it adopted a new, more streamlined scheme better designed to meet frontier realities. Departments of the East, New Mexico,
Pacific, Texas, and West now provided basic administrative structure. Goods
imported through coastal depots at Indianola, Corpus Christi, and Brazos
Santiago supplied the Department of Texas (generally including all of Texas
except Fort Bliss, which was attached to the Department of New Mexico to
ease supply difficulties). But to Davis's chagrin, these administrative adjust-
ments could not overcome geographic realities. In the mid-1850s, forage costs
alone at Fort Davis averaged nearly six thousand dollars per month. Grain
had to be imported by private contractors, who charged shipping fees of $1.70
per one hundred pounds for every one hundred miles. Wastage added to the
army's miseries. During the year ending May 1856, for example, inspectors
condemned 10 percent of the 2,000 barrels of pork, 8 percent of the 300,000
pounds of bacon, 13 percent of the 5,500 barrels of flour, and 21 percent of
the 280,000 pounds of bread delivered to posts in the Department of Texas.[16]

Efforts to resolve the crisis took an unusual twist in 1855, when Secretary Davis secured funds to import seventy camels from the Middle East to
Texas. In theory, the hardy camels would be a cheaper alternative to oxen and
mules. In July 1857, Lt. Edward F. Beale led twenty-five of the beasts through
the Trans-Pecos on a major field trial of their suitability to the American
West. The exotic caravan reached Fort Davis about sunrise on July 17. In a
dramatic understatement, Beale acknowledged that "we were kindly treated
by the officers." Indeed, they must have been, for the wondrous sight of the
camels, their Arabian handlers, and the exhausted escort surely shattered the
monotony of a West Texas summer. Another diarist probably came closer to
capturing the true spirit of the moment, noting that many expedition members returned from Fort Davis to camp in the wee hours of the night "with a
gait that denoted a slight indulgence in alcoholic stimulants" before pressing
on the following afternoon.[17]

Further tests reconfirmed the camels' extraordinary abilities. In 1859,
Lt. Edward L. Hartz and a squad from Fort Davis escorted an expedition of
camels, horses, and mules seeking to chart a more direct route to San Antonio. "The horses and mules nearly exhausted," marveled Hartz in his report,
"the camels appeared strong and vigorous." The following year, Bvt. Lt.
William H. Echols, thirty-one soldiers, several mule teams, and a camel caravan blazed a trail from Fort Davis to Presidio del Norte, then along the Rio
Grande and across country to San Carlos. The hardy camels easily out-
stripped the mules, which nearly died for want of water before limping back
to Fort Davis.[18]

Every field test demonstrated that the camels could carry larger loads and needed less water and food than oxen or mules. Yet the camels found it difficult to negotiate muddy or slippery ground, and soldiers detested the beasts' acute halitosis, bad odor, and voluminous sneezing. The army also failed to establish a breeding program, and the dromedaries lost their most powerful champion in 1857 when Davis left the War Department. Amid the growing sectional crisis, the army lost interest in the camels; they had been sold, lost, or forgotten by the time of the Civil War.[19]

The army's size and composition further inhibited its effectiveness as the nation's agent of empire. Although a million square miles had been added to the national domain during the 1840s, following the war with Mexico the army totaled just over ten thousand officers and men—about the same size as it had been in 1815. Only three of its fifteen regiments were mounted, a serious deficiency given the western terrain and the habits of many of its Indian foes. Sen. Sam Houston, longtime regular army critic from Texas, claimed that "the infantry dare not go out in any hostile manner for fear of being shot and scalped!" In his classic travelogue on antebellum Texas, Frederick Law Olmsted, who would go on to become one of the nation's leading urban planners, compared the infantry's efforts to "keeping a bulldog to chase mosquitoes." But it cost two to four times as much to equip and supply a cavalryman as his infantry counterpart, so increasing the mounted arm was always problematic.[20]

Many in the Lone Star State believed they had a ready answer to the Indian question—use the Texas Rangers instead of regulars. Claiming that such volunteers would be acquainted with the frontier environment and the habits of their Indian enemies, Texans attributed almost mythical qualities to their Rangers. "The U.S. troops don't understand the character of these Indians, nor are they acquainted with the character of the country," growled one West Texan. Rarely acknowledged was yet another advantage: controlled by the state, Rangers meant jobs, political patronage, and money for the frontier. The army vigorously counterattacked, asserting that Texans exaggerated the number and magnitude of Indian depredations and pointing out that volunteer units were much more expensive to maintain than the regulars. The ill-disciplined actions of the Rangers, according to these critics, created rather than prevented hostilities. As one regular declared, "Take one of the lowest canal drivers, dress him in ragged clothes . . . utterly eradicate any little trace of civilization or refinement that may have by chance been acquired—then turn him loose, a lazy, ruffianly scoundrel in a country where little is known of, less cared for, the laws of God or man, and you have the material for a Texan Mounted Ranger."[21]

Such jealousies made cooperation between Rangers and regulars problematic. In one incident, Maj. John S. Simonson, based at Fort Davis, was slated to lead a mixed detachment of mounted riflemen and state troops against suspected Mescalero haunts in the Guadalupe Mountains. The troubles began even before the volunteers reached Fort Davis. West of San Antonio, the drunken men of a Ranger company pillaged the unfortunate little hamlet of D'Hanis. Upon learning of the incident, Simonson promptly arrested the company's captain and eleven others. Neither the Davis-based expedition nor another column from Fort Bliss encountered any Indians; although the remaining two Ranger companies gave Simonson no trouble, the exercise had been a complete failure.[22]

Public perceptions about the regulars contrasted sharply with public expectations of the range of services they could provide. Westerners often needed more federal assistance than those in longer-occupied eastern states; in the absence of other, more specialized agencies, government officials usually turned to the thin ranks of bluecoats, who thus found themselves employed in a remarkable array of nation-building activities. Regulars explored much of the West, protected the mails, built roads, restored law and order, and offered succor to needy travelers. Arguing that a larger force was necessary to perform these diverse tasks, Pres. Millard Fillmore proclaimed manpower levels to be "entirely inadequate." Bowing somewhat to the realities of the new domain, in 1850 Congress expanded the size of companies stationed on the frontiers, allowing the army to grow to about thirteen thousand.[23]

Even so, soon after taking office, Secretary of War Davis proclaimed the army's size to be "manifestly inadequate." In order to repress Indian attacks in threatened regions, soldiers had to be transported at great expense from other forts. As troops left one area to go to another, the former point lay open to Indian attack. To make matters worse, the army rarely met its authorized force levels, with desertions, discharges, and deaths typically exceeding recruiting supplements. Detached duties further depleted the effective force. Officers were liable for service on courts-martial, boards of survey, and recruiting details; enlisted men were often used to construct and repair post facilities. Frontier garrisons, then, remained pitifully small. June 1853 figures were typical. Although the army's authorized strength was 13,821, only 10,417 soldiers were actually serving. Just over 7,000 were present at the fifty-four western posts, whose garrisons averaged only 128 men.[24]

In 1855, Congress responded to the secretary's prodding by adding two cavalry and two infantry regiments to the two dragoon, one mounted riflemen, four artillery, and eight infantry regiments already in existence. A colonel, assisted by a lieutenant colonel and two majors, commanded each regiment. Infantry and mounted regiments were divided into ten companies, each of which included a captain, a first lieutenant, and a second lieutenant. Each company boasted four sergeants and four corporals; those stationed on the frontiers could have as many as seventy-four privates. Including its allotment of one sergeant-major, one quartermaster sergeant, two chief musicians, and twenty musicians, an infantry regiment deployed in Texas could number 878 officers and enlisted men.[25]

Army personnel reflected the ambiguous nature of the antebellum society from which they had come. Personal jealousies, often fostered by unfulfilled ambitions and sectional tensions, could be tempered by notions of self-interest. Among commissioned officers, the tedium of frontier service and shared misery of uncomfortable living conditions usually encouraged a sense of group solidarity. As one astute student of the nineteenth-century army has explained, "In the closely knit society of officers, so dependent on each other's fellowship, extremes were to be avoided." But even the strongest families squabble among themselves, and the officers were no exception. "I have heard more scandal since I have been in the army than I ever heard before in my life," complained one contemporary. Sectional rivalries and bitterness over real and imagined grievances concerning favorable details and leaves of absence proved disruptive. Slow promotions and jealousies stemming from the use of brevets, which could be given for merit, gallantry, or ten years' continuous service in one rank, further exacerbated differences among officers. Brevet promotions sometimes, but by no means always, allowed the holder the authority and pay of the higher rank. Fort Davis–based James V. Bomford, for example, boasted Mexican War brevets to major and lieutenant colonel for gallantry at the battles of Contreras, Churubusco, and Molino del Rey, yet was ranked according to his regular commission—a captain. His quest for command according to his brevet status joined those of countless others in a sea of bureaucratic paperwork.[26]

Many antebellum officers seemed uncomfortable with their role as agents of western empire. Upon observing the Indians at one of the temporary Texas reservations, Bvt. Maj. Earl Van Dorn concluded: "It cannot reasonably be expected that they, as wild and as free as the eagle, would voluntarily shut themselves up in such a coop, or that they would be driven there without a violent struggle. Who would?" Almost all officers expressed contempt for the average frontiersman, and many tried to avoid service in the Lone Star State. These ambivalent views were undoubtedly influenced by their wives, who often accompanied them in their western journeys. The West seemed both a garden and a desert, an ambiguous wilderness of untold happiness and opportunity, filled with dread and evil. Wife of a lieutenant in the Regiment of Mounted Riflemen, Lydia Lane landed in Texas amid an outbreak of yellow fever. "It was dreadful news to us, as there was no escape, no running away from it, nothing to do but land, take the risk, and trust in Providence," she wrote. "I had 'gone for a soldier,' and a soldier I determined to be."[27]

In the end, the officers followed the orders of their president and their government, however distasteful some found them to be. The brutality of frontier warfare magnified the dangers. The element of surprise was crucial; upon locating an enemy, both sides usually launched an immediate attack, fearing that a more deliberate approach would allow their foes to escape. Sparing women and children from these confused melees was always inconvenient and often impossible. Traditional rules of warfare also paled in light of customary Indian treatment of prisoners. Mutilated bodies and recollections of former hostages, multiplied by storytellers and gossips and dramatized by lurid captivity narratives, provided gruesome reminders of the fate awaiting those who fell into the hands of Indians. One Fort Davis officer described his feelings this way:

> The war on this frontier is one of extermination. In the worst sense of the word these tribes are savages. They are *devils* and the coldest blood must boil at the narration of the manner in which they have treated prisoners who have fallen into their hands, not men, alone, taken with arms in their hands, for *they* can but die, but innocent women and children. Orders are now issued to the troops to take no prisoners; to spare no one; to listen to no terms for peace until the race is cowed by their punishment.

One Davis-based soldier admitted that he had been part of an expedition that had taken matters into its own hands. Burdened by a captive teenage girl who had reportedly tried to seize a pistol from one of her captors, "the men reasoned and agreed among themselves that it was better to kill this prisoner than to take the risk of having one or more of their number killed by her." She was summarily executed. "Nothing was said about it," the soldier explained.[28]

The army, many officers concluded, was caught in the middle, left to implement an inconsistent policy made by an ungrateful government against a dangerous enemy. Low pay added to their sense of martyrdom. Basic salaries were pitifully small (since 1802, for example, in infantry and artillery regiments, colonels had received $75 per month; lieutenant colonels $60; captains $40; first lieutenants $30; and second lieutenants a mere $25), but supplemental allowances for rations, servants, forage for animals, experience, and extra responsibilities could nearly treble the base pay. In fiscal year 1853, for example, Lt. Col. Washington Seawell, who would serve as commander at Fort Davis for much of the decade, netted a total of $3,497.65 (roughly $81,000 in 2004 dollars). Few junior officers, however, could take full advantage of such bonuses. For eleven months' service, Lt. Edward D. Blake, also destined for duty at the post on the Limpia, earned only $953.12 (about $22,000 in 2004 dollars). Across-the-board pay raises of $20 per month in 1855 only partially alleviated the problem.[29]

The experiences of Lt. Edward L. Hartz, a Pennsylvania native who had graduated from the U.S. Military Academy in 1855, were probably typical. Fort Davis was Hartz's first station, and the spectacular beauty of the Davis Mountains, pure water of Limpia Creek, and quaint romance of nearby prairie dog towns initially captivated the young officer. "I am heartier, healthier, happier, better contented and stronger than I have ever been in all the twenty-four years of my life," he reported in June 1856. Yet the romance of garrison life eventually lost its luster. Four years of hard service in West Texas had produced a bored, lonely bachelor with little hope of professional advancement. Falling victim to a depression common among antebellum officers, Hartz begged his father to use his political influence to secure his transfer to a station nearer "civilization." As the lieutenant reasoned, "You will only be doing what is done every day."[30]

Officers frequently bemoaned the quality of their enlisted personnel. Instead of the sturdy, native-born farming stock envisioned by War Department officials, immigrants and city dwellers dominated the ranks. An army study of the early 1850s concluded that more than 70 percent of incoming recruits were foreign-born. Ireland alone contributed nearly 43 percent of the total, with the Germanies also providing more soldiers than any single state in the Union. Many officers attributed this to the low salaries offered enlisted personnel; infantry privates, for example, received only $11 a month. "The material offered in time of peace is not of the most desirable character, consisting principally of newly arrived immigrants, of those broken down by bad habits and dissipation, the idle, and the improvident," concluded Assistant Surgeon Richard H. Coolidge.[31]

But such criticisms were probably more indicative of the class and ethnic biases of the officers than they were an accurate description of the enlisted men. Eleven dollars per month (about $256 in 2004 dollars) indeed seemed low, but the army offered a wide range of extra bonuses and emoluments. Soldiers in mounted regiments received another dollar per month. A second enlistment merited a monthly bonus of $2, with each additional five-year stint adding another dollar to the total. Those men performing extra duty as clerks, mechanics, or laborers received additional compensation, usually between twenty-five and forty cents per day. The army also offered job security, an especially compelling factor when considering that most recruiting offices were located in the competitive job markets of eastern cities. Indeed, the army had ample stocks of prospective recruits, as inspectors rejected four out of every five applicants. Instead of offering a dead-end job attractive only to the outcasts of society, the antebellum army offered a reasonable option for a newly arrived immigrant or an unskilled laborer.[32]

Even so, high rates of desertion—which had reached 16 percent annually before the pay raises of 1854—would plague the army throughout the nineteenth century. The problem was particularly acute in the West, where civilians could expect higher wages. Common laborers in Texas, for example, could expect 20 percent higher pay than the national average. At Fort Davis, the fifty dollars a month paid to civilian blacksmiths (four times the basic pay of a buck private) must have surely attracted the eye of many a skilled laborer who had joined the enlisted ranks. Even the payments of twenty dollars a month to teamsters must have made civilian life seem attractive to soldiers seeking more independence than allowed by the military.[33]

The difficulties of responding to western realities were also reflected in the army's halting efforts to feed, arm, and clothe its soldiers. Army food was ample in quantity if not quality. The daily ration, which cost the War Department between twenty and thirty cents, provided for twenty ounces of beef or twelve ounces of pork and eighteen ounces of bread or flour, twelve ounces of hard bread, or twenty ounces of cornmeal per day. Rice, peas or beans, coffee, and sugar were also part of the ration, as were vinegar, salt, tallow, and soap. To vary the diet, efficient cooks could sell excess foods to local residents and use the proceeds to purchase other items. An individual soldier could also supplement his ration through private purchases from the sutler, who paid a small fee for the privilege of running a mercantile store on post. Payday often led to a frenzied run on the sutler's delicacies. "When payday does come, you should see the life!" wrote one private. "The rations are not touched. The men live on dainties until their money is gone."[34]

In a cost-saving measure, uniforms were worn on dress parade as well as on fatigue and field duty. Although the dark blue 1851 regulation frock coats, which featured stand-up collars, shoulder epaulettes, and color-coordinated trim, facings, and piping, lent a martial demeanor, they seemed bizarrely out of place in the blazing West Texas sun. Similarly, the six-inch-tall official shako, though inspiring in its Napoleonic appearance, scarcely served the western soldier's needs. Its narrow leather visor neither shaded the eyes nor protected the neck. Official relief for the beleaguered infantry at Fort Davis finally came in 1857 and 1858, when the Quartermaster Department began issuing sky blue fatigue jackets and dark blue forage caps.[35]

Improved ordnance was also on its way, but it took time for the latest uniforms and weapons to reach western posts. Rifled weapons boasting new primers began replacing older smoothbore flintlocks. The .58 caliber Model 1855 Rifled Musket was also being phased in. For mounted troops, the army began phasing in new rifled carbines and revolvers in place of aging musketoons and single-shot pistols. But during his 1856 inspection, Col. Joseph K. F. Mansfield found that only 33 of the 442 muskets at Fort Davis had the newest primer system. Mansfield also found the six companies of Eighth Infantrymen there in possession of a grand total of three rifles and one carbine. None of the forty soldiers in Company A had the army's latest uniforms (officially adopted five years earlier!). Company C, though not in uniform, presented a "neat" appearance. Companies D and G were short of pants. Five men of Company F and thirteen in Company G had no canteens. Of the 251 men who turned out for parade, 149 did not have their official shakos. And regulations notwithstanding, frontier troops routinely shed their uniforms for more practical garb while in the field. Hunting shirts, slouched hats, and white pants supplanted the official woolens, leaving many soldiers wearing costumes more serviceable than military.[36]

The antebellum army's mixed record in supplying, equipping, and clothing its western garrisons reflected the nation's ambiguous attitude toward most things military. The army never possessed the men, horses, or equipment it believed necessary to defeat the Indians. Too, the government failed to establish a clear, effective Indian policy, an oversight that the army's lack of strategic planning only exacerbated. Although almost all non-Indians believed that they had the right, even the duty, to remove Indians from their traditional lands, logically conceived, adequately funded, and consistently applied measures that might have reduced frontier violence were neither formulated nor implemented. An essential paradox thus characterized the frontiers of Texas and much of the West. The United States wanted to settle the region with farmers of Western European stock, yet refused to fund adequately the single most important agency assisting that development—the regular army. The Eighth Infantrymen who provided the bulk of the garrison at antebellum Fort Davis thus enjoyed only the lukewarm support of their government and nation.

CHAPTER THREE

FRONTIER OUTPOST

Often-contradictory American beliefs, societal mores, and cultural practices frequently intersected at antebellum Fort Davis. The post's physical structures revealed the country's reluctance to adequately fund the most visible agent of its growing empire. At the same time, its existence reflected the nation's confidence in the righteousness of its western expansion and would serve as the genesis for a new frontier community. Its inhabitants brought with them the customs of a people who venerated liberty while simultaneously enslaving one out of every eight Americans. Immigrants manned its garrisons and served its needs but sometimes found their opportunities restricted. In sum, Fort Davis was becoming a frontier crossroads of nineteenth-century America, an intersection of nationalistic expectations, social dynamics, and western realities.

Construction of Fort Davis began in October 1854. Beautiful though the position was, Lt. Col. Washington Seawell, the first post commander, always thought it a poor choice. Echoing the sentiments of many, Seawell feared that Indians could approach unobserved and fire down into the post from the overlooking cliffs. He instead favored a less exposed position outside the mouth of the canyon. Department officials overruled Seawell's objections, however, and the first buildings went up in the shadows of the canyon walls. Like most frontier posts, Fort Davis would have no wooden palisades, its structures instead forming a rough square around an open parade ground. "There is nothing to prevent Indians or anyone else, from riding through the posts in any direction. They are built simply for quarters, and their localities for defence is [sic] seldom thought of," remembered one officer. "They are placed so as to have a level place for a parade, convenient to water & c., without any expectation that they will ever have to stand a siege."[1]

Construction reflected the nation's ambiguous attitude toward the frontier and the army. The West must be conquered, but at minimum cost to taxpayers. In accord with contemporary practice, the soldiers of the Eighth Infantry Regiment were pressed into service as carpenters, lumbermen, masons, and laborers to save the expense of hiring civilians. Chronic shortages of money and bureaucratic red tape also slowed progress. Old army hands reconciled themselves to the inevitable delays. Lt. Albert J. Myer, post surgeon at Fort Davis from January to November 1855, reported that "a man gets used to taking things cooly [*sic*] after a little service with the army." Built from locally available timber, early "jacal" structures consisted of oak and cottonwood slabs set up lengthwise about a rude frame; mud and prairie grass chinked the gaps, with even officers' quarters offering only the barest protection from the elements. Lt. Zenas R. Bliss's cramped billet, for example, was fifteen feet square and six feet high. Its canvas roof and warped walls provided an unanticipated source of ventilation, convenient until rain and snow seeped through the cracks. The first enlisted men's barracks, each fifty-six feet long by twenty feet wide, were of similar makeshift assembly, as were the guardhouse and the laundresses' quarters. A tent and a small wood shanty constituted the post hospital, and the wooden bakery was of only slightly more substantial construction. The blacksmith's shop, powder magazine, and quartermaster's storehouse were made of stone, although the latter two buildings had only canvas roofs. One passerby put it succinctly: "Davis is a poorly built fort."[2]

Reservations about the costs of securing the land upon which the post lay partially explained these ramshackle early structures. Hoping they might find cheaper land elsewhere, department officials considered relocating the fort to a site between Leon Hole and Eagle Springs. But the garrison was bulging; with eight officers and 397 enlisted men by June 1856, Fort Davis stood among the army's biggest western posts (the largest that year, Fort Riley, Kansas, boasted 529 men). In late August, Capt. Arthur T. Lee, temporarily commanding the post during Seawell's absence, seized the opportunity to request "permission to erect such structures as will protect the comd. [command] during the approaching winter." Reminding Lee "of the contemplated removal of the post," Bvt. Capt. Don Carlos Buell, the department's assistant adjutant general, allowed that only the "absolute want of shelter" could justify new construction.[3]

Buell's protests notwithstanding, soldier-laborers at the post on the Limpia threw themselves into their work with a vengeance, relying on locally available resources for almost all their materials. In January 1857, in what signaled a tacit approval of Lee's expansion program, departmental headquarters promised to give "favorable consideration" to a new hospital. That same month, Lee reported that six stone barracks for enlisted men had replaced the old jacales. Located near the rocky cliffs overlooking the right side of the canyon, the barracks, each sixty feet by twenty feet, had thatched roofs, flagged stone floors, and thick limestone walls. The commanding officer now occupied a fine frame house, with two rooms and two glazed windows. The powder magazine, blacksmith's shop, and bakery all had stone walls. But federal officials rejected department commander Bvt. Maj. Gen. David E. Twiggs's effort to secure an extra ten thousand dollars for permanent facilities at Davis; the lack of additional monies, combined with the absence of any master plan, rendered the new construction program incomplete. Thirteen rundown shanties, each sixteen feet by fourteen feet, housed the married enlisted men and their families, and the quartermaster's storehouses still had canvas roofs. The green wood used to build the seven sets of officers' quarters along the left side of the canyon had warped. "The condition of all of them is bad," concluded the regimental quartermaster. "They are altogether uncomfortable and insufficient quarters."[4]

The new building program had begun amid a continuing feud between Lieutenant Colonel Seawell and Captain Lee. In December 1854, Seawell had brought court-martial charges against Lee, an eighteen-year veteran who dabbled in art, history, music, and engineering. The captain responded with three formal complaints of his own, the third timed to coincide with his request to expand the buildings at Fort Davis. Seawell returned the favor with another charge against his subordinate, this time insisting that the matter be forwarded to Washington. Reluctantly, department commander Twiggs did so, but with the sensible endorsement that "the interests of the service do not require a court martial to investigate the enclosed charges." Wisely turning a blind eye to the bickering, War Department officials took no action.[5]

Though often feuding with each other, officers drew a strict line between themselves and their enlisted men. As Lieutenant Hartz explained, "We have no society apart from the officers." Army hierarchy and social custom demanded it. Indeed, the gulf between officers' row and the enlisted barracks was much wider than the steps it took to cross the parade ground. Most officers took little interest in routine military drill, leaving such matters to their sergeants. Whereas commissioned personnel liked to enjoy a drink in the genteel surroundings of sutler Alexander Young's shop on post, enlisted men favored the unofficial saloons outside the military reservation. Enlisted men seemed to accept this social stratification, ostracizing their comrades who acted as servants for their officers, derisively referring to such men as "strikers" or "dogrobbers." Zealously guarding their own prerogatives, sergeants meted out informal punishment to enlisted transgressors. "The training and

Lt. Col. Washington Seawell, a veteran of the Second Seminole War, commanded Fort Davis for most of the 1850s. He was awarded a brevet brigadier generalship in 1865. Courtesy Library of Congress.

discipline of the companies are left in their hands entirely and they are held strictly accountable for the conduct of their men," recalled one sergeant.[6]

As they did at all western posts, officers at Fort Davis spent most of their time in a world of their own. Jealousies and infighting existed within that society, but most understood that it was in their best interest to limit their squabbles to recognized boundaries. They had too much in common with one another not to do so. Eighty percent of the commissioned officers stationed at Fort Davis before the Civil War were West Point graduates, a figure closely approximating that for the army as a whole. Mexican War veterans undoubtedly felt a similar unity—at least ten officers at Fort Davis during the 1850s had served in the conflict. The tedium of frontier service, shared misery of uncomfortable living conditions, and unceasing struggle for respect from a nation that rarely recognized their military endeavors also fostered class solidarity. In a public demonstration of collective action in October 1855, nine Fort Davis officers petitioned Congress for financial relief. Noting "the total inadequacy of our present pay to our respectable support," they called for a daily increase of twenty cents in the commutation of each officer's ration.[7]

Commissioned personnel employed a variety of slaves, servants, and enlisted men. At Fort Davis, Assistant Surgeon DeWitt C. Peters and his wife owned the only slave enumerated in the census of 1860, a twenty-four-year-old woman who lived in the detached kitchen behind their quarters. Officers also hired men from the ranks to act as their servants. Cooking, cleaning, cutting firewood, and performing other routine tasks, they greatly eased the labors and responsibilities of those who could afford such assistance. The practice was not without some risk, as Lieutenants Edward L. Hartz and John G. Taylor discovered when they hired Privates Walter Scott and Samuel Thompson. In May 1856, the lieutenants found that their former workers had disappeared, along with the officers' clothes and firearms. One of the criminals was apprehended still lurking about the post; the other was tracked down at Presidio. Fortunately for Hartz and Taylor, most of the stolen goods were recovered.[8]

Some officers brought their wives, who, like their husbands, thought of themselves as superior to the enlisted men, laundresses, and civilian laborers. Although the vigorous efforts of antebellum spokespersons for expanded rights and roles for women must not be forgotten, most middle-class women of the period conceived of a broadly defined ideology of domesticity in which their primary responsibilities lay with homemaking and the family. Popular culture and social controls reinforced traditional norms distinguishing the spheres of men from those of women. Men, held to be stronger and more capable of practical decision making, worked outside the home and provided public leadership; women, believed to be more virtuous, dominated domestic affairs and set society's moral guidelines.[9]

Children and a vast menagerie of animals frolicked about the area. Frontier parenting was, however, fraught with tragedies. Captain Lee's infant child died en route to Fort Davis. Lieutenant Colonel Seawell also experienced the trials of fatherhood. From 1848 to 1853, he sent three of his sons to a private school in Shelbyville, Kentucky, but tuition and board consumed nearly half of his regular salary. Unwilling to continue the uneven struggle, Seawell brought two of his children to the post on the Limpia. There, a fellow officer frowned upon his lax parental discipline, complaining that the commander "is rather too indulgent & makes these children his equals."[10]

Enlisted personnel at Fort Davis were a remarkably cosmopolitan lot. Nearly 90 percent of the ninety-five enlisted men present during the census taker's 1860 visit had been born outside the United States. As was the case for the army as a whole, Ireland (42 percent) and the Germanies (26 percent) contributed the most garrison members. New York, with four native sons at Fort Davis, provided more soldiers than any other state in the union. Their average age was roughly twenty-five; despite official minimum age requirements, Thomas Ryan of New York listed his age as fourteen. John Flourly (England) and Peter John (Switzerland), each aged forty, shared the distinction of being the oldest enlisted men present. Nineteen soldiers owned property; although most valued their personal estates to be worth between fifty dollars and three hundred dollars each, the hospital steward claimed one thousand dollars. Seventeen property holders were foreign-born. Six of those living in the barracks listed their occupation as farmer (or gardener); shoemakers, clerks, musicians, laborers, and blacksmiths added to the list. A baker, a chandler, an apothecary, a stonecutter, a student, a seaman, a painter, a plasterer, two carpenters, and a butcher rounded out the occupational register, with the rest simply referred to as soldiers.[11]

Fort Davis recruits had come from the infantry's "school of instruction" at Governors Island, New York. Theoretically, the new soldiers received the rudiments of military instruction here; in practice, enlisted personnel were dispatched to their units without even the most basic of training. Large recruiting classes bound for West Texas were dispatched in 1854, 1855, and 1860. The three-week sea voyage from New York to Texas sorely tested those officers assigned the thankless task of shepherding the rabble to their appointed destinations. Lieutenant Bliss, destined to serve at Fort Davis both before and after the Civil War, admitted that his efforts to distribute rations on board during the 1854 journey met "with very poor success." Bliss continued, "As the barrel of pork was opened, someone gave a push and they all piled on top of the pork and in a minute it was gone. I finally got it issued, but I am not quite sure that it was a very equitable division." Fires, fistfights, and a near riot between soldiers and ship's crew added to the lieutenant's "rough experiences." Upon landing near Corpus Christi, the men promptly got drunk on bootleg whiskey. Desertion rates soared as Bliss and other officers herded the mob to San Antonio before embarking on the final march to destinations in western Texas and New Mexico.[12]

Harsh, often capricious discipline awaited the new arrivals. The informal punishment dispensed by company sergeants prevented small-time offenders from having their records smeared by petty crimes. But if abused, the unregulated disciplinary process could result in cruel and arbitrary treatment of enlisted personnel. Officially, a garrison court of three officers handled minor cases. General courts, with between five and thirteen officers, considered more serious crimes and all trials involving commissioned personnel. Punishment varied wildly. Absence from drill might result in a five-dollar fine. One soldier found guilty of leaving his post while on guard duty was, because of his "previous good character," given what the court considered a lenient punishment: a nine-dollar fine and three months of hard labor. Pvt. William Gould forfeited eighteen dollars of his pay and was confined to hard labor for two months for falling asleep while on guard duty. For a similar offense, a different court fined Pvt. William Morris fifty dollars and sentenced him to carry a twenty-four-pound pack around the post once every three hours from reveille to retreat for a month. Offenses often involved the abuse of alcohol, which local purveyors happily supplied in ample quantities. As one officer recognized, "Men that will get drunk, can get drunk." In March 1857, a court found Company F's Pvt. Peter Fay guilty of being drunk on guard duty. It sentenced him to forfeit his pay for the next two months and put him on bread and water for ten days. Two years later, Fay, now in Company D, committed the same offense. This time the punishment involved six months of hard labor in the guardhouse; for two weeks of each alternate month, he was placed in solitary confinement on a diet of bread and water.[13]

Some soldiers were reluctant to inflict the punishment assessed by their officers. As officer of the day, Lieutenant Hartz once ordered that the hapless Private Gould be whipped. In rapid succession, five men refused to lash Gould to Hartz's satisfaction. One of the men accused of insufficient zeal was the semiliterate Pvt. Lewis D. Brooks, who explained that "i was detailed to flog a man witch [sic] i did it seems not quit [sic] hard enuf witch [sic] god knows i have floged [sic] others the same and nothing was said to me. . . . god knows i did not intend to fail to do my duty." Hartz would have none of that. "Humanity is a commendable virtue," he wrote, "but must give way to the voice of law and the ends of justice." The reluctant castigators were each fined seventy dollars.[14]

Those not on labor details or in the guardhouse carved out a daily routine that would have been familiar to virtually every soldier of the West. Reveille sounded at daybreak, rousting the enlisted men for early-morning roll call. Drill started half an hour later. Coffee, bacon, bread, and molasses were served at the enlisted men's mess halls at seven A.M., followed by the daily guard mounting. Officers of the day then began their appointed rounds and relieved the old guard of its duties, an event that highlighted the average day. "We listen & watch this important measure," wrote one melodramatic observer, "for here on hangs our safety from the visitations of Indians who surround us in hordes." Inspection of company barracks began at nine o'clock. Most officers then returned to their quarters, where they slept, read, wrote, or played cards until the afternoon. The officer of the day oversaw the garrison's routine duties, policing the grounds, mounting sentinels, and supervising guardhouse activities. Officers were also liable for service on courts-martial and boards of survey and examination, which performed a thousand mundane tasks essential to the post's good order. Following time-honored tradition, junior officers invariably found themselves appointed secretaries of such boards. For the enlisted men, selection to the guard meant closely supervised duty yet merited minor privileges such as early meals and the chance to skip drills. Fatigue details, especially in the early years, were also burdensome. Other soldiers tilled the post garden, a by-product of Secretary of War Charles Conrad's cost-cutting measures of the early 1850s.[15]

Lunch call relieved fatigue parties about noon, when soldiers sat down to the day's major meal, a hearty portion of beef, whatever vegetable or starch was available, bread, and the ever-present coffee. Ill-equipped cooks, drawn from the ranks with no special training, hampered all efforts to improve the diet. The ersatz chefs at Fort Davis found baking bread, an essential element of the regulation diet, especially mysterious. Fortunately, soldier-farmers garnered bumper harvests from the post garden. Spearheaded by Bvt. Maj. Larkin Smith, who managed to wrangle a shipment of experimental seeds from Washington, the men cultivated cabbages, celery, and sugarcane. Corn, beans, and fruits imported from Mexico afforded the garrison another means of diversifying the daily fare. Hunting and fishing offered additional variety, although the threat of Indian attack limited all but the largest parties to the immediate vicinity of Fort Davis.[16]

Fatigue call reassembled the work parties about one o'clock. Two hours later, company and battalion drill began. Retreat sounded at sunset, followed by a light supper of warmed-over beef, bread, and coffee for the enlisted men. As always, officers supplied their own rations and ate in their own quarters separate from the enlisted men, combining their resources to form mess pools. Tattoo ended the day about eight thirty. On Sundays, dress parades gave the fort an unusually martial appearance.[17]

Military exercises at antebellum Fort Davis were much better than those at the typical frontier post, whose garrisons often went months without such training. In 1856, Inspector Mansfield complimented the six companies in garrison for having displayed a "handsome" battalion drill and a smoothly executed skirmishing maneuver. The garrison's marksmanship was especially impressive in an army whose soldiers were more accustomed to swinging an ax or hammering a nail than aligning a gun's sights; 20 percent of the men of every company at Davis had hit a target one hundred yards away with at least one of two shots. Three years later, Lt. Col. Joseph E. Johnston was similarly impressed. Although now only 107 strong, Fort Davis's garrison and commander had continued their exemplary habits:

> The appearance of the company under arms was very handsome—the men strong, healthy & well "set up"—the arms, accoutrements & clothing in excellent order—their movements accurate & ready both as infantry of the line & skirmishers—their progress in the bayonet exercise handsome—& from the record of their target practice, the improvement in that respect decided. I have great satisfaction in finding a commanding officer who appreciates the importance of military exercises. . . . There is more evidence of attention to discipline & instruction at this than at any other post I have inspected.[18]

Off duty, some reveled in the remote post's isolation, whereas others found the loneliness almost overwhelming. "We had no amusements outside of the Post but what we could invent with our limited means," explained Lieutenant Bliss, "and had to resort to almost every device to kill time." Mail was always welcome, and readers hungrily exchanged newspapers and magazines from back east. Enterprising enlisted men built a horse-racing track, a theater, a library, a reading room, and a bowling alley. Fortunately, the Eighth Infantry's regimental band was also stationed at Fort Davis. Officers occasionally assumed religious responsibilities before makeshift congregations as their beliefs permitted. To break the monotony, three officers organized "a flying trip to Mexico" in early 1858. Commissioned personnel also enjoyed a rudimentary billiards table in the sutler's back room. "We can surely amuse ourselves with such opportunities," proclaimed one satisfied surgeon.[19]

With a garrison with assigned strength averaging fourteen officers and 242 enlisted men between 1854 and 1861 (see appendix 1), Fort Davis also brought rudimentary law and order, government jobs, federal contracts, and service-related employment to the Trans-Pecos. Presidio County had officially been created in 1850, but the region's sparse civilian population led the state to attach it to El Paso County for judicial purposes. With law enforcement virtually nonexistent, civilians turned to army officers to settle disputes. Frontier entrepreneurs, attracted by the promise of providing services to a garrison that generated about fifty-five thousand dollars per year in salaries (nearly $1.2 million in 2004 dollars), also relocated to Fort Davis. Post officials usually hired a guide, and blacksmiths and teamsters occasionally found temporary employment. The local mail and stage station promised additional income. And although the army imported most of the supplies for the garrison from outside contractors, West Texas businessmen often secured small contracts for beef, corn, hay, and wood.[20]

Clearly, there was money to be made at the post on the Limpia, with Alexander Young, a Pennsylvania native who held the Fort Davis sutlership from 1855 through the onset of the Civil War, leading the way. Attempting to ensure that soldiers had some of society's amenities, the army allowed regimental and post commanders to permit selected individuals to serve as sutlers, regulated by boards of officers, on army posts. Paying a monthly tax of five cents per man to the post fund for the official recognition, the enterprising Young also secured contracts for supplying the Davis garrison with wood, hay, and corn; picked up the sutlership at Fort Quitman in 1860; and acted as an erstwhile banker between the army paymaster's infrequent visits. Although one critic charged that Young hawked his wares "at enormous prices," an army inspector reported that he kept his store "well supplied with all the requisites for the troops & gives satisfaction." Whatever his ethics, by 1860 he was easily the wealthiest man in the Fort Davis community, valuing his estate at twenty-eight thousand dollars.[21]

Laundresses and hospital matrons, who joined the sutler in enjoying official military status, also did quite well at antebellum Fort Davis. Company commanders appointed and dismissed the laundresses, who charged fees set by local councils. In 1856, no less than fifteen laundresses resided at the fort; reflecting the decline in the number of troops present, by October 1860 only six such workers remained, living in flimsy jacal structures officially referred to as married men's quarters. Some may have supplemented their incomes by prostitution, a practice tolerated, if not officially sanctioned, by the military. By 1860, these women who resided on post were quite prosperous. The hospital matron, identified only as "M. Kelly," was a native of Puerto Rico who had assembled an estate of $1,500 (nearly $35,000 in 2004 dollars), fully one-third larger than that of the hospital steward listed in the same household. Similarly, the six laundresses declared estates averaging just over $880 each. Mary Powell claimed $1,800, which made her, at least according to the census, the second-wealthiest person at Davis. Six children lived with the laundresses, four having been born in Texas. Five of the six laundresses on post seem to have been married (four to soldiers). Despite policy that frowned upon such unions, strong economic incentives were present, as a laundress drew another government ration along with the income from her washing. The only Hispanic laundress there lived with her husband in a shack behind commander Seawell's home, acting as maid and servant for the post commander and his two children.[22]

A sensational incident involving a laundress fueled camp gossip in July 1857, when Pvt. Edward Eagan declared to laundress Jane McDermott his determination "to get some woman to sleep with." Several days later, Eagan returned to her quarters brandishing a butcher knife and threatening to kill Jane's husband, Pvt. James McDermott, so as to "have the pleasure of sleeping with you yet." Upon learning of this, McDermott grabbed a pistol and tracked down Eagan just outside the camp theater. The two exchanged insults; after McDermott fired a shot into the air, his adversary charged him with his knife. McDermott then shot and killed his tormenter. A good soldier before the incident, he was thrown into the guardhouse for ten months until a garrison court-martial convened. The court found McDermott guilty of having shot Eagan but attached no criminality because of the extenuating circumstances. However, it went on to assess the hapless McDermott a thirty-dollar fine and six months of hard labor for having illegally discharged a firearm on the post. The long-suffering private protested the penalties, noting his "suffering . . . at having his wife alone during that time without a protector." On the advice of the court, Fort Davis authorities later remitted McDermott's sentence.[23]

By 1860, two communities—Wild Rose Pass and Las Limpias—had developed near Fort Davis (see appendix 2). The former, a bustling settlement serving the overland trail, had a population of forty-nine, which defied stereotypical characterizations of Anglo dominance of mid-nineteenth century Texas. Nineteen residents had been born in Mexico, two in Ireland, and one in Saxony. Twenty-three were natives of slave states (including a colony of ten from Arkansas), but only four hailed from states north of the Mason-Dixon line. Most of the hamlet's eleven dwellings housed a station keeper, cook, and hostler. Housing patterns reflected a degree of racial and ethnic integration. Six households each had a single Hispanic cook; all of the residents of three other houses were white. But the two wealthiest households were those headed by Gregario (aged sixty) and Lauriano (aged thirty) Carrasco. A farmer, Gregario Carrasco boasted an estate of more than $2,100 (roughly $49,000 in 2004 dollars); Lauriano, a laborer and presumably Gregario's son, had another $700. All members of the two Carrasco households listed Mexico as their birthplaces. By contrast, the wealthiest white man in Wild Rose Pass was an Irish station keeper, James Frances, who claimed $500. At Wild Rose Pass, at least, the most successful Mexican immigrants had outpaced their European rivals.[24]

Las Limpias nestled closer to the fort, its 116 residents including forty-four women and thirty-five children. Employment at Las Limpias centered upon serving the military garrison's various needs—the census enumerator logged seventeen laborers, thirteen laundresses, eleven servants or housekeepers, eight seamstresses, five cooks, three tailors, a merchant, a grocer, a clerk, two bookkeepers, a printer, a guide, a carpenter, and a sutler. Seven others were associated with the overland stage and transport service. Three farmers, a farmhand, three herders, and a miner rounded out the occupation list. Ninety-three residents of Las Limpias had been born in Mexico; seven children, including three of Mexican descent, were born in Texas. Foreign-born included four from Ireland, three from Germany, one from Belgium, and one from France. Indiana, New Jersey, New York, Massachusetts, and Pennsylvania were also represented among the community's inhabitants. Everyone seemed to have come recently to Las Limpias, drawn by the military post's employment opportunities, relative security from Indian attacks, and the transport business.[25]

Racial stratification characterized housing patterns and society at Las Limpias. Of the village's thirty-seven households, two were all white and thirty entirely Hispanic. Only one interracial marriage—that of Belgian native, Dietrick Dutchover, to a Mexican national, Refugia—was evident from the census records of 1860. And whereas Hispanics at Wild Rose Pass were wealthier than their white counterparts, the reverse was true at Las Limpias. Thanks largely to the four wealthiest inhabitants—Pennsylvania-born sutler Alexander Young ($28,000), Irish-born merchants Daniel Murphy ($11,500) and Patrick Murphy ($6,000), and the aforementioned Dutchover ($5,900)—the fifteen whites claiming property there averaged more than $3,500 per person in 1860. By contrast, the twenty-six Hispanics listing property averaged only $111, with the wealthiest being farmer Victoriano Hernandez ($600) and carpenter Adolfo Anver ($550). Indian attacks had driven away another prosperous settler, Manuel Musquiz, from his ranch six miles from the post.[26]

Outside the little settlement at Wild Rose Pass, frontier opportunities in this corner of the Trans-Pecos favored whites. None of the army's ante-bellum contractors for Fort Davis had a Hispanic surname. The state identi-fied the original claimant to the Fort Davis site as one A. S. Lewis, with no apparent recognition of the previous claims of José Ronquillo's heirs. By 1854, John James, a prominent West Texas surveyor, land agent, and specu-lator, had secured control and leased the 640-acre tract to the government for twenty years at three hundred dollars per annum. James also successfully sued to secure his claim to the post timber lease, a suit that eventually re-sulted in the government compensating him an additional one thousand dol-lars for improperly cutting timber there. Fearing personal liability for their roles in having drawn up the original timber contract, the four officers in-volved (including Seawell and Lee, who presumably managed to set their per-sonal differences aside in the face of this external threat) hired their own legal counsel. Fortunately for the beleaguered officers, the government eventually agreed to cover the costs of James's reimbursement and the court costs.[27]

Much like antebellum American society as a whole, the outpost of Fort Davis thus represented a contradictory mix of egalitarianism and inequality, opportunity and disappointment, racial segregation and ethnic diversity, and hierarchy and social mobility. A diverse civilian population had come to the post on the Limpia. The promise of government jobs and contracts, as well as the opportunity to capitalize on the steady incomes of garrison members, seemed especially attractive in light of the added security promised by the army's presence. Successful Mexican, American, and European-born entre-preneurs had all benefited from these advantages. Individual initiative had been a key factor in the growth of the Fort Davis community; rarely ex-pressed, but always understood, had been the federal government's indis-pensable role in stimulating frontier development.

CHAPTER FOUR

IMPLEMENTATION OF EMPIRE

he task of conquering the Trans-Pecos rested with the U.S. Army, and Fort Davis had become a focus of operations against Indians even before it officially opened. In late September 1854, Bvt. Maj. Gen. Persifor F. Smith had left El Paso en route to selecting the site for the new post on Limpia Creek. Smith's command included a hundred members of the Regiment of Mounted Riflemen, a mountain howitzer, and a dozen handlers. Upon reaching Eagle Springs, about 120 miles east of El Paso, the party encountered a group of immigrants herding cattle to California, who reported that Mescalero and Lipan Apaches had recently stolen a number of their stock. On October 1, Smith dispatched Capt. John G. Walker and forty-two Mounted Riflemen after the marauders. Four civilians accompanied Walker's regulars.[1]

A Missourian, Walker had been appointed an officer in 1846 and brevetted for gallantry during the Mexican War. Second in command was Lt. Eugene A. Carr, who would later be awarded the Medal of Honor for his Civil War heroism at the Battle of Pea Ridge, Arkansas. Fortunately, one of the Mexican civilians, José Policarpo ("Polly") Rodriguez, was an experienced tracker. After a day and a half's march of seventy miles, Walker's troops spotted two Indians. Captain Walker split his remaining forces with Lieutenant Carr. Racing ahead, Carr's section stumbled into the middle of an Apache encampment of sixty to seventy lodges. Suddenly, an unseen party of Indians swept out of a protected gorge and fell upon Carr's platoon. Walker's arrival with the rest of the command drove away the Indians after a sharp, confused fight. "The sides of the mountains were literally covered with mounted and dismounted warriors," Walker recalled, "and with the women and children escaping from the village near which we were." But as the soldiers began destroying the camp lodges and food supplies, the Indians re-formed and began raining down arrows from the surrounding heights. Prudence seeming the better part of valor, the captain withdrew. Lieutenant Carr had been severely wounded; the guide, Polly Rodriguez, had taken an arrow wound just above his hip, and a hail of arrows had killed a private. Walker estimated Indian losses at six or seven killed and double that number injured.

Seeking professional attention for Carr's wound, Walker broke off the pursuit and on October 5 rejoined General Smith, seven miles west of Dead Man's Hole. Walker praised his entire command: Carr's gallant conduct had been "worthy of his profession"; the soldiers had eaten hardtack for three days "without a murmur of discontent." Guide Rodriguez earned recognition for his "good service as a trailer and as a good rifle shot in the fight." Smith agreed with this assessment; noting that several arrows had left the captain's shirt in tatters, he added that Walker's "spirited action there is highly to his credit and that of his command."

A flurry of operations in western Texas and eastern New Mexico followed the Walker fight. Majors John S. Simonson and James Longstreet scoured the Trans-Pecos that winter. They found good water sources in the Guadalupe Mountains and at Pine Spring, 125 miles northwest of Fort Davis, but failed to locate any Indians. Perhaps the leadership had been uninspired. Although Longstreet later became one of Robert E. Lee's ablest corps commanders during the Civil War, the aging Simonson, a veteran of the War of 1812 and once described as "a simple, but kind old fellow . . . deficient in reason, cramped in his understanding, and warped in his judgment," was long past his prime. The presence of several companies of mounted Texas volunteers had undoubtedly added to the beleaguered old officer's predicament.[2]

Meanwhile, columns led by Capt. Richard S. Ewell and Lt. Samuel D. Sturgis combed southeastern New Mexico. In a series of running battles in the Sacramento Mountains that winter, Ewell's command, including twenty-nine dragoons and fifty infantry, killed fifteen Mescaleros and destroyed an Indian village. Yet they had not inflicted a crushing blow. Exhausted by the terrain and the winter season, Ewell's troops limped back to the cover of the federal forts in New Mexico. The lack of forage had hit the dragoon horses particularly hard. "The infantry were of valuable service," Ewell concluded, "and towards the end of the campaign were able to outmarch the dragoons." On January 19, 1855, Lieutenant Sturgis struck another party of Mescaleros 175 miles southeast of Santa Fe. The bitter cold making it difficult for his men to reload their firearms, Sturgis ordered a saber charge. He and three of his men were wounded, one mortally; three Indians were killed and four others wounded. That April, the regulars established Fort Stanton in the heart of Mescalero country.[3]

Bvt. Maj. Gen. Persifor F. Smith, commander of the Department of Texas from 1853 to 1856, picked out the original site for Fort Davis. Courtesy Fort Davis National Historic Site.

As the recent campaigns had demonstrated, qualified scouts were essential to any successful patrol. Although one army bureaucrat, safely ensconced at San Antonio, sniffed that "but little importance" should be attached to the guides, frontier veterans knew better. "The necessity of a few such men on every scout among Indians cannot be too highly estimated," wrote one officer. The respected guide for Walker's 1854 expedition, Polly Rodriguez, continued to work for the army until the outbreak of the Civil War, after which he eventually converted to Methodism and became a lay preacher. At Fort Davis, the army frequently paid guides Jesus Aguilera, Sam Cherry, and José Maria Bill thirty dollars a month.[4]

Even with experienced scouts, the prospect of chasing mounted Indians through the Trans-Pecos with the infantrymen who garrisoned Fort Davis scarcely inspired optimism. "Infantry on foot after Indians on horseback," muttered one soldier in assessing an infantry detachment's attempt to track down horse thieves. "They were near enough, at one time, to fire and they did so, injuring, they say, two warriors, very badly, but after a long race in a broiling sun they came back utterly exhausted and the sixty horses were thenceforth missing." Even so, the lack of mounts should not in itself have doomed the efforts of the command at Fort Davis. Feeding the army's grain-fed horses always posed enormous logistical challenges. Winter offered special opportunities for infantry columns willing to dare nature's wrath, for without forage, Indian ponies lost their endurance and speed. As Captain Ewell had discovered during his 1855 winter campaign in the mountains of New Mexico, energetically led foot soldiers could penetrate the securest Indian haunts even as cavalry mounts wore out.[5]

Natural, logistical, and geopolitical hazards did more than the lack of horses to confound the efforts of the foot soldiers at Fort Davis. The terrain was ideally suited to Indian tactics, honed by wisdom gleaned over several generations. Watering holes, isolated campgrounds, and rocky outcroppings of the Guadalupe, Davis, Chisos, Glass, Sierra Diablo, and Sierra Blanca mountains offered countless opportunities for ambush. Shortages of water and the intense summer heat compounded everything. Enormous distances—it was three hundred miles from the Pecos River to El Paso—posed another fearsome difficulty. An officer in the field thus faced a cruel logistical dilemma. Should he take enough stores to provide for a long campaign through the vast Trans-Pecos, in the process reducing his command's speed? Or should he strip his men of all but the barest essentials in hopes of gaining more mobility, thus risking starvation or dehydration?[6]

Geopolitical constraints also rendered irrelevant what was usually the army's most effective tactical maneuver during its long wars against American Indians—the surprise strike directly against their homes and villages. Just as Indians often ambushed unwitting travelers, so could the bluecoats catch Indians unaware, forcing their enemies to protect loved ones rather than to adopt their more favored choice of fleeing to fight another day. But such was rarely the case in the Trans-Pecos, for the Comanches, Lipans, and Mescaleros who operated there usually kept their dependents in Mexico or on reservations elsewhere, far from the probes of U.S. troops garrisoned in the immediate vicinity. International rivalries prevented joint U.S.-Mexico campaigns against the Indians during the 1850s; similarly, political pressures between the Indian Bureau and the army normally kept the troops stationed in the Trans-Pecos from striking reservations in the United States. Free of the burden of protecting their wives, children, and elderly, the Indians of far western Texas thus became an even more formidable threat.

Popular culture and pseudoscientific claims of Indian inferiority gave Americans a subhuman villain to whom they attributed all of their problems. Murders, raids, thefts, and unexplained incidents were invariably attributed to Indians. Potential federal compensation to victims of Indian depredations also encouraged such tendencies. As Lieutenant Bliss put it, "The Indians were so many, and killed so many people on the road, that whenever a murder was committed, the perpetrators always endeavored to leave the impression that it was done by the Indians." Not surprisingly, inexperienced soldiers found it difficult to distinguish between real signs of Indians and other sounds. All too often, jittery young watchmen unnecessarily rousted troops from their slumber. Frontiersman Edward Beale summed up what must have been a popular sentiment among veterans of one too many unwarranted alarms. "This evening many of our party have seen Indians, but for me, 'Ah! sinner that I am, I was not permitted to witness so glorious a sight,'" he wrote. "I encourage the young men, however, in the belief that deer, bushes, &c., which they have mistaken for Indians, are all veritable Comanches, as it makes them watchful on guard at night."[7]

Large, properly equipped, and carefully led parties had little to fear from Indian sorties, but overconfident or inexperienced groups could pay for their lack of wariness with their lives, even within the immediate vicinity of Fort Davis. In one such incident shortly after the post had been established, guide Sam Cherry and a four-man escort set out in search of lumber suitable for building. A twelve-year-old drummer boy also slipped away to join the fun. Indians ambushed the party near Wild Rose Pass. The four soldiers died fighting; Cherry, apparently suspecting a trap, had spurred his mount and raced past the warriors. His horse stumbled and fell, however, pinning the guide beneath it. After a brief struggle, Cherry shot himself to avoid capture. The next day, a detachment from the fort found the mutilated bodies of the missing wood party. The Indians captured and later killed the little drummer boy.[8]

The army did achieve occasional successes. On July 22, 1855, Lt. Horace Randal, just a year out of West Point, spotted signs of Indians near Eagle Springs while leading a patrol of twenty Mounted Riflemen. Raised in East Texas, Randal was no scholar, having been delayed for a year because of poor grades before graduating next to the bottom of his Military Academy class of forty-six. But the Eighth Infantry officer knew how to fight. Leaving six men to guard the horses, Randal posted seven men in the canyon's mouth and led the remaining seven soldiers around to the rear entrance. His own small command drove fifteen surprised Indians into the waiting party at the opposite end of the canyon. Eight Indians, including four women, fell dead; two others were mortally wounded. Two of the remainder jumped off a sixty-foot precipice, presumably to their deaths, and the soldiers captured a young boy. Only two Indians escaped. Having earned his combat spurs, Randal, who scalped one body, secured a much-coveted transfer to the Second Dragoon Regiment the following year.[9]

But things rarely went so well for the regulars at Fort Davis. In one embarrassing incident, half a dozen Mescaleros almost made off with the horses of four companies of the Regiment of Mounted Riflemen temporarily stabled there. The attacks were particularly bad in 1856. In April, Indians drove off the post sutler's livestock. Two months later, raiders seized several head of the post's cattle herd, grazing just a quarter of a mile from the post. Pursuit teams rarely caught the marauders. In a typical incident, a mule-mounted chase team led by Lieutenant Bliss went three days without water. The report summarizing Bliss's effort explained matter-of-factly that "of course [he] could keep on their trail, but after following them 200 miles he had to strike El Paso almost starved."[10]

Determined to end such assaults, Department of Texas officials ordered Capt. Robert Maclay to take seventy-five men, "as lightly equipped as possible," to follow the heavily used path between the Horsehead Crossing of the Pecos River and the Rio Grande. Carrying twenty days' rations, the column should "attack any Indians it may meet," then locate a good site for a new post on the Rio Grande. Assigned to map the expedition's movements, Lieutenant Hartz took news of the pending campaign philosophically. "I shall probably be absent a month or so and have some rough times," he wrote his father. "But as I am paid for seeing rough times as well as easy ones I am bound to 'put up' with the roughness and atone for it by making the most of my ease when it presents itself." The results were meager. From mid-December 1856 to mid-January 1857, the Maclay scout combed the region but found neither Indians nor a good site for a new post on the Rio Grande. As had earlier patrols, the group found the terrain foreboding and available resources limited.[11]

Other obligations frequently stymied the army's efforts to concentrate enough troops to seize the initiative against the Indians of the Trans-Pecos. The army often purchased supplies in Chihuahua; furthermore, it had some responsibility to protect U.S. citizens south of the border. Yet the unsettled nature of Mexico's internal affairs strained U.S. relations with its southern neighbor and precluded effective international cooperation. Department commander Smith complained that Mexican bandits crossed into the United States "to murder and rob," then "carry back their booty for sale in sight of our frontier." Thus, detachments from Fort Davis patrolled the road to Presidio during the 1850s, foreshadowing what would eventually become one of the garrison's major duties. But these efforts depleted the garrison's resources.[12]

Davis-based troops also supported attempts to locate underground water supplies in the Pecos River valley. In fall 1857, the luckless Lieutenant Hartz was tabbed to lead a seventy-five-man escort for the Topographical Engineers assigned to the task. Hardly eager to spend several more months in the field, Hartz admitted, "The prospect before me is bleak." Commanding the project, Capt. John Pope, who would achieve much greater fame during the Civil War, put Hartz's men to work improving a road from the artesian drill site to Fort Davis. Unfortunately, bad luck and poor equipment bedeviled Pope every step of the way. Pipes, drills, and the steam-powered boiler all broke down. The escort–road-building team turned positively mutinous during the winter, which was unusually severe. Pope admitted defeat the following summer. The surveys did, however, discover two Mexican boys who had eluded their Comanche captors while crossing the Pecos River.[13]

Protecting the U.S. mails demanded even more resources. From Fort Clark, the mail route followed the immigrant trail for nearly 180 miles before reaching the Horsehead Crossing of the Pecos River. Exhausted by the long, dry trail, diarists vied for the best means of describing the brackish Pecos water. "Hot discussion tonight . . . as to whether the Pecos water would or would not cook beans," joked Burr G. Duval. "I am now able to state that Pecos water will not cook beans soft. Boiled them ten hours. They were edible but by no means choice." Another writer described his efforts to choke down a little moisture: "It is cool and unodorous [sic], and its disagreeable taste is quite vanquished by holding the nose as you drink."[14]

From the Pecos River crossing, the trail ran nineteen miles past the Escondido and Tunis stations and Comanche Springs before reaching the stage stand at Leon Holes. Barrilla Springs was the next station, thirty-four miles from Leon. The final twenty-eight miles to the "Las Limpias" stage stand

near Fort Davis, which wound through Wild Rose Pass, was especially per-
ilous. "This pass is considered the most dangerous of the rout [*sic*]. . . . ten
Indians could give a large party great trouble," wrote one traveler. Like the
proverbial oasis in the desert, travelers could rest, refit, and replenish their
supplies at Fort Davis. "It was a pleasure to us when we reached an army post
where we were safe, and for that day, at least, could relax our vigilance," recalled an army officer's wife. "We met with kind friends everywhere, who
supplied us with many small comforts which could not be purchased." The
post sutler sold other merchandise; wagons could be repaired at the blacksmith's shop. Travelers might also procure fresh eggs, milk, and butter, virtually unobtainable elsewhere on the trail.[15]

On leaving Las Limpias, mail parties traveled to Barrel Springs, which
boasted good water, fair grass, and sufficient wood. Nineteen more dangerous miles lay ahead to the next major stop—El Muerto, or Dead Man's Hole.
Here stood a bleak adobe corral and small combination sleeping quarters,
storeroom, and kitchen. A lone stationmaster tended the animals and cooked
meals for stage passengers. Van Horn's Well lay thirty-two miles ahead. The
site itself offered only water, although forage and firewood could be found
two miles to the east. Twenty miles farther was Eagle Springs, notorious as
the scene of frequent Indian attacks. The San Antonio–El Paso road then
wound its way for another thirty-two miles, passing Fort Quitman before
striking the Rio Grande. Hugging the river for the remaining eighty-five
miles, the road continued to Fort Bliss, where travelers and mailmen could
again relax their guard.[16]

The mail companies expected military protection, but quarrels with the
regulars made for an uneasy relationship. In August 1855, for example, troops
at Fort Davis filed "grievances in connection with the escorting of the mail"
from Fort Clark. More trouble came in 1857, when postal inspector Isaiah Z.
Woods failed to return thirty-six mules he had borrowed from Fort Davis. Post
commander Washington Seawell charged that Woods had falsely claimed that
a number of animals had "strayed" when in fact he had taken them all the way
to Tucson, Arizona. Seawell also accused Wood of using his dual role as postal
worker and company agent to skim illegal profits. "Besides being the super-
intendent," the lieutenant colonel contended, "I have it from pretty good
authority that Mr. Woods is also a secret partner in this mail contract."[17]

But the army–mail company rivalries paled in comparison to the very
real dangers of the road. On January 31, 1857, Indians killed four soldiers escorting a mail express near Fort Lancaster. Another dramatic attack came
that July, when Ernest Schroeder and six privates of the Eighth Infantry
made up the mail escort from Fort Lancaster. Having enlisted two years ear-

lier, the twenty-seven-year-old Schroeder, a native of Germany, had already become company sergeant. Six First Infantrymen from a wood-gathering party led by Sgt. John H. Libbey, a tough veteran in his second enlistment, also accompanied the train. Encountering about sixty Indians near the Pecos River around dusk on July 24, the soldiers unhitched the mules and took cover behind the wagons. As the two groups surveyed one another warily, the Indians held up a white flag. While several Indians exchanged insults (in Spanish) with Sergeant Libbey, another group crept closer up a small ravine, hoping to get a better line of fire on the soldiers.[18]

Suddenly, shots rang out. The two sergeants steadied their isolated command, pointing out enemy positions to the privates. As Schroeder scurried about behind one of the wagons, Libbey exclaimed: "Look out Sergt [*sic*] for the sons of bitches they will get the advantage of you if they can & dont [*sic*] put yourself in danger." The warning came too late, for the next volley felled Schroeder with a shot through the heart. The soldiers returned fire, dropping two Indians from their horses. Surrounded and badly outnumbered, Libbey ordered his command to abandon the wagons and began a fighting retreat, half the men firing while the others reloaded. They carried Sergeant Schroeder's limp frame for over a mile until the Indians made another charge, forcing Libbey to order his men to abandon the body "& look out for ourselves." Fortunately for the outnumbered soldiers, the warriors gave up the chase when dark fell. The escort limped back into Fort Lancaster about three o'clock the next morning. "Sergeant Libbey did all he possibly could; he was perfectly cool & behaved with courage & discretion," remembered one private. Another recalled that, despite the fearful odds, the command had never panicked, killing five Indians in the skirmish. A board of inquiry agreed, complimenting the "gallant and judicious" conduct of the sergeants.[19]

In response, Lt. Edward Hartz led out forty infantrymen, most of whom were on temporary mail-escort duty from their home base at Davis, from Fort Lancaster. Because his foot soldiers could not catch their mounted foes in a short summer campaign, Hartz set a trap. Exposing only a dozen regulars as "escorts," he kept most of his men hidden in accompanying wagons. The ruse worked. Thinking that the column was a regular supply train, about thirty Mescaleros attacked the convoy forty-five miles west of Lancaster. Surprised by the soldiers scrambling out of the wagons, the Indians lost one or two of their number in the ensuing firefight and withdrew, setting the prairie afire to cover their retreat. Hartz had done well, luring his opponent into an ill-advised attack against his own strong command. Yet his inability to catch his mounted foes was galling. "The impunity with which attacks against the bands at present infesting the road," the lieutenant reported, "show[s] conclusively that the Indians are in virtual possession of the road . . . having the power to retire beyond the reach of chastisement at their pleasure."[20]

The episode highlighted a recurring army dilemma. Only a few months before the skirmishes between Schroeder, Libbey, Hartz, and the Mescaleros, Fort Davis officials had requested twenty horses to mount a portion of the garrison. Although sympathetic to the problems, department officials had insufficient resources to fill the request, suggesting instead that all available mules be mustered to form a flying detachment. Thus the frustrations continued. On May 31, 1858, Mescaleros stole the mules from a government mail party. In response, Seawell ordered Lt. William B. Hazen to "overtake and chasten" the Indians. Hazen had come to Texas from Oregon three months earlier; eventually, his long and illustrious military career would leave him a major general of volunteers. The twenty-eight-year-old West Pointer left Fort Davis on June 4 with thirty soldiers, two Mexican guides, twelve horses, and several pack mules. He followed an Indian trail to the northwest for four days. With water supplies running low, Hazen broke off the exhausting chase to make a forced march to a water hole north of Eagle Springs. He and his men then pushed on to the Guadalupe Mountains, where on the evening of June 10 they discovered a Mescalero encampment of fifteen lodges. Lieutenant Hazen struck immediately. Surprised, the hundred-odd Indians fled for cover up a canyon. The weary bluecoats killed one man and captured a woman but could not catch the others. They did, however, round up twenty-nine horses and government mules and most of the Indians' camp—lodges, pelts, horse gear, arms, ammunition, and a huge cache of prepared food. Among the spoils were fifty scalps.[21]

After burning everything they could not carry, Lieutenant Hazen and his command began the long trek back to Fort Davis. His troops wilted in the broiling Texas heat. The dozen grain-fed horses had long since broken down, so everyone was on foot. Gun barrels were too hot to touch. A few desperate men drank urine, with predictably agonizing results. At nightfall on the third day after the attack, they found a small salt spring, but horses and men fell ill after consuming the briny sulfur water too greedily. That night's sentinel, Pvt. Michael Kellett, fell asleep on duty in a nearby patch of grass. Assuming that Kellett had gone to bed, his relief blazed away without first issuing a challenge when he heard nearby rustling. Kellett fell dead and the camp panicked. Another panicked watchman, Pvt. Michael Hyers, rushed blindly into the campsite, firing and screaming as he came. Several wild shots from his surprised comrades killed Hyers as the horses stampeded. Only with great difficulty did Hazen restore a semblance of order.

William B. Hazen, who led the 1858 expedition from Fort Davis against the Mescaleros, eventually reached the rank of major general. Courtesy Library of Congress.

Having marched four hundred miles in sixteen days, the badly shaken detachment limped back into Fort Davis on June 20. Lieutenant Hazen commended three soldiers and the two scouts but damned the other twenty-seven infantrymen. "I never saw so worthless a set of men thrown together before in my life," wrote Hazen. "While in the Indian country they were much frightened, ready to fire at any time, on anything, and it was with peril that I could visit the sentinels at night." All but three of his horses had died in the Trans-Pecos, a country he described as "perfectly worthless for agricultural purposes." He found building stone, lime, and salt in the Guadalupes, but concluded that the remote location meant that the mountains "must remain valueless."

In spring 1859, department commander Twiggs redoubled efforts to protect the San Antonio–El Paso road. To harass Indians moving cattle and horses stolen from Mexico through Texas, regulars established Fort Stockton at the junction of the Comanche trail, eighty miles east of Davis. Three companies were transferred from Davis to garrison the new post. Similarly, Capt. Albert G. Brackett conducted a major scouting expedition from Fort Lancaster that April. Formerly an officer in the Fourth Infantry, Brackett had been lured back into the army in 1855 with a prized commission in the newly formed Second Cavalry. His command, including sixty-six cavalrymen, Fort Davis scout José Maria Bill, and a pack train, left Fort Lancaster on April 19 with fifteen days' rations. Water and grass grew increasingly scarce as the column moved south and west past Comanche Springs, reaching the Rio Grande on April 30 opposite the deserted Spanish presidio at San Vicente. Discovering a large Indian camp, Brackett immediately attacked, his men killing two Indians and wounding another without loss.[22]

Though victorious, Brackett was now running low on food and was seventy-five miles from Presidio, the closest town of any size on the U.S. side of the border. In an illegal move born of desperation, he splashed across the Rio Grande into Mexico and headed for San Carlos. He and his men arrived hungry but safe on May 5, most of them having had no rations whatsoever for the last two days. The broken-down pack train arrived a day later. Without any means of carrying the supplies needed to make the hazardous journey back up the Comanche trail, Brackett pushed west to Presidio del Norte before finally heading north to Fort Davis, where he arrived on May 15.[23]

Brackett's efforts notwithstanding, Indian attacks continued to plague the West Texas mails. An especially daring strike came on August 28, 1859, when Mescaleros stole nine mules and a horse from the El Muerto stage stand. The raiding party, it was claimed, had come from New Mexico. Reporting the attack from Fort Davis, Washington Seawell added caustically that the tribe was theoretically "at peace" and "taken care of by the government." He also noted that "if it had been possible for a foot command to overtake them," he would have dispatched a pursuit squad. Deeming the situation hopeless, Seawell contented himself with a request that troops from Fort Stanton search the reservation for the stolen animals.[24]

Seawell's inaction betrayed his growing personal malaise. It had been thirty-five long years since his graduation from West Point, and the lieutenant colonel had tired of the outpost on the Limpia, his station for most of the past five and a half years. Called to San Antonio to take temporary command of the Department of Texas in early 1860, Seawell seized the opportunity to request transfer of his regimental headquarters to the Alamo city. "Though I think this change in the Head Quarters of the 8th Inf. is required by the interest of the service, I also ask it as a favor if it should be considered that my services entitle me to such an indulgence," explained Seawell in his position as head of the regiment. Not surprisingly, temporary department chief Seawell favorably endorsed the request. Secretary of War John B. Floyd also approved the transfer; accordingly, the headquarters staff and band left Fort Davis in July. Presumably, such a move eased Seawell's task as regimental commander and department head by consolidating the positions in San Antonio. In reality, the transfer of the Eighth Infantry headquarters from Fort Davis had been made to enable Seawell to escape the Trans-Pecos.[25]

Conditions at Fort Davis deteriorated badly in Seawell's absence. On St. Patrick's Day in 1860, bartender William Graham stabbed and killed Pvt. John Pratt in a post-reveille scuffle at Daniel Murphy's saloon, located a quarter mile southeast of the fort. Bent on revenge and full of alcohol, Pratt's comrades from Company G fired a ragged fusillade into Murphy's establishment, where they believed the culprit lay in hiding. In the darkness of the night, one of their number, Pvt. Michael Powers, was mortally wounded. Upon the arrival of Lt. William M. Dye, Graham, fearing for his life, admitted to having stabbed Pratt. Graham was escorted to the stockade under a heavy guard. The next night, the men of Company G broke into the jail, seized the prisoner, and hung him from a nearby tree. When asked about the culprits, the dazed guard replied, "The whole company have done it."[26]

Company commander Lt. Theodore Fink, a German-born former enlisted man who had won his commission during the war against Mexico, attributed the lynching to his soldiers' determination to revenge "the death of a beloved comrade." Dissatisfied by such a tepid response, Secretary of War Floyd demanded action. Bvt. Col. Robert E. Lee, who had by this time replaced Seawell as department commander, dissolved Company G, distributing its men among the rest of the regiment, and ordered Company H back from Fort Quitman to restore order. Lee also ordered Seawell to head a board of inquiry to investigate the matter. But the enlisted men stonewalled the court. One acknowledged that he had been "quite drunk" on the evening of March 17; another allowed that his fellow soldiers had threatened him with physical harm if he testified. The other forty-six men claimed ignorance of anything related to the crime. Not deterred by the refusal of the enlisted men to turn evidence against one another, the Seawell court delivered seven suspects to the nearest civilian court at El Paso. But a local justice of the peace quickly acquitted them. Members of the guard who had allowed Graham to be taken from the stockade received stiff punishments; once again, however, investigators had not cracked the ring of silence.

Several factors had contributed to the disintegration of Company G. Its captain, Joseph Selden, had been absent, sick, or on detached duty for the past twelve years. Lieutenant Fink was frequently detached as recruiting officer; several officers, including Seawell, thought that he had been an overly lax disciplinarian. Lt. James J. Van Horn held the other commissioned slot. Though described as "a highly meritorious officer" who "performs his duty well," Van Horn had less than two years' experience. Detached service, extra duty, sickness, and crime further divided the unit and reduced morale. Company discipline suffered accordingly. With little oversight from their officers, the soldiers had grown accustomed to looking out for themselves. Uncertain that Graham would be punished, they had taken matters into their own hands, in the process terrifying superiors who recognized the tenuous nature of frontier military discipline.[27]

Col. Joseph K. F. Mansfield's return inspection that October gave further evidence of the deterioration at Fort Davis. The sawmill was out of order; fearing that its shingled roof would catch fire and the munitions explode, wary garrison members kept a healthy distance from the magazine. The enlisted men's barracks needed glass windows, and Mansfield recommended that the flimsy kitchens and mess rooms be "burned for firewood." The hospital, "a worthless building of posts set on end, and shrunken in, & rotten," would "soon fall down, or be blown down," he predicted. Commanding officer Seawell was absent. Twenty-three officers and men were on detached duty at Fort Quitman; another officer was at San Antonio. This left the garrison at Fort Davis with one commissioned officer, one sergeant, two corporals, one musician, and twenty-six privates, seven of whom were in the guardhouse. Such a tiny force could barely prevent the theft of government property, much less assist in the military conquest of the Trans-Pecos. As one immigrant put it, although military posts were as welcome to travelers "as the oasis in the desert . . . a parade of the entire force would sometimes diminish our feeling of security."[28]

Abandoned was any pretense of adopting a more aggressive stance in West Texas. Twiggs admitted as much, ordering his command "to resort to the defensive system again." Not surprisingly, the list of real and imagined Indian depredations grew accordingly. In early February 1861, Indians attacked a wagon train hauling copper ore through the Fort Davis area and drove off one hundred mules.[29]

The American empire had yet to fully consolidate its hold over the Trans-Pecos. Inconsistent Indian policy and poorly conceived military strategy explained many of the difficulties faced by the Davis regulars, whose efforts were further complicated by outdated equipment and ill-suited uniforms. On the other hand, troops from the outpost on the Limpia could claim several successes. Of the sixty-two army-Indian engagements in the Lone Star State between 1854 and 1861, Fort Davis had played a significant role in ten. Troops led by John G. Walker (1854), Horace Randal (1855), Edward L. Hartz (1857), William B. Hazen (1858), and Albert G. Brackett (1859) had each inflicted stinging defeats on various Indian bands; although not enough to eliminate Indian opposition, these skirmishes certainly made hostile tribes more cautious.[30]

Those who garrisoned Fort Davis in the 1850s probably gave little thought to such imperial concerns. Many would have concurred with Lieutenant Hartz, the young West Pointer who had become one of the garrison's most experienced campaigners. "Quarters are decidedly pleasant when returning fagged out from constant travelling, bivouacking and hard feeding," explained Hartz. "They offer you a comfortable bed, a roof to shelter, and the enticements of a tolerably well spread table." But in spite of the simple pleasures of garrison life, Hartz enjoyed the "excitement, adventure, and constant novelty" of active campaigning. "Life in the field," continued Hartz philosophically, "is in the main more desirable than being immured within the walls of the cañon attending to the humdrum routines of garrison duty."[31]

CHAPTER FIVE

CRISIS OF EMPIRE

he recent problems at Fort Davis were soon overshadowed by the growing storm clouds of secession. From the moment of their incorporation into the Union, Texans had criticized the federal government's failure to prevent Indian attacks. Not surprisingly, the state's secession convention would list this as one of their justifications for leaving the Union in 1861. The ensuing Civil War thus not only forced garrison members to examine their loyalties but also tested the ability of state officials to raise, equip, and train replacements for the regulars in blue. The state of Texas, rather than the federal government, would now assume responsibility for guarding the Davis Mountains outpost. Shorn of the money and troops that had once come from Washington, Texans were now on their own.

The dilemma of secession sorely challenged the fidelities of the frontier regulars. Two officers destined to serve at Fort Davis had ruminated about the potential division as early as the 1856 presidential election. Each rejected extremists from both North and South in favor of the Democratic candidate, James Buchanan. "If he [Buchanan] is elected & our machinery does not work smooth the only thing to be done is to put Massachusetts & South Carolina in ruins," wrote Assistant Surgeon DeWitt C. Peters, a native of New York. Similarly, the Pennsylvania-born Lt. Edward L. Hartz damned both the Republican Party's "accursed fanatical interference in slavery" as well as "the fanatic portion" of the South. Four years later, as news of South Carolina's secession swept through Texas, U.S. Army officers voiced mixed reactions. Rhode Island's Zenas R. Bliss still dismissed talk of secession as more of the bluster that had characterized recent national politics. On the other hand, Lt. Col. Robert E. Lee wrote from Fort Mason: "I can anticipate no greater calamity for the country than a dissolution of the Union." Yet Lee, a native Virginian who had faithfully served his country for thirty years, resolved to "return to my native State and share the miseries of my people" if his beloved Dominion left the Union.[1]

In late January 1861, a state convention assembled in Austin to consider relations with the U.S. government. Although many Texans, including Gov. Sam Houston, opposed disunion, the convention voted 166–8 to secede, a decision later ratified by a popular vote. Heavily dependent on federal protection and the local military establishment, residents of Fort Davis and Presidio had voted 48–0 and 316–0, respectively, against leaving the Union. However, the more populous El Paso precincts overwhelmingly supported secession, thus ensuring that the measure passed El Paso County by a healthy majority. The outcome led Fort Davis's Daniel Murphy to predict that "there is a poor chance for us for getting any protection in this section of the country."[2]

Bvt. Maj. Gen. David E. Twiggs, who had on the eve of secession returned from a leave of absence to command the Department of Texas, had responded to the situation with dispatch if perhaps not loyalty. A native of Georgia, Twiggs had devoted his life to the service of his country, having opposed the South Carolina nullifiers of 1832 and fought in three wars. Yet the election of Abraham Lincoln had disillusioned the old warhorse, weary of his long quarrels with commanding general Winfield Scott. Frustrated by the War Department's failures to provide specific guidance during the secession crisis, Twiggs had initiated correspondence with the governor of Georgia for a position with that state's militia and begun negotiating the army's possible withdrawal with representatives of the Texas secession convention. Rightly suspicious of his loyalties, in early February 1861 the War Department had relieved Twiggs of command, belatedly ordering troops in the Lone Star State to concentrate in anticipation of evacuation to Kansas.[3]

But the orders from Washington arrived too late. In mid-February, Twiggs surrendered all federal posts in Texas. By virtue of the agreement, the twenty-six hundred troops in the Lone Star State, composing nearly 15 percent of the entire U.S. Army, were allowed to keep their small arms and assured of safe passage to the Union. In conjunction with the surrender, Twiggs ordered post commanders to prepare for a march to the coast. Startled by the abrupt capitulation, officers and men contemplated their loyalties. Twiggs returned to a hero's welcome in New Orleans and a major generalship in the Confederate army. Lieutenant Colonel Lee placed his fate with that of his native state, resigning his federal commission after Virginia declared for secession. Farther west, Edward Hartz cast his lot with the Union even as he blasted "Black Republicans" as "fanatics who regard the principles of a political party as paramount to the interests of their country and the welfare of a few miserable negroes of more importance than the perpetuity of the American Union." Hartz also reserved a few parting shots for the Lone Star State: "Texas has already cost the U.S. Government millions upon millions and has never brought anything into the Union but her worthless self, her quarrels and her debts." From Fort Davis, Assistant Surgeon Peters joined a chorus of officers criticizing Twiggs's surrender as "humiliating." In contrast to Hartz, however, Peters wished no ill will upon Texans, many of whom "are poor beyond means."[4]

Of the thirty commissioned personnel who had served at Fort Davis before the Civil War, ten ultimately joined the Confederate army. Six of those ten had been born in states that seceded; John G. Taylor and Edmunds B. Holloway hailed from Kentucky, a slave state that attempted to remain neutral. Robert P. Maclay (Pennsylvania) and Philip Stockton (New Jersey) completed the list of those who joined the gray. Three—Maclay, Thomas M. Jones (Virginia), and Horace Randal (Tennessee)—became brigadier generals. On the other hand, twenty officers who had served at Fort Davis remained loyal to the Union. Seventeen had been born in Northern states; another, Theodore Fink, hailed from Germany. Washington Seawell and Richard I. Dodge came from slave states but continued their federal service. Of those remaining in the U.S. Army, ten eventually won general's stars; two, William Hazen and Zenas R. Bliss, became major generals.[5]

The Union evacuation of West Texas went by stages. On March 31, troops abandoned Fort Bliss, falling back to Fort Quitman, which followed suit six days later. The evacuees then continued their eastward march to Fort Davis. There, post commander Capt. Edward D. Blake, a native South Carolinian who subsequently joined the Confederate service, nonetheless cut down the flagstaff in a final act of defiance. The combined forces abandoned Fort Davis on April 13. Unable to transport all their property, local merchants sold many of their wares at ruinously low prices. Dietrick Dutchover and E. P. Webster remained behind in a vain effort to protect federal property from vandalism. A civilian guide, two stage keepers, and a handful of Mexican families joined Daniel Murphy and Victoriano Hernandez as the only other remnants of the once-thriving civilian community.[6]

News of the firing on Fort Sumter shattered the uneasy truce in the Lone Star State. More than 1,300 regulars had already left Texas, with 800 others en route to Indianola, where they hoped to rendezvous with naval transports. Bvt. Lt. Col. Isaac V. D. Reeve commanded the Federals from western Texas, now totaling 366 rank and file. Twenty-two miles west of San Antonio, Reeve's command encountered 1,500 Texans and six cannons led by Col.

Earl Van Dorn, himself recently resigned from the U.S. Army. In the face of this overwhelming force, on May 9 Reeve surrendered his command. Assistant Surgeon Peters immediately accepted the parole offered by Confederate authorities. Denouncing the Southerners as "crazy as loonies," Peters decided that his own poor health and the need to protect his wife demanded that he leave the enlisted men and return North. After initially rejecting any favors offered by their Confederate captors, other officers gradually followed Peters's lead and accepted parole over the ensuing fifteen months.[7]

The treatment of those regulars who remained in confinement remains an issue of debate. "They were subjected to degrading labors, supplied with scanty food and clothing, and sometimes chained to the ground, or made to suffer other severe military punishments," according to the Eighth Infantry's nineteenth-century historian. A Confederate guard, however, remembered a far different story. Assigned to oversee prisoners at Camp Verde, he recalled that he "had a friendly feeling for the poor old soldiers and did what I could to make their confinement as light and pleasant as possible." He claimed that the captives received the same rations as did the Confederates, were allowed to supplement their food supplies by hunting, and could leave camp on parole to attend miscellaneous needs. Whatever the case, on February 25, 1863, the 278 enlisted men still under Confederate authority gained their freedom via a prisoner exchange. The men returned to active service with the Eighth Infantry, their extended stay in Texas finally over.[8]

The regulars gone, Texans found themselves responsible for their own protection. The Knights of the Golden Circle, a secret military society formed in 1855 to secure new lands for slavery, had provided much of the manpower and material for occupying western Texas in the immediate aftermath of secession. Lt. Col. John R. Baylor, a noted frontiersman and second in command of the Second Texas Mounted Rifles, oversaw the first occupation forces as he organized the Confederate Territory of Arizona. Soldiers led by Capt. Trevanion T. Teel, himself a Knight, occupied the old federal positions of Forts Clark, Duncan, Lancaster, and Stockton and Camp Hudson. A handful of others, led by Capt. James W. Walker and Lt. Samuel W. McAllister, were subsequently dispatched to Fort Davis for six months' service. Indians warily investigated the new occupants of the Trans-Pecos, trading mescal cakes, bows, shields, arrows, lances, and clothing for scrap iron, ore, and liquor. One Mescalero leader, Nicolás, allegedly offered the hand of one of his daughters in marriage to a Confederate. On May 31, another chief, Espejo, came in for a "confab" with McAllister. Supposedly more than one hundred years old, Espejo spoke excellent Spanish, recounting not only the old days during Mexican rule but also his tribe's conflicts with the Comanches. One dubious Confederate, however, suspected "that the old rascal came in for the purpose of reconnoirtering [*sic*] and finding out our numerical strength."⁹

Life along the Limpia, far from the comforts of home, quickly bored the new residents. Trousers were in particularly short supply; fortunately, Daniel Murphy's wife, Sarah, was the only woman on post. "By keeping out of sight of the Murphy residence we could get along fairly with our shirts," a Confederate diarist explained. Only by fashioning wagon sheets into ersatz trousers was the clothing crisis resolved. Some garrison members whiled away the time hunting for copper, silver, and big game. Others celebrated July 4 by firing off a few rounds from the unit's cannon. Unfortunately, the festivities nearly ended in tragedy. One of the boys "did not elevate the piece quite enough" to ensure the projectile cleared the surrounding canyon wall, explained one Rebel, for the shell struck the edge of the bluff and ricocheted back down the mountain before exploding. Observed the diarist nonchalantly, the gunner "had cut his fuse too long."¹⁰

Meanwhile, state and Confederate authorities set out to complete their control of what they hoped would become a new western empire. Lieutenants William E. White and Reuben R. Mays soon took over command at Fort Davis. But difficulties in organizing, equipping, and training recruits continued to plague Confederate efforts. Brig. Gen. Paul O. Hebert, Van Dorn's successor as commander of the Department of Texas, complained that "the people are poor and the state without money or apparent credit. . . . arms, ammunition, provisions and equipments are wanting." Disciplining the independent-minded Rebels seemed futile. Gambling, horse racing, and theft were endemic; "if any gamblers come to the posts or about them to filch the troops of their earnings [you] will order them to stop their gambling or require them to leave at once," insisted one frontier adjutant.¹¹

Undaunted, Lieutenant Colonel Baylor, physically a giant of a man at six feet three inches tall and 230 pounds, pressed ahead. On July 12, 1861, he ordered most of the Davis garrison forward to Fort Bliss, leaving only twenty men behind. Realizing that this might invite Indian attack, Baylor unsuccessfully sought a truce with Nicolás, but the shaky armistice was quickly shattered. "We have just com [*sic*] from a five days scout yesterday we kild [*sic*] two Indians and tuck [*sic*] one with us a Life [alive] he is hear [*sic*] with us now," scribbled a semiliterate Fort Davis trooper, who believed that two hundred Indians lurked nearby. On the night of August 4, Apaches killed three herders at the old Musquiz ranch. Lieutenant Mays set out in pursuit with six soldiers, two Hispanic guides, and five Anglo civilians. On August 10, his patrol captured several dozen Apache horses, only to blunder into an ambush the following day. Only one of the guides escaped. Pursuit columns dispatched from Forts Davis and Stockton failed to catch the suspected raiders.[12]

The Mays disaster forced Baylor to reinforce the Trans-Pecos outposts. By the end of September, the Fort Davis garrison included Capt. William C. Adams, Lieutenants White and Emory Gibbons, five privates left behind as sick by other companies, and sixty-three Second Texas Mounted Riflemen. The next month, while Adams was away raising additional recruits, orders from Baylor arrived demanding the arrest of A. F. Wulff, an alleged Union spy who had been selling hay, corn, and wood to Fort Davis from his store in Presidio del Norte, Mexico. "I want him enticed over on this side of the river and taken prisoner and sent to these headquarters [Dona Ana, New Mexico] in irons," wrote Baylor. In Adams's absence, Lieutenant Gibbons assumed responsibility for carrying out the task. About three o'clock in the morning of October 15, five Confederates from Fort Davis joined Joe Leaton, son of the deceased land baron Ben Leaton, in rousting Wulff from his store at Presidio del Norte.[13]

As the Texans dragged their prisoner through the streets, Wulff's brother-in-law organized a posse and tracked down the kidnappers. Shots rang out in the streets of Presidio in the early morning; when the smoke cleared, two Confederates and an unidentified Mexican were dead. Wulff escaped unharmed. "Providence seems to protect me," noted a relieved Wulff. "This time I did not expect to see my family again." Wisely, the former contractor advised his friend and partner, Daniel Murphy, that "we might just as well give up furnishing Fort Davis." The misadventure indeed cost Murphy the Fort Davis sutlership, the San Antonio–based firm of Moke and Brothers assuming this position in his place. Back at Fort Davis, Adams arrested Gibbons for having bungled the Wulff kidnapping.[14]

By the end of October, Confederates at Fort Davis had settled into more routine duties. "I think when ever I git [sic] home," speculated a weary soldier, "I will be able to bye [sic] me a farm and settle myself for life for I think the war will be all over by that time and if it is not I know not what I shel [sic] do." Corn and hay were plentiful, but the men had gone without pay for months. Although the garrison had only twenty-five rounds of ammunition per man, at least one of their number remained confident of victory, noting that the Yankees were "all Greasers or one half of them." Already bloodied by the loss of several acquaintances in the fighting, this Confederate urged friends back home to "do soum [sic] thing for [their] country."[15]

Help was on the way, in the form of a column commanded by Brig. Gen. Henry H. Sibley. Armed with Pres. Jefferson Davis's permission to raise two regiments (later increased to three) and a battery of howitzers to invade

New Mexico, Sibley had spent the summer and early fall preparing to move west. Proceeding in small parties to ease supply difficulties, elements of Sibley's command pushed through Fort Davis in November and December. Poor discipline and inadequate planning marked their journey. One enlisted man observed that two officers had "tanked up considerably" while at Fort Davis; ignorant of the terrain, their beleaguered company was forced to make a dry camp. Further misfortune awaited a group of unfortunate Texans at Van Horn's Well—an earlier wagon train had taken all the water. The men of another column mutinied after their bread ran out. In an effort to mollify the restless troops, officers from the latter party issued passes to Fort Davis, where the poorly clad soldiers snapped up all available clothing from the post sutler and seized the chance to "get tight."[16]

Normalcy returned to Fort Davis as Sibley's troops departed. Now sporting an exotic array of uniforms, materials purchased from the sutler, and garments supplied by friends, relatives, and citizens' groups back home, the tiny garrison, which averaged less than thirty men in spring 1862, was too small to undertake much formal military training. The variety of their arms rivaled the wide assortment of clothing: musketoons, Springfield muskets, Sharps carbines, and Colts pistols were the most prevalent weapons used by the Confederates. Fortunately, the firm of Moke and Brothers was now importing sizable stocks of merchandise; between August 1861 and January 1862, in addition to his normal rations, Captain Adams purchased tobacco, a washbowl and basin, a pitcher, shoes, socks, envelopes, a pocketknife, sugar, tea, a tin pan, and a wool hat from the sutler. Canned delicacies included pineapples, sardines, preserves, green peas, pickles, oysters, and strawberries. Cognac, two bottles of brandy, and four bottles of champagne rounded out Adams's grocery list, which totaled $72.60. Enlisted men favored Patrick Murphy's shop, with one prodigal private ringing up $119.67 in bills.[17]

The fate of Fort Davis now lay with Sibley's twenty-five-hundred-strong Army of New Mexico. Notorious for his heavy use of alcohol, Sibley, whose graying hair reflected two decades of distinguished service in the U.S. Army, had expected to find sufficient local resources to supply his men. But it was now too late in the season. Stuck in New Mexico in midwinter, his army ran short of food, ammunition, and clothing. Federal opposition, organized by Col. Edward R. S. Canby, also proved stronger than anticipated. Although victorious at the Battle of Valverde (February 21, 1862), the loss of the Confederate supply train at Glorieta (March 28, 1862) forced Sibley to abandon his dreams of conquest. From Mesilla, Baylor's last-ditch efforts to exterminate the Indian threat also failed. Upon learning of his ruthless policy, Confederate authorities stripped Baylor of his command.[18]

Sibley's column disintegrated as it fell back into Texas. As one Rebel put it, "Every man for himself and the wagons take the hindmost." Another man complained angrily: "Sibley is heartily despised by every man in the brigade for his want of feeling, poor generalship, and cowardice. Several Mexican whores can find room to ride in his wagons while the poor private soldier is thrown out to die on the way." Indians multiplied the rabble's plight by filling water holes with dirt and sheep carcasses. Only eighteen hundred men returned from New Mexico, which a chastened Sibley denounced as "not worth a quarter of the blood and treasure expended in its conquest."[19]

Fort Davis served as a receiving station for the sick and wounded as Sibley's broken command retreated east. One thankful soldier remembered that his party "'gourmandised [sic] sumptuously' on fat beef, the first for many a long day." Garrison duties at Fort Davis temporarily fell to Capt. Angel Navarro, who instructed prospective recruiters to secure volunteers who "have a horse and if possible good armament." But Sibley's rout had convinced Confederate authorities to abandon the Trans-Pecos. Once again, Dietrick Dutchover led the small civilian contingent that tried to remain behind. Apaches soon looted the fort, forcing Dutchover and the other refugees to hide on the roof of one of the buildings. After two days and nights atop the roof, the Dutchover party abandoned one of their sick comrades and began the ninety-mile trek to Presidio. The escapees arrived safely in the border town; one arrow-ridden body, apparently that of the man left behind, was later discovered back at Fort Davis.[20]

On August 22, 1862, advancing Union troops from New Mexico hoisted the Stars and Stripes over Fort Quitman. Rumors that a "company of troops of Mexican heritage" was lurking to the east led to the dispatch of Capt. E. D. Shirland with a company of the First California Cavalry to investigate the situation. Arriving at Fort Davis five days later, the Federals found the post ransacked. Shirland's little command departed the abandoned site on August 30. The following day, a mixed party of Indians, some mounted and others on foot, tried to ambush the Union troops about ten miles west of Dead Man's Hole. "Wishing to get rid of the footmen, I made a running fight of it, expecting the mounted men to follow," reported Shirland. "Finding it too hot for them, they returned," leaving behind four dead. The captain also claimed twenty Indians wounded. His losses numbering two wounded, Shirland resumed his retreat to El Paso.[21]

Commanding Federal troops in the region, Brig. Gen. James H. Carleton praised Shirland's gallantry and execution of orders. But Carleton turned his attention from the Davis Mountains to New Mexico, where Navajo and Mescalero attacks had increased since the outbreak of the Civil War.

Establishing his departmental headquarters at Santa Fe, he discounted the possibility of another Confederate invasion; should such an offensive occur, Carleton vowed to implement a scorched-earth policy in West Texas.[22]

Though focusing his efforts elsewhere, Carleton did seize upon the opportunity to clean up the "ruffians" near Presidio who had attempted to kidnap A. F. Wulff. Among the gang's reputed ringleaders was Edward Hall, a former Federal contractor who had been selling property looted from Fort Davis. Seeking assistance from any quarter, Carleton authorized the governor of Chihuahua to cross the river and deal with the outlaws. Hall "should be dealt summarily with," contended Carleton. "A stern example should be made of such a ruffian." But nothing was done until April 1864, when Capt. Alfred H. French and twenty-five First California Cavalrymen marched to Presidio del Norte. On April 15, French surprised Skillman's "Texas spy and scouting party" at Spencer's ranch. The Federals routed the astonished Rebels, who lost three killed (including their commander), two others mortally wounded, four men taken prisoner, and nine animals captured. French reported no losses.[23]

Carleton's assessment of the Confederacy's inability to launch another western thrust proved correct. Sibley's brigade had returned from New Mexico an unarmed mob, and Union threats to the Gulf Coast precluded any Texas efforts to organize another offensive. Victoriano Hernandez and a few hardy Hispanic families had remained in the central Trans-Pecos, but the Indians had reclaimed military superiority west of San Antonio. Confederate resistance in Texas finally collapsed in early June 1865, when Gen. E. Kirby Smith surrendered the Trans-Mississippi Department.[24]

The war's end returned responsibility for safeguarding the non-Indian presence in the Trans-Pecos to the U.S. Army. Mustering out the massive volunteer forces that had won the Civil War, Congress would by 1870 reduce the number of enlisted men to thirty thousand, divided into ten cavalry, twenty-five infantry, and five artillery regiments. Of the forty regiments in the reorganized army, four—the Ninth and Tenth Cavalry, and the Twenty-fourth and Twenty-fifth Infantry—would be reserved for black enlisted personnel. As their congressional supporters pointed out, black troops were far less likely to desert than their white counterparts, a trend that would continue for the rest of the century. Maj. Gen. Philip H. Sheridan assumed command of Federal forces in the Lone Star State. A crusty veteran of some of the Civil War's hardest fighting, the pugnacious Sheridan was skeptical of rumors of Indian attacks and doubted if Texans had genuinely accepted the North's victory. "Texas has not yet suffered from the war and will require some intimidation," he asserted. Assaults on blacks and Unionists by groups such as the Ku Klux Klan reinforced the general's determination to maintain domestic order. Over the protests of many conservative whites, Sheridan initially deployed his units among the state's more populous interior communities rather than along the frontiers.[25]

Congress supported Sheridan's determination to restore federal authority in the South, eventually establishing military rule over most of the former Confederate states. Resentful of the army's presence, many white Texans seized upon every opportunity to revile the Reconstruction forces. As interest in the regions west of San Antonio was rekindled, envisioning an Indian attack around every corner proved a popular pastime. Some of the reports, however, were genuine, and several wagon trains crossing the Trans-Pecos reported run-ins with Indians. Two attacks, attributed to Lipan and Mescalero Apaches led by Espejo and José Cigarito, occurred near abandoned Fort Davis. Newspapers recorded the deaths of thirty-four men between Fort Quitman and El Paso in a period of only a few weeks. Gov. James Throckmorton demanded action.[26]

To avert a call-up of state volunteers and to display the power of the federal government, in spring 1867 Sheridan readied several units, including the black soldiers of the Ninth Cavalry, for frontier service. Stationing the regiment in the sparsely settled Trans-Pecos would help reestablish American dominance while at the same time ease the rivalries between the regulars and conservative whites in the Southern heartlands, who resented the black cavalrymen in their midst. The Ninth Cavalry's colonel, Edward Hatch, was a garrulous, tolerant Iowan who had compiled a fine Civil War record. Second in command was the trim, boyish-looking Lt. Col. Wesley Merritt, a fighting cavalryman who had been brevetted for his activities at Gettysburg, Yellow Tavern, Haw's Shop, Winchester, and Five Forks. Reflecting the regiment's Kentucky and Louisiana recruiting grounds, more than 60 percent of its enlisted personnel had been born in these two states. Nearly 40 percent had fought in the Civil War, providing the unit with a solid cadre of veterans. But all was not well, for the racial prejudice that characterized most of nineteenth-century American society was reflected in the lily-white officer corps. To make matters worse, low literacy rates among black enlisted men burdened officers with additional clerical duties. Ominously, only eleven of the regiment's thirty line officers were present as the regiment prepared to move into West Texas, far too few to ensure good discipline.[27]

The problems exploded in Lt. Edward M. Heyl's E Troop. Born in 1844, Heyl had enlisted as a quartermaster sergeant at the onset of the Civil War, securing his commission in 1862. But Heyl's horizons were extremely limited. When asked by a postwar examining board to "give the principal

Lt. Col. Wesley Merritt commanded the Ninth Cavalry, who reestablished Fort Davis in 1867. He was brevetted to major general for his exploits on the eastern front during the Civil War. Courtesy Fort Davis National Historic Site.

rivers of Europe," Heyl responded simply, "Nile." "How is the pres. of the U.S. selected by the Constitution?" inquired the board. "He is chosen from the Senate," replied the befuddled lieutenant, whose application for promotion to captain was denied. A heavy drinker who had named his black horse "Nigger," Heyl proved a terrible match for the Ninth, erratically meting out brutal punishment to his unfortunate troopers. Following a drunken escapade just outside San Antonio during which Heyl had slashed two soldiers with his saber and fired several shots at a group of others, his company rebelled. One sergeant was killed and two officers wounded in the resulting melee. Lieutenant Colonel Merritt concluded that the sadistic lieutenant was "much to blame" for the incident, and the Judge Advocate General's department remitted the death sentences of two men found guilty of mutiny.[28]

Amid the controversy engulfing Heyl's company, Lieutenant Colonel Merritt oversaw the reoccupation of Fort Davis. On June 29, 1867, Merritt and four troops of Ninth Cavalrymen rode into the crumbling remains of the post on Limpia Creek. By August 1868, elements of the all-black Forty-first Infantry (soon to be merged with the Thirty-eighth to form the Twenty-fourth Regiment) had joined the garrison. Other regulars reoccupied Fort Quitman and staked out Fort Concho, a new post at the present-day city of San Angelo. Meanwhile, Colonel Hatch was setting up regimental headquarters at Fort Stockton. Federal authority had returned to the Trans-Pecos.[29]

CHAPTER SIX

RETURN TO THE FRONTIER

The return of the regular army brought order—federal-government style—to the Trans-Pecos. Although traditional histories sometimes reviled Reconstruction's impact on Texas, non-Indians of the Fort Davis region found that economic opportunities and greater security accompanied the renewed military presence. But changes in the old routine were also apparent. Whereas Washington Seawell's controversial tenure during the 1850s had provided a semblance of command stability to Fort Davis, over the next decade and a half the post had no fewer than six permanent and thirteen temporary commanders. The troops stationed there also shifted about more frequently. Soldiers from a single regiment, the Eighth Infantry, had formed the permanent garrison from the fort's inception to 1861; between 1867 and 1882, however, members of six different regiments guarded the post on the Limpia (see table 6.1 and appendix 1).

The soldiers at Fort Davis after the Civil War differed significantly from their antebellum predecessors. Whereas the typical soldier had once been a white emigrant from Ireland or the Germanies, he was now black, probably a former slave, and had been born in the upper South or a border state. Analysis of the enlisted personnel enumerated in the 1870 and 1880 censuses, for example, reveals that nearly 25 percent of all troops stationed at Davis had been born in Kentucky; another 16 percent hailed from Virginia. Collectively, 88 percent of garrison members were natives of slave states. Only six men listed as "soldier" had been born abroad, listing Mexico (three), Canada, Jamaica, and Bombay as their places of birth. At age thirty-nine, Henry Wiley, a Kentuckian, was the oldest enlisted man on post in 1870; he was married to forty-year-old Jane Wiley, who had been born in Maryland. Their eight-year-old child, Laura, had been born in Louisiana. In 1880, John

TABLE 6.1

Permanent Commanders at Fort Davis, 1867–82

Name	Rank	Unit	Dates of command
Wesley Merritt	Lt. Col.	Ninth Cavalry	July 1–Nov. 29, 1867
			June 1, 1868–Sept. 3, 1869
Edward Hatch	Col.	Ninth Cavalry	Nov. 26, 1869–Dec. 15, 1870
William R. Shafter	Lt. Col.	Twenty-fourth Infantry	May 18–June 18, 1871
			July 9–Oct. 5, 1871
			Nov. 1–12, 1871
			Jan. 1–May 26, 1872
George L. Andrews	Col.	Twenty-fifth Infantry	May 26– July 31, 1872
			Aug. 8, 1872–Mar. 4, 1873
			Sept. 8, 1874–Apr. 25, 1876
			Nov. 26, 1876–Aug. 30, 1878
Louis H. Carpenter	Capt. and Bvt. Col.	Tenth Cavalry	Aug. 30, 1878–May 29, 1879
			June 13–July 27, 1879
			Sept. 14–Oct. 20, 1879
Napoleon B. McLaughlin	Maj.	Tenth Cavalry	Oct. 20, 1878–June 18, 1880
			Oct. 15, 1880–Mar. 12, 1881
William R. Shafter	Col.	First Infantry	Mar. 12, 1881–May 13, 1882

Adapted from Greene, *Historic Resource Study*, 344–49.

Thomas and Edward Berry, both of whom lived in the barracks and were forty-two years old, tied for the honor.[1]

Considerable debate accompanied the arrival of black troops in West Texas. Black soldiers were "of little or no use on the Texas Frontier," claimed Lt. Col. John S. Mason, acting inspector general of the Department of Texas. Brig. Gen. Edward O. C. Ord, department commander from 1875 to 1880, asserted that "a feeling of hostility" marred relations between black regulars and Hispanic civilians. Others resorted to the racial stereotypes of the day. "Every fellow seemed to be an expert on the banjo or violin," wrote one, and "they all carried a razor about their person as their favorite weapon of defense."[2]

Racial tensions occasionally exploded. In the early morning of November 21, 1872, the sound of glass breaking in her bedroom window awakened Mrs. Frederic Kendall, wife of a Twenty-fifth Infantry lieutenant who was on temporary assignment elsewhere. Mrs. Kendall raised the curtain to find Cpl. Daniel Talliferro, Ninth Cavalry, trying to force his way into the house. Shouting a frantic warning, Mrs. Kendall seized a revolver and killed the intruder with a bullet through the head. News of the incident spread like wildfire, for threats by a black enlisted man upon a white officer's wife challenged the foundations of military society. George L. Andrews, the bespectacled post commander and himself colonel of the all-black Twenty-fifth Infantry, complained to department headquarters that such incidents were becoming more frequent. Married officers were now reluctant to leave their families alone after dark; detached service, claimed Andrews, had become "a positive cruelty."[3]

Andrews's prejudices notwithstanding, racial divisions occasionally threatened army discipline and order. In July 1873, black troops at Fort Stockton nearly mutinied in response to a surgeon's alleged mistreatment of a sick patient. Other ugly confrontations occurred at San Antonio and Fort Concho. "The fact cannot be disguised, that there is anxiety at every post garrisoned exclusively by colored troops," concluded the normally fair-minded Brig. Gen. Christopher C. Augur, who commanded the Department of Texas during 1872–75 and 1881–83. "They are so clannish, and so excitable—turning every question into one of class, that there is no knowing when a question may arise which will annoy in a moment the whole of the garrison against its officers not as officers, but as white men."[4]

Others, however, defended black troops. Lt. Charles J. Crane, assigned to the Twenty-fourth Infantry upon his graduation from West Point, professed that although he "had not desired the colored infantry," he had "never regretted my service in that regiment." Elizabeth Custer, that romantic chronicler of army life, defended the qualities of blacks in combat: "They were determined that no soldiering should be carried on in which their valor was not proved," she explained. Lt. Robert Smither, a Tenth Cavalryman who had seen four long years of Civil War, contended that his black troopers "exhibited the noblest courage" in their frontier service. Responding to criticisms of black soldiers, Smither argued that "the taunt of cowardice illy suits a class of men who generally expose themselves unnecessarily to the fire of the enemy."[5]

The racial discrimination that permeated American society had left the army an attractive choice for many black men. The steady income (even on a private's salary of thirteen dollars per month), food, clothing, and opportunities seemed especially attractive to those with limited employment options. Explaining his decision to enlist, one black soldier put it simply: "I got tired of looking mules in the face from sunrise to sunset." Blacks deserted far less frequently than their white comrades. In 1867, for example, when desertion rates for the army as a whole reached an astonishing 25 percent, only

Artist and illustrator Frederic Remington often used black soldiers as his subjects. His *A Pull at the Canteen* offers a classic image of a black cavalryman. Courtesy Frederic Remington Art Museum.

4 percent of blacks deserted. Indeed, one officer serving with black troops in Texas concluded that "if a garrison like the one here could be introduced into every northern town for six months, the opponents of universal suffrage would be few."[6]

For Lieutenant Colonel Merritt and the black garrison at Fort Davis, establishing government authority in the Trans-Pecos was the first order of business. Amid continuing controversies in state and local government, the military garrison provided needed stability at Fort Davis. Complaining that Justice of the Peace Patrick Murphy had been "almost inaccessible" and had demanded "extortionate" fees for taking affidavits, Merritt, using the authority given to military officials in former Confederate states to oversee local government during Reconstruction, secured Murphy's removal. And in 1872, quarrels between local election officials led the Republican district judge, Simon B. Newcomb, to recommend that all votes cast in the Davis precinct be rejected. Fierce partisan struggles added to the turmoil. Dominating state government in the late 1860s, Republicans contemplated efforts to establish a separate Presidio County. Their success would undoubtedly have meant the election of another Republican state senator from this strongly Unionist district. But the evenhanded Judge Newcomb admitted that such machinations were "a dam [sic] fraud," since the proposed new district lacked the requisite minimum of 150 prospective voters.[7]

By 1872, Trans-Pecos Democrats had wrested sufficient control over the vastly more populated El Paso and San Elizario precincts to oust Republicans from power in El Paso County. Fearful for his safety, the Republican Newcomb declared that he would not hold court again without a military escort. Yet even as Democrats swept back into state and county offices, the Fort Davis region, with its dependence upon the federal government and influx of discharged soldiers, tended to vote stubbornly Republican. A separate Presidio County was finally organized in 1875, with Fort Davis designated as the new county seat.[8]

The Democratic Party's resurgence also brought the Texas Rangers to the Fort Davis region. In 1874, Richard Coke, the state's first Democratic governor since the Civil War, convinced the legislature to create a 450-strong "Frontier Battalion." In May 1879, the notorious Jesse Evans gang robbed several prominent Fort Davis businessmen. One Fort Davis resident explained their easy getaway: "It is so common for strangers to come in on horseback and well-armed that no one took any account of seeing them around." Responding to the crime wave, in early June Sgt. L. B. Caruthers arrived with a squad of Rangers. Cornering the outlaws in a mountain refuge eighteen miles from Presidio, the Rangers forced Evans and two henchmen to surrender after a bloody gunfight. The episode convinced state authorities to station a company of Rangers at Fort Davis.[9]

The army's return reinvigorated civilian efforts to occupy the Davis Mountains region, which had been largely deserted during the Civil War. By 1870, in addition to the 61 civilians living on post, 247 others resided off base at a community now known as Fort Davis (see appendix 2). Federal dollars once again provided the village's economic livelihood. In 1876, for example, the garrison's twenty-four officers and 274 enlisted men drew salaries of well over $100,000; federal contracts for forage and heating fuel let out that year at Davis totaled another $44,463 (in 2004 dollars, this represented an injection of well over $2 million into the region's economy). Although the largest contracts went to merchants from San Antonio or Fort Stockton, transporting the thousands of tons of grain and forage consumed by the garrison meant numerous jobs (see table 6.2). Fort Davis residents William Lampert, Joseph Sender, and Otis Keesey submitted successful bids to furnish the garrison with hay,

TABLE 6.2

Civilian Occupations at Fort Davis by Race/Ethnicity, 1870

Category	Total workforce (%)	White (%)	Spanish-surnamed (%)	Black/mulatto (%)
Agriculture	7	55	36	9
Stage and transport	3	20	80	0
White collar	12	89	5	5
Skilled mechanics	18	68	11	21
Semiskilled	15	17	74	9
Unskilled	45	3	63	34
% of Total workforce	**100**	**31**	**47**	**22**

SOURCE: U.S. Manuscript Census, 1870, Presidio County.

NOTE: "Agriculture" includes farmers, shepherds, herders, gardeners, and ranchers; "Stage and transport" includes drivers, wagoners, station keepers, and teamsters; "White collar" includes merchants, clerks, bar keepers, restaurant keepers, and bakers; "Skilled mechanics" includes masons, plasterers, shoemakers, blacksmiths, saddlers, painters, mechanics, brick makers, and carpenters; "Semiskilled" includes cooks, hucksters, tailors, seamstresses, spinners, and waiters; "Unskilled" includes domestic servants, laborers, and laundresses; $n = 153$.

wood, and charcoal. Two former sutlers at the post on the Limpia also won army contracts during the 1870s. Hardy frontier veterans, including businessman and rancher Daniel Murphy and the intrepid Dietrick Dutchover, had returned, as had Victoriano Hernandez, who once again emerged as the wealthiest Hispanic in the immediate region. By 1871, Hernandez's personal estate, which included 4 horses, 140 cattle, 300 sheep, and 600 acres of property, had an estimated value of $2,720 (more than $40,000 in 2004 terms).[10]

Civil-military relations at Davis were not always cordial. Few civilians remained ambivalent when dealing with officers such as the domineering Lt. Col. William Shafter, post commander in 1871–72 and 1881–82. Some respected his severe efficiency; others found him impossibly rigid. In one instance, the burly Shafter ordered a drunken Presidio County sheriff found in the sutler's store to leave the post. When the inebriated civil servant threatened Shafter, the lieutenant colonel offered to throw the lawman off the fort by force or slap him in the stockade. The sheriff slunk away, with Shafter demanding that he obtain special permission to enter the military reservation again. And upon finding another drunken civilian in the post billiards room, Shafter dispensed his own brand of justice. "As there was no enlisted man convenient to enforce my order," he explained gruffly, "I took him by the collar and led him to the door and upon his turning to come in kicked him so as to keep him out."[11]

Meanwhile, the regulars scrambled to construct suitable quarters at the post on the Limpia. As several officers had suggested throughout the 1850s, Lieutenant Colonel Merritt now opted to rebuild the fort farther away from the canyon walls. Once again, most of the wood and stone used in construction came from local sources. Unlike the first fort, however, civilian laborers initially spearheaded the new building projects. Between May 1867 and June 1868, more than seventy-two thousand dollars was spent on wages at Davis, more than at any other fort in Texas. Employees included a clerk, two foremen, an engineer, a sawyer, twenty-eight masons, thirty-six carpenters, a wheelwright, a blacksmith, nine quarrymen, a lime-burner, a wagon master, two teamsters, and ten laborers.[12]

But the construction bonanza was short-lived, hampered by shortages of wood and disinterested civilian mechanics. One worker admitted that most of his fellow employees spent most of their time "loafing a round the lumber pile at the back of the shop." One man, he claimed, was hired because he had bribed an officer with "fore [four] game cocks and too [two] bull dogs." The pace of construction slowed discernibly in spring 1869, when sharp budget restrictions forced the department quartermaster to cut the number of civilian workers to twenty. A frustrated onlooker described the result:

> The vast multitude of mechanics gathered here in the past two years, to assist in rebuilding their post, have been dismissed and dispersed; and the role of economy and reform has been fully inaugurated here, by the presiding genius at Washington. To my mind it is a question capable of much doubt, whether, or not, it was genuine economy to abandon the buildings nearly completed to the drenching rains and driving storms, and witness the unprotected adobe walls slowly but surely returning to a shapeless heap of mother earth. Had the work on the unfinished buildings progressed during the past Spring and Summer, the early Autumn would have found the Post completed, and most truly it would have been the pride of the frontier; but, looking upon it to-day, with its bare and roofless walls, the passer-by is forced to exclaim, "what a masterly failure." It is truly a melancholly [sic] abortion of what was intended to tower aloft, as a monument to martial pride and architectural vanity.[13]

Fort Davis's dilemmas were hardly unique. Dismayed by the deplorable conditions at many frontier posts, commanding general William T. Sherman acknowledged that "the huts in which our troops are forced to live are in some places inferior to what horses usually have." Because there was little money to hire civilian labor, impetus for continued construction fell to soldiers in the Fort Davis garrison, forcing many troops to spend more time laboring than soldiering. By January 1870, nine officers' quarters formed a north-south line across the mouth of the canyon. Front and rear porches graced each set of officers' quarters, which all had separate rear kitchens. Largest was the commander's residence, a seventeen-hundred-square-foot structure that featured limestone walls, a shingle roof, and two chimneys. Three sets of captains' quarters, smaller than those of the commanding officer, also lined officers' row. The captains each had two front rooms, separated by a wide entranceway, and a rear wing. Lieutenants' quarters lacked the latter extension.[14]

Across the parade ground from officers' row, six companies of enlisted men crowded into two completed barracks by 1869, each 186 feet long by 27 feet wide. A passageway separated each barrack into two equal sections and led to a rear wing that included a mess room, kitchen, and storeroom. Sergeants' quarters and offices occupied small closets at the far ends of the squad rooms. A communal sink lay behind each barrack. As in the officers' quarters, open fireplaces provided the heat. Older veterans quickly staked out the bunks closest to the three windows at the front of each section. Although the dirt floors rendered the barracks "very untidy, dirty, and disorderly," the quarters must have seemed quite cozy to the envious cavalry troopers still living in tents, as two additional barracks would not be completed until 1877.[15]

Numerous other structures dotted the landscape. Near the north side of the canyon bluffs lay two magazines that held the garrison's ammunition for small arms, two 3-inch field guns, and two Gatling guns. The limestone guardhouse, commanding the south side of the parade ground, was universally criticized as being too small—by January 1871, for example, an average of forty-six prisoners, many of whom had been sent from Forts Bliss, Quitman, and Stockton to await courts-martial, were crammed into its small holding tank and three tiny cells. An executive office building stood on the north side of the parade. Company and quartermaster stables and corrals lay behind the enlisted barracks. North and south of the corrals stood the quartermaster's and commissary storehouses, respectively. Observers praised the bakery, which produced "the best" bread, but the hospital remained problematic. The temporary buildings that served as the first postwar Fort Davis infirmary had a leaky roof and no glass windows; workers had cobbled together the hospital kitchen from condemned adobe bricks and scrap lumber. Complained Assistant Surgeon Daniel Weisel, "It, like the remainder of the Hospital being only built for temporary purposes, is rapidly decaying."[16]

The guardhouse, enlisted barracks, and quartermaster corrals and storehouses of the second Fort Davis, about 1871. Courtesy Fort Davis National Historic Site.

Doubtful of the permanency of the Federal presence at Fort Davis, post commander Shafter repeatedly rejected Weisel's attempts to requisition new funds for the hospital. The existing building, Shafter reasoned, had "answered the purpose very well for several years and is as good now as it ever was." Following Shafter's departure in 1872, plans for a new twenty-four-bed structure proceeded up the ladder of military bureaucracy, only to be vetoed at Division of the Missouri headquarters in faraway Chicago. Remarking that the Fort Davis climate was "very healthful," Lieutenant General Sheridan, commanding the division, insisted that half the number would suffice. Construction for a smaller twelve-bed infirmary, centerpiece of a nine-room adobe medical complex, finally began in October 1874.[17]

Controversies concerning the Fort Davis hospital highlighted the tensions that frequently divided surgeons and line officers at frontier posts. Company officers wanted to retain their best soldiers for regular duty, so they responded to the surgeon's pleas for help by dispatching their least capable men to the hospital. Post commanders almost inevitably sided with their company officers, thus alienating the doctors. Relations were further complicated in late 1869, when the War Department directed surgeons to conduct regular inspections of the station's physical properties, water supply, and cooking equipment. Not surprisingly, doctors often compiled an impressively long list of problems; in an army where the slightest criticism was interpreted as a deep personal affront, such a system was guaranteed to stir resentment.[18]

At Fort Davis, relations between Assistant Surgeon Weisel and Shafter's successor, Col. George Andrews, typified the larger problem. A native of Maryland, Weisel and his bride, Isabel, had arrived at Fort Davis in December 1868. The new doctor made an immediate impact. Collecting locally available watercress and introducing sauerkraut, onions, pickles, and citric acids into the ration, Weisel helped prevent another outbreak of scurvy, which had ravaged the garrison the previous spring. He also encouraged the men to bathe in Limpia Creek. Reasoning that "innocent and healthful amusements" would curtail the average soldier's "inducements to seek pleasures farther away and more injurious," Weisel hounded officers to show more concern for the health of their troops. The campaign worked, reducing sick rates by 42 percent. Deaths, sicknesses, and medical discharges at Fort Davis were less than half the national average.[19]

But not everyone appreciated the energetic young surgeon's work, with Colonel Andrews spearheading the criticism. In the post's official medical record, the doctor had complained that the general police of the post was "not done as regularly as it should" and noted the "very bad condition" of the sinks. Upon Weisel's transfer, Andrews fired back, charging that the surgeon's hospital records "have been irregularly and improperly kept." Weisel, according to Andrews, had used the official post medical history "as a means of expressing personal spleen." Gleefully immersing himself in the details of the hospital books, Andrews ferreted out numerous accounting discrepancies and implied that the doctor had used medicinal alcohol for his private consumption.[20]

Supplying the frontier garrison, which between 1867 and 1880 averaged nearly 390 officers and enlisted men (see appendix 1), confounded efforts to cut costs and improve military efficiency. Inadequate storage facilities and the enormous distances between ports of entry (Corpus Christi and Indianola), department headquarters (usually at San Antonio), and Trans-Pecos forts such as Davis frequently overwhelmed the system. In 1872, a Fort Davis board of survey concluded that nearly one-quarter of the recent shipment of bacon, along with 263 pounds of rice, 187 pounds of sugar, and 129 pounds of soap, had been lost to "natural waste" during the hard journey. Three years later, another board charged "that old and an inferior quality of stores are often sent to this post . . . and others are packed so badly that in their arrival here are totally unfit for issue." Within the past six months, 2,357 pounds of bread, 900 pounds of hominy, 384 pounds of hay, 151 pounds of crackers, 97 gallons of molasses, 208 pounds of vermicelli, 256 pounds of macaroni, 588 cans of condensed milk, 9 heads of cheese, 49 hams, 154 cans of sardines, 20 gallons of onions, 198 cans of sweet potatoes, 120 pounds of creamed tartar, 143 cans of onions, 508 pounds of lard, and 848 cans of lima beans had spoiled.[21]

Frustrated officers sometimes attempted to take matters into their own hands. In early 1871, a Fort Davis board held quartermaster officials in San Antonio responsible for the loss of 2,500 pounds of spoiled bacon. Rumor held that the board's officers would be court-martialed for their temerity in having challenged department authorities. Defending his subordinates against possible retribution, Lieutenant Colonel Shafter sought to soothe relations. The board of officers had "intended to do their duty," he assured the brass in San Antonio. "I believe their judgment in the case to be erroneous," Shafter contended, "but I do not think they ought to be humiliated by being brought to trial for it." For good measure, Shafter added that "they are all good officers and I think will be very careful in the future that their recommendations are more carefully made."[22]

The post garden afforded some relief from the bland official rations. In 1870, a garden had been established at the old Musquiz ranch, but as one skeptical inspector put it, "Twelve miles out and back over a rough road is a long ways to go for a head of lettuce or a bunch of radishes." Accordingly, the troops planted a new five-acre plot just southeast of the post, producing Irish potatoes, sweet potatoes, and melons. Later in the decade, soldiers were detailed to a garden established in Limpia Canyon for up to six weeks at a time. Of course, unforeseen impediments occasionally bedeviled the soldier-farmers. In 1873, for example, grasshoppers destroyed almost the entire crop; ten years later, civilian livestock broke into the garden and ravaged much of the produce.[23]

Purchases from the sutler further supplemented regular rations. Responding to highly publicized abuses during the Civil War, during the late 1860s the army allowed several traders to operate at a single post; competition, it was hoped, would improve the quality of services to the troops. By October 1868, Fort Davis boasted three official traders—Jarvis Hubbell, R. G. Hurlbut, and C. H. Lesnisky & Co. Two years later, Congress again revamped the post trader system, authorizing Secretary of War William Belknap to appoint sutlers. Belknap, who brazenly used the patronage to line his own pockets (and who would be forced to resign for having done so), named Simon Chaney for the position at Fort Davis. Post residents protested the choice, lambasting the new sutler as "unreliable" and maintaining "an inferior stock of goods." Secretary Belknap transferred the appointment to Chaney's brother, A. W., but the latter also failed to meet the garrison's demands. On the advice of Rep. John L. Vance (D-Ohio), Belknap named John D. Davis to succeed the Chaneys. Despite the unusual circumstances surrounding his appointment, Davis managed to win over local skeptics, taking on George H. Abbott as his partner and expanding his compound to include a residence, bar, store, telegraph office, and two privies.[24]

Regimental bands had long been an army institution, but a cost-conscious Congress now limited appropriations to a single chief musician per regiment. Sixteen (later twenty) privates and a sergeant could be detached from their units to form a band, but musicians had to provide their own instruments. Congress "has done a wrong thing," protested one officer, and most regiments kept their bands by private subscription—at Fort Davis in 1873, for example, the regimental council of administration levied "voluntary" 1 percent salary contributions upon all officers for the purchase and repair of band instruments. Bandsmen frequently held plum staff posts and were spared service on guard and fatigue details. In addition to playing at parties and hops, the group serenaded the garrison at inspection, roll call, and special military occasions.[25]

Other leisure activities on post reflected contemporary recreational trends. Despite official proclamations threatening ruinous penalties, gambling was endemic on every military post. Good marksmen found themselves invited to well-organized hunting parties sponsored by their officers. Company and post funds supplied checkers, backgammon, and Parcheesi sets for the enlisted barracks. Soldiers throughout the West embraced baseball during the late 1880s, and the men at Fort Davis proved no exception. Contests between the Fort Davis nine and civilian or rival garrison teams frequently highlighted holiday celebrations. And like their comrades in arms throughout history, soldiers at Fort Davis took great pride in their abilities as practical jokers. On their triumphant return from a successful scout in 1868, members of the Ninth Cavalry dressed up in their captured booty and pretended to be Apaches, surprising a group of their comrades working on a stone quarry about a mile from the post. "You can imagine how fast those men ran trying to get back to the post," quipped an observer. Another diarist recorded the following prank: "A strange sight met my gaze this morning walking down the road in front of the officers row—some soldiers had dressed *a burro in white drawers on the legs*, and a white jacket round its body and an old hat upon its head, the animal's ears projecting through openings in the crown. Playing cards were pinned to the sides of the coat, and a cigar box hung from the fore shoulder. Thus attired the brute has been walking up and down the post all day to the amusement of those who saw it."[26]

The army also sponsored educational and religious activities. The library and reading room, supported by post funds and small War Department grants, provided a widely used outlet for the garrison. In a typical month, about 20 percent of the enlisted men on post visited the library. Magazine subscriptions included copies of *Scribner's Magazine, United Service, Harper's Magazine, Appleton's, Popular Science, The North American Review, Frank Leslie's Illustrated, London Graphic, The Nation,* and the *Army and Navy Register.* Daily newspapers from New York, St. Louis, Chicago, Boston, Houston, San Antonio, and Philadelphia were also available, as were an assortment of books.[27]

Shortly after the Civil War, Congress had ordered each permanent garrison to organize a school. Education at Fort Davis received an energetic boost in 1875 with the arrival of Chaplain George M. Mullins, Twenty-fifth Infantry. A Disciples of Christ minister, Mullins boasted a master's degree from the University of Kentucky. The school flourished under his tutelage, with black troops eager to acquire skills that had long been denied them. "The marked improvement the men have made in the various studies . . . reflects great credit upon themselves and is highly recommendable," bragged the post commander. With company officers supporting his efforts and average attendance climbing to ninety-two in May 1876, Mullins acknowledged that his students displayed "remarkable ambition and ability to learn." When the increasing demands of Indian campaigns forced the temporary discontinuance of the school for soldiers, Chaplain Mullins organized classes for children that met every weekday between one and three o'clock. An enlisted man was detailed as teacher; "he will have authority to inflict slight punishments, but whipping will not be permitted," explained one circular. For the first three months of 1880, attendance averaged ten of the twenty-two children of enlisted men on post; they were joined by three civilian youngsters.[28]

Mullins also found time for his more traditional religious duties. "I am humbly convinced that any interest in and influence of the preaching is but fugitive, and for the hour," the chaplain had sighed shortly after his arrival. To make matters worse, "the use of intoxicating liquors seems to be steadily on the increase." But Mullins doggedly attacked these concerns, working with fellow officers to secure more furniture and soliciting extra Bibles and hymnals from the American Bible Society. By spring 1879, a new post chapel stood ready for service.[29]

Army laundresses remained a highly visible presence, but in contrast to their relative prosperity at antebellum Fort Davis, eked out only a precarious existence after the Civil War. Sixty-two percent of Fort Davis army laundresses were black; 24 percent, mulatto; and 14 percent, Hispanic. Just over half were married to soldiers, often the corporals and sergeants who formed the backbone of the army. Still, they were typically relegated to the poorest quarters on post; in 1883, for instance, they were moved into an eight-room adobe structure located southeast of the parade ground that had already been deemed "past repair." And long intervals between the paymaster's visits often left the women, like their customers, strapped for cash. Two laundresses explained their plight to the post commander on one such occasion: "We are a lone [sic] standing women," they reasoned, "and thought best to try for your assistance." Twenty-seven soldiers owed them for five months' work.[30]

But many were unsympathetic with the laundresses' plight. Claiming that enlisted personnel could handle the chores more effectively, critics accused the laundresses of prostitution and charged that marriages between soldiers and laundresses were often strictly those of convenience, designed to allow the "husband" to live outside the barracks. Echoing commonly held Victorian ideals, supporters retorted that the presence of women had a positive moral impact upon the men; at the very least, they were necessary to keep their irreplaceable noncommissioned officer-husbands in the service. In a cost-saving measure, Congress eventually stripped the women of their government rations, but army tradition held strong, and laundresses remained on post in at least a semiofficial capacity.[31]

Only about 2 percent of the enlisted men at Fort Davis after the Civil War were married. Several had wed Hispanic women, suggesting that interaction between black enlisted personnel and Mexican Americans was tolerated on the Trans-Pecos military frontier. Their ramshackle quarters were the scene of lively, if not always reputable, activity. On June 11, 1877, for example, a Twenty-fifth Infantry private entered the quarters of Henry Ratcliffe's wife, laundress for the Tenth Cavalry. Finding her absent, the enraged infantryman kicked over a table filled with crockery, "thereby . . . disturbing the good order of the garrison." Another soldier stormed into Sgt. James Cooper's house, complaining to Mrs. Cooper about her husband. Seizing a fistful of hair, the soldier dragged her outside before the guard rescued her.[32]

A few white soldiers at Fort Davis dared to challenge racial barriers and social traditions. One married contract surgeon was accused of "cohabitating" with a Mexican woman. The former wife of Lt. Calvin P. McTaggert, Seventeenth Infantry, married a First Infantry private named Daniel Davis, a member of the Fort Davis garrison. A U.S. congressman asked the army to allow Davis's wife to join her husband there. None too happy about the unusual request, William Shafter promised to help Private Davis secure an early discharge, complaining that "I have not quarters in the garrison for Mrs. Davis. . . . if she wishes to come here and live in the town adjacent to the post, she can do so, and Davis can see her every day." But Shafter warned that "Mrs. Davis has been the wife of an officer and I think she will find it very unpleasant living near a post." Before any arrangements could be concluded, another First Infantryman raped Mrs. Davis. Although the Texas Rangers nabbed the villain (who subsequently received the death penalty), only later was Private Davis's discharge secured.[33]

But these were the exceptions, for the lines separating officers and enlisted personnel remained strong. About one-third of the postbellum officers had families living with them at Fort Davis. Their wives and children continued as the post elite, mixing almost entirely with each other or with the upper crust of the nearby civilian community. Picnics, dances, hunts, and dinner parties delighted the officers and their families. Romantic couples liked to steal away for quiet strolls into the nearby canyon. Several officers brought pianos to Fort Davis, and at least one dabbled in photography, putting on "lantern entertainments" for selected guests. Birthday parties for officers' children featured games such as pin-the-tail-on-the-donkey. At a "progressive euchre party" attended by many officers' wives and hosted by postmistress and teacher Mattie Belle Anderson, the "booby prize" consisted of "a good-sized healthy-looking frog, who croaked melodiously when handed to the winner."[34]

Bachelor officers carefully scrutinized the daughters of their commissioned comrades and Fort Davis civilian elites for their suitability as wives or girlfriends. Lt. Leighton Finley, a Princeton graduate, kept a list of "girls I have known," assigning numerical ratings to his female acquaintances as to the "degree of influence they exercised over me." Of those at Fort Davis, Mary Shafter, the post commander's daughter, rated a 4. Mary Beck (daughter of Lt. William H. Beck), initially earned only a 3, but was later upgraded to a 7. Daniel Murphy's daughters were especially popular with the bachelor crowd. Murphy's home and store, which lay several hundred yards outside the southern limits of the post, became a convenient gathering place for townspeople and officers. "The Murphys are real warm-hearted frontier people," explained one traveler. The girls, who had attended boarding school in San Antonio and often flashed imported clothes, "really 'get themselves up' very creditably." Predictably, four of Murphy's daughters married army officers.[35]

Frontier conditions compounded the difficulties of bearing and raising children for everyone, regardless of class. Childbirth on a military post far from home and friends was an especially traumatic experience. "Though I ought not to complain, this post being really lovely and home like," wrote Annie Nolan, wife of a tough old Tenth Cavalryman, admitted that she would rather have borne her child among her friends at Fort Concho, where she had been stationed for several years, than among strangers at her new home at Fort Davis. Caring for newborn babies tested even the best parents. Mary Swan Thompson, wife of Lt. James K. Thompson, handled the initial prob-

Several officers and their families posed for this late 1880s photograph overlooking officers'
row. Courtesy Fort Davis National Historic Site.

lems extremely well. Having put her baby boy to sleep, Mary allowed that
"all my nervousness has gone . . . I've not an ache or pain anywhere." With
the infant nursing at regular hours, things could scarcely have been better.
But four weeks later, an exhausted Mary replied testily to appeals by her
mother and grandmother for more frequent letters: "This is the first afternoon I've had a moment to myself in I can't tell when. . . . The baby is so
wakeful all day long and keeps me so busy—but today he has just succeeded
after trying for nearly two hours in howling himself to sleep. . . . It is two
o'clock now—and so far today he has slept just fifteen minutes, after his bath
this morning, so you can see he is an incessant scamp—and there is nobody
to take him but myself. So please stop scolding me about not writing."[36]

Nor did class solidarity preclude intraofficer bickering. Stationed at
neighboring Fort Stockton, Lt. Louis H. Orleman; his eighteen-year-old-
daughter, Lillie; and Capt. Andrew Geddes took the stagecoach together in
February 1879 to begin a short tour of temporary duty at Davis. The trip was
an eventful one, for Lieutenant Orleman later charged Geddes with having
attempted "to corrupt" Lillie "to his own illicit purposes." Tearfully, Lillie
also accused Geddes of repeatedly propositioning her. Mounting a vigorous
defense, Geddes, separated from his wife and twice Lillie's age, struck back,
accusing Orleman of "having criminal intercourse with his said daughter"

at Stockton. He also presented the affidavit of a fellow passenger asserting that Orleman had been "fondling with the breast of his daughter" on the stage trip. After sixty-eight days of scintillating testimony at San Antonio, the court-martial found Geddes guilty, a decision later overturned by Pres. Rutherford B. Hayes.[37]

Another sensational incident at Fort Davis involved the first black graduate of West Point, Lt. Henry O. Flipper. Born in Thomasville, Georgia, Flipper had overcome the ostracism of fellow cadets to graduate in 1876. He received a commission in the Tenth Cavalry and came to Fort Davis four years later. Although Maj. Napoleon B. McLaughlin, then serving as post commander, seemed to Flipper "a very fine officer and gentleman," most of the other officers were "hyenas." Conditions completely soured with Colonel Shafter's return to Fort Davis in 1881. Friends in town warned Lieutenant Flipper that Shafter and his minions were out to get him. "Never did a man walk the path of uprighteousness straighter than I did," Flipper later remembered, "but the trap was cunningly laid and I was sacrificed."[38]

Like many fellow officers, Lieutenant Flipper found the paperwork associated with routine duties—in his case, as post commissary officer—to be overwhelming. In August 1881, he was arrested for misappropriating army funds and attempting to conceal a twenty-four-hundred-dollar discrepancy in his accounts. His court-martial began the following month. Flipper acknowledged the shortfall but denied any conscious attempt to defraud the government. In light of his "peculiar situation," the black lieutenant had concluded that he must "endeavor to work out the problem alone." Unfortunately, his plan to pay off the debt went awry when projected royalties from his autobiography were delayed. Pleading for leniency, his lawyer, Capt. Merritt Barber, acknowledged Flipper's carelessness but defended his decision to cover up the matter as having been perfectly logical: "He has had no one to turn to for counsel or sympathy," argued Barber. "Is it strange then that when he found himself confronted with a mystery he could not solve, he should hide it in his own breast and endeavor to work out the problem alone as he had been compelled to do all the other problems of his life?"[39]

Without formal training as an accountant, the lieutenant had been a poor choice as commissary officer. He had doubted that his superiors would overlook his bookkeeping errors, a reasonable conclusion based upon years of overcoming racial bigotry. But from the army's perspective, the failure to render forthright reports—absolutely essential for effective military operations—was a serious offense. This, combined with his black skin, proved fatal to his military career. Local residents took up a collection to repay Flipper's debt (Shafter himself contributed to the fund), and a stream of witnesses testified to his good character. But their efforts were in vain. Unable to prove him guilty of embezzlement, the court-martial dismissed Flipper from the service for "conduct unbecoming an officer and a gentleman." The young man went on to become a successful mining engineer, spending much of the rest of his life in a futile effort to clear his army record.[40]

The regular army's return had provided the Davis Mountains region with a semblance of order and authority. A regimental band, school, and library had brought the rudiments of American culture to the refurbished post. Although providing the frontier regulars with adequate housing, supplies, and medical care continued to bedevil military authorities working within a tight federal budget, an assortment of new buildings, now located outside the canyon walls, had eventually been constructed to shelter the postbellum garrison. Forays by surgeons into the daily routine had improved health but added unforeseen tensions between the doctors and line officers. And the army now included several regiments of black troops; not surprisingly, it also witnessed the racial prejudice that plagued society as a whole. With few exceptions, white officers and their ladies continued to insist that their social worlds remain distinct from those of persons of color and those, such as enlisted personnel and laundresses, whom they deemed to belong to inferior classes. Practically speaking, however, their paths often crossed; the physical segregation they might well have desired would never be absolute. In sum, with Fort Davis came the United States to West Texas.

CHAPTER SEVEN

FRONTIER DUTIES

In reoccupying Fort Davis following the Civil War, the federal government had signaled its determination to complete its conquest of the
Trans-Pecos. Americans once again expected their army to play a leading role in this process of nation-building. A garrison afforded better security
as well as a considerable influx of federal money, both sure to attract civilian
settlement. Soldiers would also help improve communications, building the
roads and stringing the telegraph wires that would make the region more
accessible to outsiders. Finally, the army was to enforce the nation's claims
to West Texas, seeking out and crushing all who dared to challenge its man-
ifest destiny.

Such high expectations were inconsistent with the often-contradictory
relationship between the U.S. Army and the rest of American society after
the Civil War. Though eager to defeat the Indians and conquer the West,
Americans remained unwilling to provide the army with the tools needed to
quickly achieve these goals. Some—particularly many white Southerners,
who deeply resented the military's role during Reconstruction—held the
army responsible for all of society's ills. Others feared that a large standing
army threatened liberty and represented an unnecessary burden on taxpayers. The army thus suffered a political pummeling. Pres. Ulysses S. Grant,
newly elected in 1869, refused to support a move to give the commanding
general real power, ensuring that the dysfunctional line-staff relationship of
antebellum years would continue. Repeated cutbacks in the army's authorized strength—from 54,000 in 1866, to 37,313 in 1869, to 30,000 in 1870,
and to 27,000 in 1874—had been accompanied by similar reductions in pay
and emoluments, which commanding general William T. Sherman described
as being "almost fatal." In 1877, Congress's failure to pass a military appropriations bill left soldiers without pay for nearly six months. Some lawmakers

threatened to disband the army entirely. "There is an almost insanity for re-trenchment," explained one senator who allied himself with the regulars, "which ignores both reason and necessity."[1]

Even as it slashed military appropriations, Congress continued to place great faith in the army's resourcefulness. When congressional Republicans wanted to ensure that the former Confederate states abided by Congress's mandates following the Civil War, for example, they gave authority over lo-cal governments to the military. When improvements in the infrastructure of the nation's capital city were necessary, the government turned to the Army Corps of Engineers. Nowhere was the "multipurpose army" more evident than in the American West, where officers and enlisted men were expected to defeat the Indians, conduct scientific reconnaissance, construct and pro-tect lines of communication, defend international borders, bolster local econ-omies, and preserve civil order.[2]

The quality of uniforms and equipment reflected the fickle relations between the army, the federal government, and the public. In order to save money, stocks of surplus Civil War woolen uniforms, though of notoriously poor quality and ill-suited to the blazing Texas heat, had to be depleted be-fore replacements could be purchased. Subsequent changes in the regulation uniform only belatedly addressed the needs of soldiers in the arid Southwest. Cavalrymen received longer coats to replace their traditional shell jackets; for a time, infantrymen were issued loose-fitting pleated coats. For dress pa-rades, mounted soldiers added a Prussian-style spiked helmet with yellow horsehair plume, and infantrymen sported new shakos. All troops eventually secured broad-brimmed felt hats for campaign duty, but only during the late 1880s did the army introduce light cotton or muslin uniforms adapted to the southwestern climate. The constant tinkering with the regulation uniform, as well as the long delays it took to replenish western stocks with updated is-sues, left the frontier regulars wearing a bizarre mixture of styles that ap-proximated society's paradoxical views about its armed forces.[3]

Weapons were better suited to West Texas than were the official uni-forms. After considerable debate and extensive field tests (which included the men of one company at Fort Davis), military officials concluded that repeating weapons were too expensive, too prone to misfire, and too limited in range. Instead, the army adopted single-shot, 1873 model .45 caliber Springfield rifles and carbines. Although often criticized, the reliable breech-loading Springfields would serve the army well in its wars against the Indians. Mounted personnel also received the Colt's 1872 revolver, a powerful .45 caliber single-action six-shooter. Light, easily manageable, and accurate to four thou-sand yards, the Hotchkiss mountain howitzer added long-range punch. Less successful was the Gatling gun. Though its hopper-fed revolving barrels could fire 350 rounds per minute, the weapon's short range, maddening proclivity to jam, and cumbersome carriage limited its effectiveness in the American West. As one veteran put it bluntly, Gatling guns "are worthless for Indian fighting."[4]

As Reconstruction waned, the military geography of Texas changed accordingly. In 1871, the Department of Texas had been transferred to the Division of the Missouri, which encompassed the homelands of the most powerful Plains Indians. In order to better handle frontier affairs, western Texas was often further subdivided into districts, which included those of Presidio (including Forts Bliss, Quitman, Davis, and Bliss), Pecos (Concho, McKavett, Clark, and Duncan), Rio Grande (McIntosh, Ringgold, and Brown), and Brazos (Griffin and Richardson). For many years, Fort Davis served as headquarters for the Presidio command. As had been the case before the Civil War, field duties encompassed a broad range of activities that often diverted attention away from fighting Indians. In the late summer of 1875, for example, Capt. Louis H. Carpenter, a hard-bitten former enlisted man, led one of the largest columns of the period—his own troop of Tenth Cavalry and a company of Twenty-fifth Infantry carrying five days' rations and two hundred rounds of ammunition per man, supported by eight wagons, eight mules, three guides, and three packers. Finding his superiors more interested in his shortening roads, "mapping the country," and preserving government animals than in finding any Indians, Carpenter returned empty-handed after logging 1,153 miles in the field. As roadwork continued, soldiers of the Twenty-fifth Infantry became especially proficient laborers, with Capt. George Schooley reputedly the king of construction foremen. "I don't think there will be any hill in the vicinity when he gets done," quipped a fellow officer.[5]

The regulars also strung telegraph wires. In 1874, Congress had authorized the War Department to construct 1,275 miles of telegraphs in Texas at one hundred dollars per mile. Done largely under the direction of Lt. Adolphus W. Greely, who would later gain greater fame for his Arctic explorations, the laborious tasks of staking out lines, digging holes, planting poles, and stringing wires demanded prodigious amounts of military time and labor. Although the enormous effort paid off in the long run—by 1880, the army could coordinate its efforts from its telegraph stations at Fort Concho, Grierson's Spring, Fort Stockton, Fort Davis, and Fort Bliss—it had strained frontier resources.[6]

Responsibilities along the Mexican border also demanded the garrison's close attention. With the close of the Civil War, caravans resumed the profitable run between San Antonio and Chihuahua City, trading mining equipment, cotton, small manufactured goods, and cattle for bullion, hides, and hard currency. The lively Chihuahua trade also encouraged development at Presidio and Ojinaga, the twin Rio Grande settlements at Presidio del Norte whose collective population now surpassed three thousand. Both the U.S. and Mexican governments maintained customs houses along the great river, although high duties and lax enforcement led many traders to circumvent legal channels. Nightly fandangos and the colorful lifestyles of the trail hands, merchants, smugglers, ne'er-do-wells, and assorted government officials gave the towns a distinctive flavor. "To the American stranger, it is a place in which he can pass a day or two with interest," calculated one contemporary guidebook.[7]

Washington officials agreed that Comanche, Apache, and Kickapoo raiders (the latter having recently migrated from Kansas) from Mexico and New Mexico must not be allowed to short-circuit this profitable trade. At the army's behest, in 1871–72 Secretary of War William Belknap and Secretary of State Hamilton J. Fish pressed Mexico to allow U.S. soldiers to cross the Rio Grande when in hot pursuit of Indians or bandits. Mexican officials, fearing that any concessions to the *Norteamericanos* meant political suicide, rejected State Department queries. Instead, the governor of Chihuahua was authorized to help the Fort Davis garrison crush "the hostile Indians in Texas." As the violence increased, Lieutenant Colonel Shafter readied a mobile squadron of thirty-five mule-mounted soldiers and dispatched a company to garrison Presidio during the summer of 1872.[8]

Links between Fort Davis and Presidio became even more evident in 1875, when the Indian Bureau appropriated twenty-five thousand dollars to facilitate the removal of tribes along the Rio Grande to interior reservations. Thomas G. Williams, chief negotiator with the Kickapoos, attributed regional depredations to Indians from New Mexico, not those living south of the Rio Grande. At the same time, Williams, keenly alert to the interests of U.S. customs officials, recommended the transfer of the Fort Davis garrison to Presidio as a means of reducing smuggling. The Treasury Department backed Williams's proposal and Interior Secretary Columbus Delano saw to it that a copy reached the War Department. Col. George L. Andrews, commanding Fort Davis at the time, strenuously protested the projected shift. In his view, local merchants and property owners were simply angling to secure a military post in order to increase the value of their investments. Division commander Sheridan supported Andrews. Fort Davis protected the road from San Antonio to El Paso; furthermore, charged Sheridan, "the recommendation of Thomas G. Williams is probably in the interests of the town of Presidio del Norte, which wants to get a market for the sale of grain and other articles of commerce." Secretary of War William Belknap thus vetoed the proposed move from Davis to Presidio.[9]

Although the transfer had been blocked, tumultuous events along the Rio Grande continued to involve the Fort Davis garrison. In November 1876, the army reported a "pretty good gang of Indians" trading at San Carlos, Mexico. Moses Kelley, who operated businesses on both sides of the border, also requested assistance after receiving threats from Mexican revolutionaries. Leaving the band to stand guard at Davis, Colonel Andrews and a company of men from the Twenty-fifth Infantry wheeled a 3-inch cannon south to Presidio. On December 10, Andrews demanded that Mexican authorities surrender a U.S. citizen taken hostage. "I am prepared to open up on the town of Presidio del Norte, Mexico, with my Artillery, and to follow it up with Cavalry and Infantry," threatened the colonel. Upon being rejected, Andrews unlimbered his cannon and lobbed several shells onto the Mexican side of the river.[10]

Andrews's demonstration had the desired effect; apparently, the hostage was freed. The colonel then hoped to exploit the incident to secure reinforcements for his overworked regulars at Fort Davis. But Sheridan, in a sharp departure from the belligerent stance he had taken during Ranald Mackenzie's 1873 strike against an Indian village near Remolino, Mexico, now counseled caution. "I think it would be well," warned Sheridan, "to caution the officers in command along the Rio Grande frontier to avoid involving themselves in cases that belong exclusively to the State Department." Despite the stern admonition, Andrews continued to detach elements of the Twenty-fifth Infantry to Presidio when he believed the situation warranted it.[11]

Protecting the mails represented another significant commitment of resources. Although a few soldiers undoubtedly welcomed the chance to escape the drudgery of garrison life, their task was both difficult and thankless. Station keepers and stage drivers, many of whom were Confederate veterans, subjected their black escorts to a humiliating torrent of racial slurs. The work could also be dangerous, as an Apache attack on the eight men guarding an eastbound mail from El Paso had demonstrated in December 1867. Lashing his mules into a dead run, the stage driver raced toward Eagle Springs. Both sides opened up a furious fusillade, with Pvt. Nathan Johnson killed and three of the escort's horses hit during the wild chase. Hearing the sounds of the firing, Capt. Henry Carroll's company of men from the Ninth Cavalry, which happened to be camped at Eagle Springs, deployed to ambush the onrushing enemy. As the coach careened wildly toward the station, the waiting troopers unleashed a devastating volley into the unsuspecting Apaches, who promptly broke off the chase.[12]

Even so, the frontier situation seemed less onerous than it had been during the late 1850s. By 1868, the garrisons of the army's Trans-Pecos posts

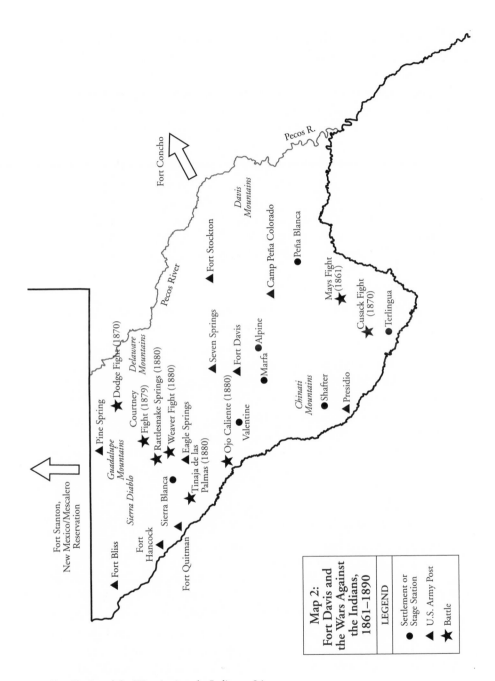

Fort Davis and the Wars Against the Indians, 1861–90

The following labels appear on the map:

Pecos R.

Fort Concho

Pecos River

▲ Pine Spring

Guadalupe Mountains

★ Dodge Fight (1870)

Delaware Mountains

Courtney
★ Fight (1879)

★ Rattlesnake Springs (1880)

★ Weaver Fight (1880)

Sierra Diablo

★ Eagle Springs

● Sierra Blanca

★ Tinaja de las
Palmas (1880)

Fort Stanton,
New Mexico/Mescalero
Reservation

▲ Fort Bliss

Fort
▲ Hancock

▲ Fort Quitman

★ Ojo Caliente (1880)

● Valentine

▲ Seven Springs

*Davis
Mountains*

▲ Fort Stockton

▲ Fort Davis

● Marfa ● Alpine

▲ Camp Peña Colorado

● Peña Blanca

Mays Fight
(1861)

★ Cusack Fight
(1870)

● Terlingua

*Chinati
Mountains*

● Shafter

▲ Presidio

Map 2:
Fort Davis and
the Wars Against
the Indians,
1861–1890

LEGEND

Settlement or
● Stage Station

▲ U.S. Army Post

★ Battle

at Davis, Stockton, Quitman, and Bliss totaled 1,209 officers and enlisted men, nearly four times the number of those stationed there in 1860. The size and scope of the army's post–Civil War reoccupation of the Trans-Pecos initially seemed to have surprised the Indians. On September 8, 1868, Lt. Patrick Cusack led sixty men from the Ninth Cavalry from Fort Davis in response to a recent theft of animals near Fort Stockton. Cusack linked up with about four dozen Mexican volunteers, who had received permission to cross the Rio Grande in pursuit of Indians who had stolen animals in Mexico. Marching at night to avoid detection, they encountered an Apache encampment ninety miles south of Davis. About seven o'clock on the morning of September 12, Cusack's column thundered through the camp, catching the inhabitants completely off guard. In a short, savage fight, the regulars and volunteers killed at least twenty Indians; wounded a similar number; captured the band's entire herd of horses, oxen, and mules; and recovered two young Mexican captives. Cusack's troopers destroyed the camp, "leaving them nothing whatever," while the volunteers scalped the dead bodies. The victory had cost only two soldiers wounded and two government horses killed. The Irish-born Cusack received a brevet promotion to captain for his exploits.[13]

A similar success came in early 1870. Leading elements of four companies of the Ninth Cavalry from Forts Davis and Quitman, Capt. Francis S. Dodge struck another Apache village in the Guadalupe Mountains near Delaware Creek on January 20. Like Cusack, Dodge was a former enlisted man who had received his commission during the Civil War. Suffering a loss of only two wounded, the cavalrymen destroyed most of the camp's winter stores, captured twenty-five horses and mules, and claimed to have killed or wounded fifty Indians.[14]

In both cases, the soldiers had surprised the Indians, complacent in the presumed safety of their Trans-Pecos hideouts. Over the next decade, however, the situation would change dramatically. The multiple expectations placed upon the army overburdened Fort Davis's limited resources. Learning from the bitter experiences of the Cusack and Dodge disasters, Lipan and Mescalero Apaches who used the region as a source of food and booty now left their families and property elsewhere. Depriving the army of its most successful tactic—the direct assault upon a band's village—small groups of mounted warriors could still take advantage of the sparsely populated vastness of the Trans-Pecos. Exploiting the many opportunities for ambush, Indians could prey upon the weak or the isolated while fleeing larger columns capable of inflicting real harm.

Defeating such enemies was not for the faint of heart. But it could be done. Just as small groups of Indians often embarrassed larger numbers of regulars, so could well-led troops—even on foot—achieve unanticipated successes. Far to the north, Col. Nelson A. Miles's Fifth Infantry would wear down the Sioux and Northern Cheyennes in their epic Montana winter campaigns of 1876–78, conquering a peace in the aftermath of the Custer disaster at the Little Bighorn. With an average of twenty officers and nearly three hundred enlisted men assigned there between 1867 and 1881, Fort Davis represented a sizable investment in army manpower and was counted upon to play a major role in stamping out opposition to the American conquest of the Trans-Pecos.

Experienced westerners knew that good scouts were essential to the success of any operations against the mobile Plains tribes. Elsewhere in the west, the army employed Indian auxiliaries to help track and defeat tribes labeled hostile by the federal government. The record at Fort Davis, however, suggests a failure to fully cultivate these important resources. The army frequently hired José Maria Bill as a guide between 1868 and 1870, but in a glaring failure of post authorities to respond to frontier realities, scouts or guides accompanied only seven of the forty-nine expeditions conducted from Fort Davis between 1871 and 1880. Only belatedly did officials initiate concerted efforts to employ Pueblo and Tigua Indians from Ysleta del Sur (near El Paso) as army auxiliaries.[15]

Inconsistent federal policies and a dearth of strategic planning aggravated the difficulties. The government vacillated between peace and war, discouraging long-range military planning in the process. Authority continued to be divided between the War Department, which was to fight Indians, and the Interior Department, which oversaw the reservations. Reservations and international boundary lines often shielded Indian raiders from their pursuers. Forts continued to be located with more regard to bowing to domestic political pressures and saving money than to carrying out effective Indian policy. A thin line of regulars manned these frontier positions, but without formalized, consistent doctrine often flailed away ineffectually at their Indian foes.[16]

Confronting a situation that demanded individual initiative and unconventional approaches, an officer stationed at Fort Davis could easily have taken the army's lack of institutional interest in developing methods suitable for the Indian conflicts as an excuse to do nothing. Indeed, many officers seemed more interested in replaying the Civil War or studying European-style conflicts than in devoting the time and thought necessary to formulate clear doctrine for frontier conditions. As one frustrated army wife proclaimed to her Indian-fighting husband, "If Indian warfare was only regarded as legitimate warfare there would be encouragement for hard work & successful campaigning such as you have done & won." Lt. Col. Emory Upton, recognized as the army's premier theoretician, confided to a fellow West Pointer "the proposition that 'bushwacking' [*sic*] and Indian fighting with one or two companies do not qualify an officer for the position as General." The haphazard intellectual approach to fighting Indians seems eerily similar to the government's failure to develop a systematic approach to western affairs. Reaction to crises seemed the order of the day; frontier officers, with their small commands stretched to the limit, often satisfied themselves with passive defense. Many found the very real shortages of horses and money to be good rationales for not pressing the attack against the elusive and skilled Plains tribes. Orders such as those to a Ninth Cavalry officer betrayed the lethargy born of such conditions. "If possible," he should punish the Indians, but only if he could do so while exercising "care and judgment" in taking "good care" of troops and government animals. Further, he should take no risks that might "endanger the safety" of his command.[17]

Thus, despite the Cusack and Dodge scouts, raids by Indians and bandits continued to threaten the Trans-Pecos. In January 1869, Indians killed two men near old Fort Quitman. That summer, they stole several stock from the stage station at Dead Man's Hole. From Presidio, rancher John D. Burgess claimed that "the Mexican thieves driven from Fort Davis . . . have taken refuge on my plantation, and are nightly committing depredations on my goat and sheep herds." In 1870, raiders killed an employee and stole four hundred sheep from Milton Faver's ranch. A late spring foray against the Fort Davis pinery snatched fifteen government mules. The garrison had launched nine retaliatory scouts by January 1871, but the problem was clearly worsening. "The sufferings of the settlers are grievous," sympathized one congressional committee.[18]

William R. Shafter's arrival at Davis in spring 1871 had seemed to herald a new regime. Energetic and imperious, the bullying Shafter halted all but the most essential construction projects in order to free up troops for offensive action. Determined not to rest on the laurels wrought by his impressive Civil War record, Lieutenant Colonel Shafter insisted upon taking the field himself. On June 16, 1871, Comanches ran off forty-four mules and army horses from the Barrilla Springs mail station. Quickly assembling all of his available mounted men—thirty-four Tenth Cavalrymen—Shafter rendezvoused at the site of the attack with a Ninth Cavalry detachment from Fort Stockton. Now leading eighty-six officers and men, he pushed north and east into the Sand Hills of western Texas, heretofore considered impenetrable by the army. Spotting an Indian village on June 30, Shafter led a headlong charge. But the Indians enjoyed too great a head start. Shafter burned the campsite and resumed the pursuit but gave up the trail on July 2 as rations ran low. On another reconnaissance in October, Shafter, two guides, and eighty troopers scoured the region south of Peña Blanca. Although Shafter found numerous signs of Indians, escape routes across the Rio Grande made it impossible to force the enemy to battle.[19]

Like most at Fort Davis, Shafter attributed the depredations to tribes from New Mexico, in February 1872 resolving to make "a long scout as soon as the grass is good through the country north of here." More horses would allow him "to thoroughly scour the country with cavalry." Brig. Gen. Christopher C. Augur, having assumed command of the Department of Texas in January, supported Shafter's resolve. Post commanders should "be not content with a mere formal pursuit of a few days . . . but see that a vigorous, determined and continued effort, even to the extent of privation to men and horses, if necessary, be made to overtake and punish the marauders." They must avoid sending expeditions "under officers who have made up their minds before starting that nothing could be done," Augur ordered. "With such leaders *nothing will be done*, and it is mere folly to send them out."[20]

But Augur had neither the resources nor the personnel to invigorate every position in Texas. The garrison at Fort Davis shrank to 110 enlisted men, and in late May 1872 Shafter was transferred to what was deemed a more critical posting on the upper Brazos River. The new post commander, Col. George L. Andrews, Twenty-fifth Infantry, had won a brevet promotion honoring his Civil War services at the Battle of Chancellorsville but seemed disinterested in fighting Indians. Four of the five expeditions sent out from Fort Davis during the second quarter of 1872 were directed against "Mexican thieves" rather than Indians, and the largest had consisted of only nineteen men. Active campaigning became even less common in the years to come.[21]

One must sympathize with the dilemma of the embattled Andrews. Local ranchers and mail and stage companies continued to expect military escorts, and in late 1872 the bespectacled colonel found his responsibilities expanded when the already-undermanned Fort Quitman was reduced to a single company. Consequently, Fort Davis now bore the responsibility for supplying guards for two additional mail stations—Van Horn's Well and the ever-dangerous Eagle Springs, both of which lay on an Indian trail into Mexico. "My men are now getting but one night in bed," complained the colonel. With nearly a third of his two-hundred-strong garrison usually on detached duty, he insisted that it was impossible to conduct proper military drills or launch effective offensives. By spring 1877, finding only fifty-eight horses on post, an inspector classified the command as "inefficient for field operations." Forced marches under the blazing sun seemed useless as Trans-Pecos

A native of Rhode Island, Col. George L. Andrews was assigned to the Twenty-fifth Infantry in December 1870. Courtesy Fort Davis National Historic Site.

warriors eluded the army's clumsy efforts. As one junior officer wrote after a particularly fruitless trek across the Panhandle, "It seems that the 10th Cavalry is particularly blessed with incompetent commanders. . . . This poor regiment has been led by damn fools."[22]

Meanwhile, local residents attributed a growing string of depredations to Indians. In June 1876, claiming that Indians had attacked his herds four times within the past six weeks, one Fort Davis rancher begged his state legislator for assistance. "For Gods sake if you can do anything toward getting 25 stand of arms for us, do so," he demanded. A stage driver and a passenger were killed at Dead Man's Hole in August 1877; despite having ten officers and 122 enlisted men present for duty, Andrews dispatched only a sergeant and ten privates in pursuit. That fall, two men were killed near Van Horn's Well. Six others were slain by Mescaleros about sixty miles northwest of Presidio the following January; six weeks later, another strike fifteen miles northeast of Davis claimed two more victims. In a rash of incidents between April 15 and 20, five men were killed, thirteen mules stolen, and a mail rider attacked within the Fort Davis defensive region. From Fort Concho, district commander Col. Benjamin Grierson tried to prod the laconic Andrews into action. "Troops sent out in pursuit of Indians must be amply provided for a long & vigorous pursuit," urged Grierson. "The Indian marauders must be attacked wherever found and severely punished if possible." Stung by the criticism, Andrews insisted that he had investigated every reported attack: "My officers are all anxious to do something and no effort will be spared to rid this section of these Indians—if I can hire two packers."[23]

A series of Fort Davis–based columns thus combed the region in 1878. Capt. Thomas C. Lebo probed the area southeast of the post that March, marching more than four hundred miles but returning empty-handed. "I saw only very old trails and camps and none at all that I consider to be recent," reported Lebo. Following the murder of a Hispanic worker near Musquiz Canyon, Lt. Robert Read, Jr., led an eleven-man search party in futile pursuit. A Tennessean who had graduated an undistinguished fifty-sixth in his West Point class only a year earlier, the inexperienced Read returned to Davis eight days and two hundred weary miles later. "I could not detect the slightest trace of anything like a fresh trail," he admitted. Despite logging more than eighteen hundred miles south and west of Fort Davis that summer, Capt. Louis H. Carpenter's thirty-three Tenth Cavalrymen had no better luck. And detachments of Twenty-fifth Infantry led by Irish-born Capt. Michael L. Courtney marched nearly a thousand miles before returning to Fort Davis with nothing to show for their efforts near the end of September.[24]

Patrols continued through the fall. In early September, Captain Lebo had taken fifty-eight enlisted men north into the Guadalupe Mountains. He returned to Fort Davis on November 30, having marched more than five hundred miles without locating any Indians. Commanding elements of Tenth Cavalry, C Troop, Capt. Charles D. Vielé undertook five expeditions from the temporary base at Eagle Springs. Never numbering more than forty enlisted men, Vielé's hardy regulars logged eleven hundred miles in experiences that epitomized the frustrations endemic in the struggle to master the Trans-Pecos. His first four attempts uncovered no recent Indian activity. On the fifth try, Vielé located a fresh trail in the Eagle Mountains. Dispatching a squad back to fetch additional rations, the captain and the rest of the men took up the chase over a waterless desert into New Mexico. The terrific pace, however, had hobbled the cavalry's mounts. Out of supplies and water, Vielé broke off the pursuit.[25]

Although winter brought a lull in operations from Fort Davis, the soldiers at the fort had now set up three subposts designed to afford the region better protection—Pine Spring in the Guadalupe Mountains, Eagle Springs on the road to old Fort Quitman, and Seven Springs twenty miles north of Davis. In another sign that the momentum might be changing, Mexican troops captured forty to fifty Indians in mid-December. Encouraged by Mexico's resumed interest in battling Indians, enthusiastic Presidio observers reported that the Indians who escaped "are rendered desperate, as they have no place they can consider themselves safe, unless it is at the [Fort] Stanton Reservation."[26]

As forage became more readily available in spring 1879, army columns once again took the field from each of the subposts. The three expeditions logged thirty-three hundred miles but captured only a few animals. That July, Captain Courtney, twelve enlisted men, and an Indian guide, who were camped at Eagle Springs, had better luck. On July 25, Courtney, twice decorated for his Civil War gallantry, discovered an enemy encampment near Sulphur Springs. Hoping to surprise his enemies, the captain left eight of his men behind with the horses, creeping up with four enlisted men and his Mexican scout on foot. Unfortunately, the scout could not understand Courtney's animated instructions and fired a shot before the others could take their assigned places and complete the trap. Still, a hurried volley forced the Indians to abandon their horses in a mad scramble for safety. Two Tenth Cavalrymen fell wounded in the ensuing pursuit; Indian casualties included two dead, one wounded, and nine horses, a mule, and assorted other goods captured. Leading a similar detachment that September, Courtney seized the horses and equipment of Indians camped near Eagle Mountain.[27]

But even this flurry of activity did not bring about complete security. In May, Indians struck an animal herd near Fort Davis; two months later, a woman was murdered in Limpia Canyon. Property losses for ranchers and merchants mounted. Daniel Murphy had been attacked three times. Dietrick Dutchover claimed losses of twenty horses and two hundred sheep. George Crosson, who had established a sheep ranch near the old Musquiz place, claimed more than eleven thousand dollars in damages even before losing another sixteen horses and three hundred sheep that September. An 1880 attack forced Crosson to give up the exposed Musquiz Canyon position; he moved to Limpia Canyon before finally settling south of present-day Alpine.[28]

Evidence suggested that the assailants had come from New Mexico. In 1877, the Warm Springs Apaches had been moved from their homelands in southwestern New Mexico to San Carlos, Arizona Territory. Dissatisfied with conditions at desolate San Carlos, Victorio and more than one hundred Warm Springs, Mescalero, and Chiricahua Apache followers had repeatedly broken away to return home. Described by one kinsman as being "the most nearly perfect human being I have ever seen," the magnetic Victorio and his allies seemed impossible to track down as they moved in and out of Arizona, New Mexico, Mexico, and Texas. On September 6, 1879, the annihilation of an eight-man army herding party at Ojo Caliente signaled the renewal of open hostilities.[29]

The army suspected that the Mescalero reservation at Tularosa, New Mexico, remained a supply depot, recruiting ground, and safe haven for Victorio. Dispatched west for a firsthand view in early 1880, John Briggs, a civilian guide at Fort Davis, judged that the government agent there "has no way of telling" how many of his charges had left the reservation. "The squaws draw the rations and the bucks could be gone a month without his knowing anything about it," he concluded. Following common army practice, Col. Edward Hatch, commanding the District of New Mexico as well as the Ninth Cavalry Regiment, decided to disarm and dismount the remaining occupants of the Mescalero reservation. Realizing the dangerous nature of the task, he convinced his superiors to dispatch troops from Arizona and Texas to coordinate a two-pronged approach on the agency.[30]

Responding to Hatch's call, Col. Benjamin Grierson set out from West Texas that April with five companies of the Tenth Cavalry and a small detachment of the Twenty-fifth Infantry. Formerly a music teacher and businessman, Grierson had volunteered for military service soon after the Civil War erupted. He went on to lead one of the conflict's most famous cavalry raids, a sixteen-day dash from La Grange, Tennessee, to Baton Rouge, Louisiana, that had diverted attention from Ulysses S. Grant's daring thrust south of

Vicksburg in 1863. Opting to make the army his career, Grierson had assumed command of the Tenth Cavalry Regiment following the Civil War. En route to link up with Hatch in New Mexico, the colonel's command killed two warriors, captured four women, and recovered a captive Mexican boy and twenty-eight head of stolen cattle.[31]

But disarming the reservation peoples went poorly, with several dozen Mescaleros eluding the soldiers to join Victorio or to form their own war parties. Publicly, Grierson defended Hatch, his brother officer, blaming the Indian Bureau for having located the reservation at "the most unsuitable place that could possibly have been selected." Privately, Grierson resented having been subordinated to another officer's machinations. Hatch, asserted Grierson, had engaged in "a systematic plan to gobble myself & command for duty in New Mexico for an indefinite but protracted length of time." Grierson returned to the Lone Star State determined to ensure that his command would no longer serve Hatch's interests.[32]

Meanwhile, Victorio had melted back into Texas. On May 12, Indians killed two persons and wounded two others, including Fort Davis's indomitable Daniel Murphy, near Eagle Springs. A month later, two dozen warriors attacked Lt. Frank H. Mills and a squad of the army's Indian scouts at Viejo Pass, near modern-day Valentine. The Mills detachment lost its chief guide, Simon Olguín, and four animals. With traditional methods having failed to stop Victorio's flight through Texas en route to Mexico, Colonel Grierson planned to establish a line of pickets along the Rio Grande to intercept the Indians as they reentered the Trans-Pecos on their return to the Mescalero reservation. Division commander Sheridan overcame his personal distaste for Grierson to approve the novel scheme.[33]

Rather than waste his efforts in fruitless chases after Victorio, Grierson stripped West Texas to deploy all available men at strategic defensive positions, especially key water holes, while the army's Tigua and Pueblo scouts patrolled the Rio Grande. But to Grierson's astonishment, on July 28 Col. Adolfe Valle and four hundred Mexican troops turned up unexpectedly at Fort Quitman, completely destitute of food. Grierson issued the hungry Mexican soldiers three thousand pounds of flour and more than eleven hundred pounds of grain; to his surprise, he learned that Valle had received permission to enter the United States in pursuit of hostile Indians.[34]

Assuming that Valle would resume the chase, the next day Grierson and a small escort left Quitman for Eagle Springs. His party soon received word that the Apaches had recrossed the Rio Grande into the United States. An attempt to run seemed suicidal and would allow the Indians to break through the line of pickets into the thinly guarded Trans-Pecos. With Lt.

William H. Beck, five privates, and his son Robert, Grierson dug in atop a ridge overlooking Tinaja de las Palmas, the only water hole for many miles. Lt. Leighton Finley and fifteen troopers galloped up at four A.M. the next morning, expecting to escort the colonel's party back to safety. But Grierson had no intention of leaving. "Being well supplied with ammunition, water, and provisions, I was confident of my ability to hold the position . . . as long as necessary," recalled Grierson, who instead dispatched couriers to summon more support. About nine o'clock that morning, the little squad observed Victorio's approach. Young Robert, "out in search of adventure," was about to have his wish granted.[35]

Though a proven Civil War combat veteran, Colonel Grierson had never before engaged Indians in battle. Frustrated by Victorio's refusal to attack his strong defensive position, he dispatched Lieutenant Finley and ten men out to engage the enemy. They met stiff opposition; quite possibly, the Indians had tried to entice Grierson to sally forth from the security of his rocky sanctuary. After an hour of long-range skirmishing, Finley ordered an attack. Just as his bluecoats seemed to be gaining the advantage, the advance guard of a relief party led by Captain Vielé arrived, only to mistake Finley's embattled troopers for the Indians.[36]

Watching the action atop the ridge with his telescope, Grierson realized that his chance to ensnare Victorio was slipping away. As Vielé sorted out the confusion, another column led by Capt. Nicholas Nolan appeared in the distance to the west. Scattering in the face of this new threat, Victorio's warriors wandered too close to the ridge, from which Grierson's hidden command finally had the chance to open fire. "Golly!! you ought to 've seen 'em turn tail & strike for the hills," wrote Robert Grierson. Nolan's appearance and the shots ringing down from Tinaja de las Palmas allowed Vielé to link up with Grierson's command, but his cavalrymen were now too exhausted to catch the Indians. The skirmishing had lasted four hours; Grierson claimed seven enemy slain and several others wounded. One officer had been wounded and one private killed; fifteen horses and mules were also lost. Benjamin Grierson, now the proud father, reported that "Robert with his Winchester and his 250 cartridges executed his post in a heroic manner."[37]

Rather than pursue the Apaches, Grierson once again reinforced his detachments at the water holes, apparently expecting Colonel Valle's Mexican soldiers to block Victorio's escape. But instead of holding the Quitman area, Valle had marched toward supplies at El Paso, thus opening a path for Victorio, bloodied but still dangerous. On August 3, Cpl. Asa Weaver, seven Tenth Cavalrymen, and a handful of Indian auxiliaries blundered into Victorio's main body between Alamo Springs and the Rio Grande about daybreak.

Frederic Remington's *Saddle Up* graced the September 4, 1886 edition of *Harper's Weekly*. Courtesy Frederic Remington Art Museum.

Badly outnumbered and deserted by his scouts, Weaver conducted a skillful fifteen-mile retreat to the safety of the subpost at Eagle Springs. By the time they reached their destination, every horse and virtually all of his men had been wounded. Pvt. George Tockes was lost, last seen as his badly wounded mount carried him into the thick of his pursuers. For having saved the rest of his command, Weaver was promoted to sergeant on the spot.[38]

The Trans-Pecos was now swarming with bluecoats. On August 3, Indians encountered troops led by Capt. William B. Kennedy; the following day, they ran into Captain Lebo, whose detachment managed to seize most of their supplies. Gaining confidence, Grierson and two companies of the Tenth raced sixty-five miles in less than twenty-four hours to the water hole at Rattlesnake Springs. Stymied by the soldiers' unexpected arrival, the Indians attacked at about two o'clock in the afternoon of August 5. The battle remained in doubt until Captain Carpenter's reinforcements turned the tide. The Apaches scattered, reorganizing in time to hit an army supply train eight miles south of the original skirmish. Escorted by a detachment of cavalry and Twenty-fourth Infantry, Company H, the column drove off the attack. Grierson claimed that four Indians had been killed in the day's fighting and admitted no casualties among his own command.[39]

Following the clash at Rattlesnake Springs, Colonel Grierson attempted to coordinate a knockout blow. But Victorio was already circling back toward Mexico. On August 9, Indians attacked a stage near Fort Quitman, killing a retired Civil War officer. "There was only one gun and one cartridge in the hands of these men—right in the center of a wild country, and during the invasion of a merciless foe," reported Texas Ranger George W. Baylor. "How men can be so blind when their lives may hang on their Winchester's muzzle passes my comprehension." Two days later, Apaches ran off the mules at Barrel Springs and cut the telegraph line between Quitman and Davis as they recrossed the Rio Grande into Mexico. Fuming over the campaign's indecisive end, Grierson attributed Victorio's escape to the failure of Mexican troops to vigorously prosecute the chase. "There seems to be an understanding between Victorio and many of the Mexicans," charged Grierson, "that so long as he does not make war upon them in earnest, he can take whatever food and other supplies he may need for his warriors."[40]

Wary of Victorio's return, the army had established a web of stations throughout far western Texas. In the District of the Pecos, troops held subposts east of the Pecos River at Grierson's Spring and Camp Charlotte. Other soldiers occupied Ojo Caliente, Fort Quitman, Eagle Mountain, Pine Spring, and Eagle Springs, the last buttressed with a mountain howitzer for good measure. A new District of the Bravo had also been created. Commanded by Shafter, the Bravo district included subposts at Faver's ranch in the Chinati Mountains, Mayer's Spring, and the mouth of the Pecos River. Shafter also kept a garrison at Camp Peña Colorado, established in August 1879 just southwest of present-day Marathon.[41]

The hard campaigning had taken a heavy toll among the regulars. The Tenth Cavalry's G Troop had participated in two battles and marched 471 miles. By August 31, only thirty-two dusty troopers (out of an authorized strength of one hundred) reported present for duty. A Troop mustered but thirty-four. And the exhaustion was now affecting military efficiency. One soldier accidentally shot a comrade through the leg on August 20. Eugene McLane, acting assistant surgeon accompanying the expedition, escorted the wounded trooper back to Fort Davis; for McLane, whose hemorrhoids had become inflamed during the sixty-five-mile dash with Grierson to Rattlesnake Springs, the chance to return to the relative comforts of the fort must have seemed particularly opportune. On the twenty-fifth, soldiers guarding two supply wagons from Eagle Springs fell asleep on duty. Two men sent to repair the telegraph line west of Quitman instead got drunk and lost their weapons.[42]

Unbeknownst to Colonel Grierson, the noose around Victorio was growing tighter. That October, Mexican troops led by Col. Joaquin Terrazas cornered the Apaches in the Tres Castillos Mountains, killing Victorio and most of his followers. Still defiant even though their leader was gone, the remnants of Victorio's band reentered the Trans-Pecos, stealing two animals from Fort Davis, snapping up a stagecoach, and killing five surprised soldiers eating breakfast at Ojo Caliente before the Indians returned to New Mexico. Another stagecoach was ambushed in Quitman Canyon the following January. Two men died in the attack. Early reports pointed to the Apaches as the culprits in the latest strike. Upon inspection, however, authorities concluded that two white escapees from the Fort Davis jail had in fact committed the murders and tried to cover up their deed by making it look like an Indian depredation.[43]

Whoever the real attackers, on January 29, 1881, the Texas Rangers exacted their revenge. Commanded by Capt. George W. Baylor, a Ranger detail hit an Apache camp near the Sierra Diablos. One warrior was killed and two others wounded; three women and two children were also slain. The Rangers recovered seven mules, nine horses, three rifles, a cavalry pistol, six cavalry saddles, and assorted goods belonging to the stage company. They escorted their captives, a woman and two small children, back to their base camp at Fort Davis for medical attention. One self-satisfied Ranger reported: "The people of Fort Davis are well pleased with what we have accomplished."[44]

A lthough no one realized it at the time, Fort Davis's wars against the Indians were nearly over. Demoralized by a series of devastating army expeditions through their traditional homelands during terrible wars of 1868–69 and 1874–75, Comanches who had once terrorized the southern plains had reluctantly accepted reservations in the Indian territory. Remnants of the Lipan Apaches had been forced into Mexico or New Mexico, where they joined their cousins, the Mescaleros, at the Fort Stanton reservation. Their days of strikes into the Trans-Pecos were over. The Davis garrison's record in this process had been mixed. Davis-based troops could claim to have been involved in more fights (twelve) against the Indians than had any other troops in Texas after the Civil War. Seven of these encounters had been Indian attacks against soldiers holding defensive positions or on mail escort duty; in most cases, these long-range skirmishes had produced relatively few casualties. The other five combat actions had resulted from the thirty-three scouts and expeditions organized against Indians from the post on the Limpia. In addition to the five offensive columns that actually brought the Indians to combat, four others either recovered some stolen property or destroyed Indian livestock. Their 27 percent success rate probably compares favorably with the record established by other frontier garrisons after the Civil War.[45]

Closer analysis of the written record reveals an instructive pattern. The Cusack and Dodge scouts of 1868 and 1870, which had caught the Indians unprepared for the army's renewed post–Civil War onslaught, had inflicted nearly one hundred enemy casualties, captured more than two hundred livestock, and destroyed two Apache encampments, at the loss of only four wounded soldiers. After these successes, however, the Indians of the Trans-Pecos seemed to have learned from their early mistakes, whereas the Davis-based troops failed to adopt the innovations necessary to retain their early edge. For the next ten years, offensives conducted by Davis-based troops had wounded just one Indian, destroyed only five lodges, and killed or recovered no more than fifty head of livestock—hardly an impressive record compared to the many Indian attacks against civilians in the Fort Davis defensive region. Only with the implementation of Grierson's new defensive tactics in the Victorio campaign had regulars from Fort Davis regained their military effectiveness.[46]

As the Indian threat wound down, in early 1881 the District of the Pecos was abolished. Although Colonel Grierson's tough veterans had not captured Victorio, they had recently performed with valor and determination in harassing the famous chieftain out of Texas. In addition, Grierson's command had strung up 300 miles of telegraph lines, built more than 1,000 miles of wagon roads, and marched 135,710 miles during the past three years. Their self-satisfied colonel reported that "a settled feeling of security" now existed in West Texas; "a rapid and permanent increase of the population and wealth," he predicted, was sure to follow. The following year, Grierson would have the opportunity to help make his forecast for the Trans-Pecos come true when he transferred his regimental headquarters from Fort Concho to Fort Davis.[47]

CHAPTER EIGHT

FRONTIER EMPIRE

he American frontiers hosted more than their fair share of capitalist enterprises, bonanzas, and money-making schemes. Fort Davis
also had its own Gilded Age booster—Col. Benjamin Grierson, who
commanded the post from 1882 to 1885. With conflicts against the Indians diminishing and the garrison regularly averaging more than six hundred officers
and troops, Grierson's tenure marked the height of Fort Davis's nineteenth-
century imperial glory.

Tragedy and bad luck had dogged the Tenth Cavalry's commander
since the Civil War. As an officer without a West Point education who commanded a black regiment, Grierson had many foes within the army, dubious
about his military abilities as well as his views on race. Personal calamities
added to his miseries. His father-in-law, John Kirk, often needed money, as
did his brother Jonathan. Alice, his wife, had lost two of their seven children
at birth, and her brother committed suicide. During the family's stay at Fort
Concho, Texas, their daughter Edith had died of typhoid fever. Charles, their
eldest son, had overcome a mental breakdown to graduate from West Point,
but second son Robert's shaky nerves had forced him to drop out of medical
school at the University of Michigan.[1]

His military career jeopardized by prejudice and petty disagreements
and his personal life marred by recurring tragedy, Grierson strove to protect
his remaining fortunes at any cost. The bearded, sharp-eyed colonel first visited Fort Davis in early summer 1878 while inspecting his District of the
Pecos. Struck by the region's natural beauty and economic potential, he re-
marked that "this appears to be a first rate country to go to sleep in." The
commanding officer's quarters were "a palace compared with our old rat trap
at [Fort] Concho," he added. In June 1882, Grierson was given the opportunity to move his regimental headquarters. The decision was easy, for as he

confided to his wife, Alice, "a change any where would be desirable." They would invest the proceeds from the sale of the five thousand acres they owned in the Fort Concho region "in a ranch in the vicinity of Davis." Such a haven might spare his youngest sons, Harry and George, from the pressures that the colonel suspected had nearly shattered Charles and Robert.[2]

Grierson's struggles to provide for himself and his family conveniently paralleled his natural proclivities as a builder. At Forts Sill (Indian territory) and Concho, the colonel had overseen major construction projects, and he would try to do the same at his new home in the Davis Mountains. Like many of his colleagues, Grierson saw no conflict of interest in mixing personal pecuniary advantage with the best interests of the U.S. Army. Fort Davis offered the perfect opportunity to establish a comfortable life for his family as well as to improve conditions for the garrison and ensure a permanent U.S. presence in the Trans-Pecos. His herculean efforts to enlarge the army's presence thus neatly coincided with equally tireless attempts to provide financial and psychological security for his family. In so doing, the colonel took actions that were hardly unique—only the scope and intensity of his ventures distinguished Grierson from the norm. Garrison members followed their commander's example: land speculation, ranching, mining, and railroad development proved fertile fields for soldier-entrepreneurs during the 1880s.[3]

With Victorio defeated and the wars against the Indians largely over, only occasional field operations from Fort Davis were now necessary. The garrison took a minor role, for example, in Brig. Gen. George Crook's 1885 campaigns against the Apaches in Arizona. Seeking to block possible escape routes into the Trans-Pecos, the War Department alerted troops at Fort Davis and its subposts to watch "all crossings . . . especially those points where Victorio crossed in eighteen hundred and eighty." Geronimo and his followers did not enter Texas, but troubles in the Indian territory that summer again put the garrison on call. Cattle thefts, sometimes attributed to Mexican soldiers, also demanded sporadic patrols between Fort Davis and the Rio Grande west of Presidio.[4]

The relative peace promised a once-in-a-lifetime opportunity for civilian development. The Southern Pacific Railroad line between El Paso and San Antonio, which ran twenty miles south of Fort Davis through Marfa, was completed by early 1883; the Texas & Pacific Railroad, which went through Dallas, connected to the Southern Pacific at Sierra Blanca, twenty-five miles east of old Fort Quitman. Having assisted the railroads every step of the way, military officials recognized that the lines would dramatically influence the placement of West Texas garrisons. Fort Quitman had been closed in 1877; its replacement, Camp Rice, was relocated to a site closer to the railroad and eventually renamed Fort Hancock. Described by one occupant as "a Godforsaken-appearing country . . . in close proximity to the supposed haunts of 'Beelzebub,'" it would nonetheless be garrisoned until 1895. Although Maj. Gen. Phil Sheridan, commanding the Division of the Missouri, opined that the expansion of railroads might force the army to abandon Fort Davis, most others disagreed. The level-headed Christopher Augur, longtime commander of the Department of Texas, acknowledged that the railroads had rendered Forts Concho, McKavett, and Stockton unnecessary. But Davis, Augur asserted, was "well located as it is," being able to support operations along the Rio Grande as well as on the railroads. Brig. Gen. David S. Stanley, who succeeded Augur as department commander in 1884, concluded that "the salubrity of the climate, the low price of wood, hay, and grass make it the best site for a military post in the wide territory of the Rio Grande and the Rio Pecos." Commanding general William T. Sherman agreed, categorizing Fort Davis as one of the "strategic points of the Texas frontier."[5]

Acquiring land sufficient to accommodate the needs of a large garrison at such an important position brought many complications. Throughout Texas, private speculators had snapped up potential military sites from the state and then leased them to the War Department at high prices. In hopes of saving money over the long run, in 1873 Congress had empowered the War Department to begin purchasing land in Texas. Accordingly, a board of survey met in San Antonio that November. Negotiations opened with landowner John James asking $15,000 for all tracts leased to the government in the Fort Davis region. The board, however, rejected James's offer, instead setting $9,000 as a fair price for the 640-acre parcel.[6]

There matters stood until 1880, when Congress appropriated $200,000 (more than $3.5 million in 2004 dollars) for the purchase of sites "on or near the Rio Grande." Finding no likely spots along the Rio Grande between the mouth of Devil's River and Presidio, in 1882 the War Department convinced Congress to allow it to use the recent appropriation anywhere in Texas. Talks concerning permanent title to Fort Davis thus resumed in January 1883. James now offered to sell the reservation and an additional 1,280 acres (known as "the pineries") for $30,000. When the army again balked, James countered by asking $27,500 for the military reservation alone. But post commander Grierson remained coy. Two of his allies, Lt. Mason Maxon (married to one of his nieces) and George Brenner (chief regimental musician), had recently paid $3,500 for lands adjacent to the post. Brenner and Maxon had laid out a town site and had already sold enough sections to recoup their original investment. Though the flurry of activity had driven up local property values,

Grierson assured superiors that "much work and quiet financiering" might still secure land at moderate rates for the government.[7]

By the time of division commander Sheridan's visit two months later, Grierson thought he had worked out a deal. Daniel Murphy had promised to sell his 300-acre tract adjacent to Fort Davis to the government for $3,500; others had pledged to follow suit at "reasonable rates." The army could purchase an additional 960 acres from the state. Such expansion, reasoned Grierson, would ensure that the garrison had enough space to conduct proper maneuvers. To help smooth the deal, the colonel explained that he had paid $1,000 for two homestead tracts west of the military reservation "to prevent the land from falling into the hands of objectionable parties," and $500 on another survey two and a half miles away from the fort. He promised to sell the land at cost to the government should it be needed for military expansion. Sheridan, however, doubted Grierson's motives and questioned the need for larger investments at Davis. Although he agreed that the purchase of Murphy's 300-acre plot was necessary to prevent the burgeoning town from completely encircling the post, the general vetoed all other expansion. No purchase was made from James, whose annual lease increased from $900 to $2,400.[8]

Although schemes to expand the military reservation along the Limpia had floundered, the big garrison still needed additional quarters. Even gruff William Shafter, habitually skeptical of the need for more building, had eventually overseen construction of five new sets of officers' quarters, extending officers' row to the south and along the base of the rocky cliffs to the north. Another enlisted barracks, a new guardhouse, and housing for the band and staff were also initiated during Shafter's latter tenure. Even so, laundresses and married men continued to occupy ramshackle structures north and east of the main parade ground, and even the officers lacked sufficient space. Indeed, the dread practice of "ranking out"—whereby senior officers forced their junior colleagues to vacate their quarters upon demand—continued through 1883. One observer described the process in this way: "Capt. Lebo came in Sunday—he chose Capt. [John T.] Morrison's quarters—Morrison [Charles L.] Cooper's, and Cooper the Vielé house." The "Vielé house" was then occupied by the ill-fated Lt. Leighton Finley, who, being away on a scout, did not learn of his eviction until he returned to the post.[9]

Such conditions ideally suited Grierson's designs, for new buildings would make Fort Davis all the more difficult for the government to abandon. In September 1882, Quartermaster General Rufus Ingalls submitted a "crude estimate" of $83,250 (some $1.46 million in 2004 terms) for additional Fort Davis construction. Seizing the opportunity, Grierson initiated a number of projects—building new commissary and quartermaster storehouses north-east of the parade ground, a spacious new forage house, another set of offi-cers' quarters, two additional enlisted barracks, and an expanded hospital, and remodeling the cavalry corrals. Conveniently enough, he had managed to find enough time to approve several Davis projects during a brief stint as acting department commander. Leaky roofs, shabby workmanship and ma-terials, and damages from natural disasters and fire added even more con-struction work.[10]

The post's water supply and drainage also required attention. The spring that lay within the reservation's limits was often fouled, so drinking water was usually hauled in from the Limpia. The floodwaters that cascaded down Hospital Canyon after heavy rains also created sanitation problems that a hastily dug drainage ditch, constructed in summer 1880, seemed inca-pable of controlling. Grierson had quickly realized that better sanitation and a more reliable water supply were essential if Fort Davis was to remain the linchpin of the army's presence in West Texas. At the colonel's behest, a pipeline from Limpia Creek to the military reservation, featuring the cost overruns that seemed to accompany every project during the Grierson years, was established during the mid-1880s.[11]

The ventures dramatically increased local employment as well as the army's stake in Fort Davis. In turn, these trends fueled demand for local products and drove up land values. To profit from these machinations, Grier-son and his cronies seemed to be everywhere. With a zeal equaling that of any Gilded Age capitalist back east, the colonel hoped to exploit the poten-tial bonanza by acquiring land throughout the Trans-Pecos. At one time or another, he claimed at least 45,000 acres in what ultimately became Jeff Davis, Brewster, and Presidio counties. He also set up his son Robert with a cattle and sheep ranch, securing for him a lucrative job with the quartermas-ter's department while he was at it. Taking no chances, Grierson saw to it that two of his confederates controlled much of the post's discretionary purchas-ing. He appointed Lt. Samuel L. Woodward, who had accompanied him dur-ing his 1863 raid through Mississippi, as post adjutant; Capt. Charles Cooper was named acting commissary of subsistence. Others followed their com-mander's example. At least seven officers stationed at Fort Davis during Grierson's years of command bought land in the vicinity, with Lt. John L. Bullis acquiring title to 53,520 acres in Pecos County alone.[12]

Veterans of frontier maneuvering, Grierson and his military family sought to match the changing defensive needs with their own personal wel-fare. Lt. William Davis, Jr., who married one of the colonel's nieces, had once owned the site of the subpost at Peña Colorado, which was given inde-

Fort Davis parade ground as viewed from the north, about 1886. Officers' row and Hospital Canyon are on the right; enlisted men lived in the barracks to the left. Courtesy Fort Davis National Historic Site.

pendent status in July 1884. Grierson also set up a temporary subpost at Viejo Pass, forty miles west of Davis and ten miles from the Southern Pacific railroad station at Valentine. Conveniently enough, the colonel had purchased 2,500 acres just north of the site, set up his son Charles with a ranch on the road between Davis and Viejo, and owned 126 town lots in Valentine. The army, however, soon abandoned the Viejo Pass subpost, undoubtedly to Grierson's economic misfortune.[13]

A railroad linking Fort Davis to the Southern Pacific at Marfa would also serve Grierson's ambition of transforming the frontier cantonment into a permanent army post. On October 18, 1883, local investors formed the Fort Davis and Marfa Narrow Gauge Railway Company. Original subscribers, who invested between two thousand and five thousand dollars each, included a mix of Grierson's coterie (Brenner, Lieutenant Woodward, and sons Charles and Robert); sutlers George H. Abbott and John D. Davis; former Texas Ranger Charles L. Nevill; and local entrepreneurs R. L. Moreno, William L. Lampert, and John M. Dean. Benjamin Grierson, though not an original stockholder, later assumed Moreno's place, having called in loans and favors to raise money for his stake. But the colonel's brother, John, manager of a Colorado mining company, had counseled caution, predicting that actual expenses would inevitably exceed predictions. With the army's departure from Fort Davis always a possibility, John urged his brother to sell the franchise immediately after the consortium had established a right of way "for more money than you could ever make out of it by building the road."[14]

Despite such warnings, Davis investors plunged ahead, seeking out guarantees that the Southern Pacific would provide materials "at fair rates." Exasperated by the slow progress of the negotiations, in January 1885 Grierson handed over the matter to Marshall P. Ayers, a banker from his wife's hometown of Jacksonville, Illinois. Ayers encouraged the colonel to manipulate shareholder votes so that the secretary of the board of directors was "one of your own side [but] not one of your sons." Preferably, one of the Griersons should be president. But the team never managed to secure solid financial backing; with the corresponding crash of the statewide railroad construction boom, Ayers nixed the entire scheme. "If the boys have good ranches, they have a good thing I expect," Ayers noted in an attempt to console the colonel.[15]

Fort Davis empire builders also hoped to find mineral resources in the Big Bend region. Rumors of lead, silver, and gold deposits abounded. Temporarily based at the subpost at Presidio, during the late 1870s Lieutenant Woodward had kept his friend and superior Grierson fully apprised of such activities. "There is certainly a big effort being made to get up mining excitement in the interest of railroads and people who own land," explained the lieutenant. As Woodward had predicted, the International & Great Northern, Texas & Pacific, and Southern Pacific rail lines, which owned huge chunks of West Texas, sponsored a major expedition. Escorted by Lt. John Bullis and a detachment of Seminole Indian scouts, the party arrived at Fort Davis in January 1880. Although they failed to turn up any direct evidence of minerals in paying quantities, Bullis must have seen something he liked, for he, Shafter, and Lt. Louis Wilhemi gobbled up land north of Presidio that they leased to what eventually became the Presidio Mining Company. The mines turned up coal, silver, and mercury. Boomtowns such as Shafter and Terlingua, established in the late nineteenth and early twentieth centuries, became centers for mining activities in the Big Bend.[16]

But the discoveries led to lawsuits rather than riches for most of the soldiers. In March 1883, the Presidio Mining Company had extended its lease without the consent of Bullis or his wife, Alice, in whose name some of the land had been purchased. A Presidio district court granted the family's injunction against new mining operations, but the company appealed the case to the Texas Supreme Court. In savage attacks, the Bullis's attorney charged that Shafter's deliberate fabrication to his clients "stamps him as a man unfit to wear the uniform." In "stabbing his brother army officer in a court of justice," asserted the lawyer, he "had betrayed Bullis in the land transaction." The court reversed the earlier decision, holding in favor of the company. But the lawsuits continued until at least 1890, when Shafter was recalled to testify in a new civil action. "We feel sure of beating him [Bullis] as he has behaved like a scoundrel from the beginning of our relations," charged Shafter.[17]

These feuds over mineral rights highlighted a larger problem. As one officer's wife remembered, "The idea of the army being 'one happy family' was a considerable exaggeration." Internal bickering could indeed be fierce. Sharp differences continued to separate those trained at West Point from those who had not attended the academy. Civil War veterans, who themselves skirmished among one another over their respective wartime glories, often scorned younger officers who had not participated in America's bloodiest war. Interregimental rivalries further divided the officer corps; slow promotion through rigid seniority only exacerbated tensions. Commissioned personnel thus eagerly scanned the pages of the *Army and Navy Journal* for army news, lines of promotion, and gossip. According to one member of the Third Cavalry, the widely circulated publication "wields more power, probably for good or bad in army matters than any other agency." Any hint of criticism was sure to touch off controversy, for as one veteran noted cogently, "In military life character and reputation is the most of our stock."[18]

Fort Davis officers joined in the internecine feuding. Of the 259 commissioned personnel known to have served there after the Civil War, 81 (31 percent) had graduated from the U.S. Military Academy. Another third had joined the service as enlisted men, most having been promoted from the ranks during the Civil War. Resulting tensions were compounded by Grierson's personal machinations and lax administrative style. "I do not admire General Grierson's ways," wrote one enemy. "He is a great talker and full of himself and his works." Maj. Anson Mills believed Grierson too easy on his regiment and too eager to promote his own personal schemes. Other garrison members claimed that the colonel discriminated against those outside his regiment. The Sixteenth Infantry's Capt. William Clapp, for example, angrily reported that he and his men "had been shamefully treated."[19]

Petty quarreling seemed the rule rather than the exception, even among Grierson's own Tenth Cavalry. "Some of the doings of these men are worse than anything I had imagined and too vulgar to be recorded in my journal," wrote one diarist. One of Grierson's allies, Samuel Woodward, described Major Mills as "a sorry excuse" and "the worse [*sic*] apology I ever struck." In return, the major criticized his antagonist as being "slow to obey." Capt. Robert Smither sparred with Mills, Grierson, and authorities in the commissary department. Lt. James Jouett remained "continually intemperate for a long time" before being dismissed from the service in 1885. Rumor held Lt. William Beck to be a gambler, a drunk, and an unfaithful husband. During the midst of the Victorio campaign, the gossipy young Robert Grierson reported that the lures of female companionship in Mexico had led Beck and an acting assistant surgeon to go, as he put it, "across the river this eve on a 'tear'—two old women and one virgin on to 14 are there. The subject demands an immediate investigation—i.e. the one 'virgin' on to 14." Another officer dismissed the entire Beck clan as little better than a plague. "Mrs. Beck is a great gossip and the boys are a bad lot," he proclaimed.[20]

A major fracas occurred in late December 1884. While Grierson was away, his nephew-in-law Lt. William Davis, while "in his usual [drunken] condition at the traders store," allegedly blasphemed the memory of Abraham Lincoln. The Sixteenth Infantry's Captain Clapp, eager to retaliate against the alleged mistreatment of his command, preferred charges against Davis. Temporary post commander Anson Mills gleefully seized the opportunity to fan the flames against Grierson by informing department headquarters of the incident. The absent colonel's defenders struck back, insisting that Mills had trumped up "petty charges" against Davis. "Mills ought to be a picket in a penitentiary," wrote one. Upon his return, Grierson convinced Davis to retract his offensive remarks. But the truce was short-lived, for Clapp and Davis soon came to blows in the sutler's store, with Davis emerging with a black eye after slapping Clapp on the face. Defiantly, Lieutenant Davis vowed to slap Mills, a brevet colonel, for good measure. In an official communication routed through regimental headquarters, Mills threatened to kill Davis if the latter dared touch him. "The Lieut. still lives, but the Colonel's [Mills's] mouth has not been slapped," quipped one wag.[21]

Even routine matters became a source of controversy. Veterans such as Grierson were content to leave military drill in the hands of noncommissioned personnel. "He left the details of the post and regiment entirely to us," complained Mills. But the old ways were gradually changing, with department and division brass encouraging junior officers to participate in professional seminars and discussion groups and to take a more active role in training their men. Similarly, regular target practice had once seemed prohibitively expensive and was believed to take too much time away from other, more immediate duties. But the disastrous defeat at the Little Bighorn in 1876 highlighted the need for a fresh approach. Weekly target practice became a habit at most forts, and company, regimental, post, department, and national competitions were organized to promote marksmanship.[22]

Still, traditional habits died hard at Fort Davis, where post officials seemed more interested in expanding the army's physical presence than in accommodating the new emphasis on target practice and military preparedness. In February 1884, the adjutant general's office demanded "a full and exhaustive report" explaining the low marksmanship scores at the post on the Limpia, where only three of the garrison's ten companies had any qualified marksmen. Another critical review came down seven months later. Although Tenth Cavalry, B Troop, had expended 22,945 rounds, Sixteenth Infantry, Companies I and K, which had spent more time in the pinery than on the target range, had each fired less than 9,000 rounds. Low shooting scores drew renewed fire from department officials in December. Indeed, the criticisms supported many of the charges against Grierson, whose easygoing style, interests in his own regiment, and desire to build a personal fortune seemed to have interfered with military duty.[23]

Although marksmanship at Fort Davis received only lukewarm support from its commander, post society reached its zenith during the Grierson years. Setting the tone was Alice Grierson. Born in 1828, she had waited until she was twenty-six years old to marry Ben, then a struggling musician. Following the Civil War, Alice had adapted to the life of a colonel's lady, loyally following her husband as he was transferred to and from Forts Leavenworth, Riley, Gibson, Sill, Concho, and now Davis. Although an accidental fall while getting out of a carriage left her lame for most of her tenure at Fort Davis, Alice enjoyed her stay, joining the other officers' wives in combing mail-order catalogs for luxuries not available from local merchants. Secure in her role as her clan's spiritual and moral guardian, she occasionally prodded her husband to accept a greater share of the burdens of raising their large family. But the patience of even this affectionate and loving woman sometimes wore thin, tested by the deaths of several immediate family members and her husband's frequent absences. "If only a little more of your energy could be transferred to me," she once complained in frustration to Ben, "I doubt if you would be any worse, and I might be all the better."[24]

Under their father's tutelage, the Grierson children played musical instruments, with the family's grand piano serving as a centerpiece for social affairs at posts from the Indian territory to Arizona. Four of their children were still alive when they reached Fort Davis. Charley, the eldest, had joined the Tenth Cavalry following his graduation from West Point. Robert, who had once declared his intention to join an Arctic expedition, was still recovering from the mental breakdown that had forced him to withdraw from medical school as his father was transferred to Fort Davis. Brought to what his parents hoped to be the calmer environment of a ranch in the Trans-Pecos, Robert soon procured a bicycle. With the huge front wheel of his

Alice Grierson. Courtesy Fort Davis National Historic Site.

newfangled contraption spanning fifty-five inches, he terrorized the garrison as he whizzed by on his "steel steed." "I often take a little start at the QM [quartermaster's] office & coast clear down to the new town on my bicycle," he told his mother, "with my legs over the handlebars."[25]

Harry and George, the Griersons' energetic younger sons, also threw themselves into frontier life at Fort Davis, joining hunting parties and engaging in typical boyish mischief. Sent ahead with company officers even be-

Benjamin H. (Harry) Grierson in the early 1880s. Courtesy Fort Davis National Historic Site.

fore his parents arrived, Harry complained good-naturedly that his mess's Chinese cook made peach pie with "more rice in it than peaches." George explained that theatrical performances at the post on the Limpia in November 1884 "brought the hole [*sic*] house down" on the first night, when reserved seats cost seventy-five cents each. Unfortunately, only about forty people paid to see the next evening's encore performance, most observers (presumably including George) opting instead to watch for free through peepholes in the walls and curtains. Daring military tradition, the two boys also nurtured friendships with enlisted men and servants. As he and his brother were being trundled off to school back at their family home in Illinois, George left behind a series of hand-drawn sketches of himself, an antelope, and several comrades, to give his friends something "to Rember [Remember] me by."[26]

Even quarrelsome families maintained social interaction, and the arrival of visitors temporarily united the officers in card parties, hops, and socials. "What an amount of kindness and goodness there is in the world," wrote one thankful traveler. Although every garrison sponsored such activities, those at Fort Davis won particular praise. "We were feted beyond all former experiences," recalled another visitor. A spectacular variety of meats, fowl, and homemade desserts could be found at such galas. The visits of outside military dignitaries provoked especially extravagant entertainments; in August 1882, the happy coincidence of an inspection by department commander Christopher Augur and a court-martial board made for particularly exciting times. "With balls, picnics, driving and riding parties, Mexican circuses and dinner parties," wrote one correspondent, "we have enough to entertain us and prevent this happy coterie from affliction with that languer [*sic*] so common to the society of a frontier military post."[27]

Christmas and New Year holidays sparked fresh rounds of festivities. Rival companies jousted with one another with competing tables laden with wild game, turkeys, chickens, pigs, pies, and puddings. Following tradition, officers and their wives inspected the enlisted men's tables before returning to their own quarters for more private celebrations. "It was quite like civilization," remembered Lt. John Bigelow of the sumptuous dinner of oysters, soup, turkey, vegetables, plum pudding, fruit, nuts, champagne, and claret that he and his wife shared with Lt. and Mrs. Charles G. Ayres in 1884. All, however, did not go as planned; Bigelow was "mortified" when Lt. James B. Hughes, a former student of his at West Point, got too drunk to attend that night's subsequent celebration of B Troop's new barracks. The regimental band, five tables overloaded with food, and two fruit-laden Christmas trees marked the occasion, during which the strict military and racial caste system was loosened but not forgotten. At nine P.M., officers and ladies commenced the dancing with a waltz and a quadrille. The strains of "Home, Sweet Home" signaled the grand finale about two thirty that morning. Similar fetes heralded the New Year, with the parties hosted by Alice Grierson, Mrs. John Davis (wife of a post trader), and the daughters of local entrepreneur Daniel Murphy highlighting the social roster. Unmarried officers seemed particularly fortunate, as custom allowed the bachelors to make the rounds of each get-together.[28]

The Tenth Cavalry had occupied West Texas since 1873. Its fractious officers had set high standards for pettiness in an army filled with ambitious men. One believed that the Tenth had degenerated into a "contest for supremacy . . . between the good element and the bad," with "the two elements . . . pretty evenly matched." Many had ventured into profit-making schemes that verged on the unethical, lax even by nineteenth-century standards. Officials would soon investigate Lieutenant Maxon's alleged mismanagement of public funds as post quartermaster; Lieutenant Jouett was being tried for a second time; two officers would shortly file charges against Lieutenant Davis. One critic claimed that several area citizens, bitter about Grierson's unwelcome competition in real estate bidding, were actively promoting his transfer.[29]

Whatever the truth of the latter rumors, the army generally attempted to rotate regiments on a regular basis, and the Tenth's turn was long overdue. "The regiment has become 'localized' to an extent as to have an effect prejudicial to the public interest," reasoned department commander Stanley in December 1884. "The localization tends to demoralization." Colonel Grierson lodged several protests, but official transfer orders arrived in early March 1885. The Tenth was to exchange positions with the Third Cavalry, currently stationed in Arizona.[30]

Tenth Cavalry units from Concho and Stockton rendezvoused at Davis in preparation for the westward march. On the afternoon of April 1, 1885, the troopers passed out of Fort Davis in a grand review. The band, mounted on dapple gray horses, preceded the column. Two abreast, the eleven companies made an impressive sight never matched in community annals. I Troop joined the column near Camp Rice, marking the only time prior to the Spanish-American War that the entire regiment had assembled together. Colonel Grierson and regimental adjutant Mason Maxon remained at Davis for another eight days, cleaning up loose ends of a military as well as a personal nature. Local workers were hired to help Robert with the family ranch, but Benjamin leased out one large section to Jonathan A. Jackson, retired from the Tenth Cavalry. "Fort Davis is like 'the deserted village' now," wrote Robert following his father's departure. But not all was grim—profits from the sale of the ranch's eggs to Fort Davis took a dramatic turn for the better. The temporary post commander, Captain Clapp, "has had all the chickens removed from the officers' line," noted Robert contentedly. "There is a great fight going on between the people and the bugs."[31]

On May 12, 1885, Col. Albert G. Brackett, Third Cavalry, assumed command of Fort Davis. A veteran cavalryman and author of a widely used history of U.S. mounted troops, Brackett quickly forbade commissary sales to civilian employees, thus closing Robert Grierson's source of cut-rate food. "Of course I can't afford to run my mess at the prices you have to pay outside," reported Robert indignantly. In his view, the tighter restrictions antagonized all of the workers. Robert later asserted that General Stanley was "not at all pleased with Col. Brackett's administration." Indeed, Stanley, upon his own transfer from Texas, recommended that Grierson replace him as department commander. But politics and rules of seniority prevailed—Grierson remained on station in Arizona. An era of frontier empire had closed.[32]

CHAPTER NINE

THE CLOSE OF THE MILITARY FRONTIER

The military post on the Limpia had long been the developmental engine for non-Indian settlement of the central Trans-Pecos. The army, attracted by the position's strategic importance, physical beauty, and locally available supplies of water, timber, and building stone, had invested considerable resources in developing and maintaining the site. With its large garrison, influx of federal money, and promise of security, Fort Davis offered attractive opportunities for frontier entrepreneurs from Mexico and the United States. Civilians had thus followed the military and reestablished their presence at Fort Davis after the Civil War. Although not always in harmony, the two groups had developed a mutual dependency—the army providing protection, law enforcement, and business opportunities to the local community in exchange for labor, entertainment, and essential services.

But military conditions were changing. Indians had been shunted aside, and the railroads had bypassed Fort Davis proper. Thus, despite the machinations of empire builders such as Benjamin Grierson, reassessments of the post's strategic value were sure to come. As a Fort Davis correspondent for the *San Antonio Daily Express* predicted ominously in 1881, "We are no longer the frontier, for we will have fallen into the embrace of the iron monster and will possibly perish beneath its wheels." In addition, the fort's physical structures were aging, and the demands on the region's finite natural resources were mounting. In an army where every dollar was precious, Fort Davis would need to offer something else, such as cheap, healthy quarters to house the nation's regulars, to maintain its status as one of the largest and most valuable western posts.[1]

But such forebodings of doom were rare during the postwar boom years. By 1880, the civilian population exceeded five hundred, having nearly doubled in the past ten years (see appendix 2). Economic prospects looked bright.

Although San Antonio- or Dallas-based firms typically won the largest hay, corn, and oats contracts let at Fort Davis, local businesspeople found supplying the federal government a lucrative source of income. In 1883, for example, L. B. Caruthers, a Fort Davis resident, supplied more than a thousand dollars' worth of corn to the post. That same year, Missouri-born Edgar Glenn, an accountant who had come to the Davis Mountains during the 1870s, supplied hay ($31,318), charcoal ($713), and hardwood ($10,144). The enterprising Glenn also landed the charcoal contract (another $213) for Camp Peña Colorado, along with the hay and charcoal contracts (totaling $4,396) for Camp Rice. Daniel Murphy held the right to provide transport between the railroad and Fort Davis. That year's garrison, which averaged thirty-nine officers and six hundred enlisted men, was paid nearly $200,000. Assuming the men spent their money locally, the federal government had pumped in roughly $250,000 that year into the Fort Davis economy (more than $4.4 million in 2004 dollars).[2]

Development was evident throughout the region. Following the extension of the Southern Pacific Railroad through the Trans-Pecos, the burgeoning settlement of Marfa began to rival the older community at Fort Davis. In a bitterly fought 1885 election, county voters, by a 392–302 margin, moved the seat of local government to Marfa. Fort Davis retained the jail as a consolation prize until March 1887, when it was made county seat of a newly created Jeff Davis County. Methodist, Baptist, Presbyterian, and Catholic ministers now offered civilians a choice of Christian faiths. Mattie Belle Anderson had opened a popular private academy, and Whittaker Keesey had donated land to the county to support a new public school. Local chapters of various fraternal organizations, including the Masons, Good Templars, Oddfellows, and Grand Army of the Republic, evidenced further civilian development. James Kibbee, future owner and proprietor of the Limpia Hotel, edited a local newspaper, the *Fort Davis News* (formerly the *Presidio County News*).[3]

Although one observer remembered that "there was not a well-defined street in the whole place," a new residential and commercial zone, referred to as North Fort Davis or New Town, now extended west and north of the military reservation. Private businesses also dotted the surrounding area. By 1884, a drugstore, lumberyard, clock shop, dressmaker, bakery, butcher, stable, dairy, and liquor store were present. Two saloons, two groceries, two hotels, and seven dry goods/general merchandise stores also competed for customers. Many still catered to the military community, but the local economy had assumed a measure of self-sufficiency. The growth of regional agriculture and animal husbandry, fueled by the coming of the railroads and the huge land grants given those companies by the state, had reduced the community's federal dependency. Indeed, by 1887 Jeff Davis County was home to nearly fifty thousand cattle, more than twenty-five thousand sheep, four thousand goats, and eleven hundred horses and mules. Army spending from that year's garrison (twenty-two officers and 292 enlisted men), along with the contracts won by community residents at Fort Davis (charcoal and wood), Camp Nevill's Springs (oats, corn, charcoal, wood, and hay), and Camp Peña Colorado (wood, hay, and transportation) had fallen to about $120,000.[4]

Lured by the employment opportunities offered at the military post and the nearby ranches, Mexican immigrants—mostly from Chihuahua—composed more than two-thirds of the population. Still, Euro-Americans controlled the local economy (see table 9.1), owning or managing virtually all of the area's large ranches and claiming 99 percent of the sheep, 95 percent of the cattle, and 96 percent of property owned by Jeff Davis County residents. White businessmen continued to run the town's largest mercantile establishments. They had also assumed control of the profitable stage and transport business, once dominated by Hispanics. Many whites also expected to govern civilian society. A white diarist, for example, recoiled when he spotted his black servant buying some luxury goods at the local drugstore. "The colored people are nothing unless they are spending money freely like the white folks," complained the diarist. Another white man complained about the "nondescript, hybrid population" at the village. Echoing the racism of the times, an army report noted that the Hispanic population was "content with little and generally not well to do in a worldly point of view." Lt. John Bigelow stopped attending the Hispanic-dominated local Catholic Church "in view of the various maladies one is liable to catch from the congregation."[5]

Despite the continuing inequalities and prejudices, racial and ethnic lines were hardly absolute. Republican Party loyalties remained strong, and several black former soldiers won election to minor local offices. A few Mexican Americans served on juries. At least one saloon sold alcohol regardless of the patron's color, and school segregation did not become official until 1904. Nor was there a strict pattern of residential segregation. Further, although violent racial riots blotted civil-military relations near several Texas military posts, there were no such confrontations between black soldiers and Anglo or Hispanic civilians at Fort Davis. Between 15 and 20 percent of community marriages during the 1870s and early 1880s were between white men and Spanish-surnamed women. Local society continued to accept these relationships, with several government officials, including Henry Tinkham (elected sheriff in 1871), Abraham Tibbetts (elected treasurer in 1875), Frank Duke (justice of the peace in 1880), and longtime county servant Otis Keesey, having married Mexican immigrants. Several Mexican women also wed black

TABLE 9.1

Civilian Occupations at Fort Davis by Race/Ethnicity, 1880

Category	Total workforce (%)	White (%)	Spanish-surnamed (%)	Black/mulatto (%)
Agriculture	26	17	77	6
Stage and transport	13	85	15	0
White collar	17	64	30	6
Skilled mechanics	8	55	41	5
Semiskilled	10	8	69	23
Unskilled	23	5	87	8
Others	4	36	18	45
% Total workforce	**100**	**34**	**57**	**9**

SOURCE: U.S. Manuscript Census, 1880, Presidio County.

NOTE: "Agriculture" includes farmers, shepherds, herders, gardeners, ranchers, miners, hunters, woods-men, stockmen, and dairymen; "Stage and transport" includes drivers, wagoners, station keepers, team-sters, and hostlers; "White collar" includes merchants, clerks, bar keepers, restaurant keepers, bakers, barbers, shopkeepers, dance hall keepers, county superintendents, overseers, musicians, cake peddlers, teachers, candy peddlers, judges, lawyers, deputy sheriffs, bookkeepers, traders, telegraph operators, and butchers; "Skilled mechanics" includes masons, plasterers, shoemakers, blacksmiths, saddlers, painters, mechanics, brick makers, carpenters, machinists, and silversmiths; "Semiskilled" includes cooks, huck-sters, tailors, seamstresses, spinners, waiters, and messengers; "Unskilled" includes domestic servants, la-borers, and laundresses; "Others" includes gamblers, idlers, smugglers, and prisoners; $n = 271$.

enlisted personnel, and one of the town's most prominent Anglo residents openly cavorted with his Hispanic mistress. In a community where there were virtually no eligible black women, only a slightly smaller pool of eligible white women, and relatively few prosperous Hispanic males, love, sexual desire, the dream of settling down and starting a family, or the quest for economic security often outweighed ethnic and racial barriers.[6]

Many—but by no means all—Hispanics lived east of the central busi-ness district in a community known as Chihuahua, probably because so many immigrants had come from that Mexican state. Chihuahua was described by one critic as a "squalid little Mexican settlement about half a mile from the garrison," and its saloons, gambling houses, and brothels attracted enlisted men thirsting for action of a nonmilitary nature. The local Catholic church, which lay southeast of the post on the main road to the county courthouse, served as a cultural and social center. And although poorer on a per-capita basis than their white counterparts, Hispanics had enjoyed some successes. They had, for example, made some inroads into the white-collar and skilled

After the Civil War, almost every western military garrison made extensive use of civilian labor. Here, at Fort Davis, Hispanic wood haulers return from a successful expedition. Courtesy Fort Davis National Historic Site.

labor jobs once almost completely dominated by whites. Spanish-surnamed taxpayers also owned 80 percent of the donkeys, 20 percent of the wagons and carriages, and 16 percent of the goats declared by county residents.[7]

The Chihuahua community's greatest individual economic success story was undoubtedly that of Fabricio Granado, his wife, Felicia, and their ten children. Fabricio first appeared on the census as an unpropertied laborer in 1870; ten years later the enumerator promoted him to farmer. Their eldest son, Porfirio, earned the title of stockman. By the late 1880s, the family had accumulated 160 acres of land, a wagon, four horses and mules, fourteen cattle, two donkeys, and eighty-five sheep. With an estate valued at more than thirteen hundred dollars, the immigrant family had become the second-wealthiest Hispanic household in town (Benancia Mahle, who had apparently married an Anglo landholder, was the wealthiest Hispanic taxpayer). The Granados' eldest daughter, Ramona, married Edward Hartnett, an Irish immigrant who frequently worked as a foreman for civilian labor teams on the military base. The Hartnetts lived next door to Ramona's parents.[8]

Race and ethnicity were nonetheless vital factors in predicting a woman's entrance into the public workforce. Census takers at Fort Davis in 1870 and

1880 classified about two-thirds of adult women—including every white female—as "keeping house" or some other similar term. Of those Tejana and black women accorded occupations, an overwhelming majority (sixty-six) were listed as laundresses. Sixteen seamstresses, nine cooks, five domestic servants, three teachers, two laborers, a teamster, and a tailoress were also present. Jesusia Sanchez received the unceremonious label of "idler." Dominga Lerma was a widowed shopkeeper, and Manuella Urquedes "keeps a dance house," according to the enumerator. Another female Hispanic divorcée oversaw the town's most exclusive brothel.[9]

As the army made few provisions for discharged soldiers, a number of former garrison members remained at Fort Davis after leaving the service. Archie Smith, a Tenth Cavalry veteran, married a Mexican woman and by the late 1880s owned more than one hundred head of cattle. John Jackson served as a local freighter and small landowner. George Bentley, a Kentucky native whose father was the illegitimate son of a white man and a black woman, also married a Hispanic woman and settled at Fort Davis; by 1887, the Bentleys boasted property valued at more than two thousand dollars. Irish native Charles Mulhern, a twenty-five-year veteran who had served at Fort Davis during the late 1870s, returned there with his Swiss-born wife and four children following his army retirement, taking up a new career as local agent for Lt. Mason M. Maxon and owning four hundred cattle and fourteen hundred acres of his own. Mulhern's ranch house, situated three miles southeast of the post, served as a popular social center.[10]

The Grierson family also remained active in Fort Davis life. Managing the ranch, Robert continued to appear at post and civilian functions and was elected county commissioner. George and Harry Grierson returned in 1887; following his military retirement in 1890, Ben Grierson divided his time between the ranch near Fort Davis and his family in Illinois. The family investments fell upon hard times, however, as drought and the overstocking of the ranges devastated the local cattle industry. Robert, long the backbone of the operation, again collapsed, depressed over his mother's death and overwhelmed by the pressure stemming from the county treasurer's embezzlement of nearly two thousand dollars. As a county commissioner, Robert had promised sureties on the treasurer's personal bond and was held personally accountable for the loss. His brothers eventually placed him in a mental institution in Illinois.[11]

Over time, the increasing civilian presence inevitably disrupted the traditional ways of the military community. Brandt C. Hammond, a Methodist-Episcopal minister appointed post chaplain in April 1885, was rebuked for having become too closely associated with the local newspaper. Long accus-

Robert Grierson, about 1887. Courtesy Fort Davis National Historic Site.

tomed to treating civilians as well as garrison members, Fort Davis surgeons also sold prescription drugs to townspeople. Civilian pharmacists George W. Geegge and A. B. Legard believed the competition hurt their businesses and complained to their congressman, S. W. T. Lanham (D-Texas). In response, post officials ended sales of army supplies for private purposes and trans-ferred Surgeon Paul Clendenin and steward Richard Dare to other posts.[12]

As the town evolved, garrison members struggled to overcome the challenges of western military life. Nothing seemed to be able to dam the tide of alcoholic beverages; official rates of alcoholism at Davis, 54.72 per 1,000 troops, ranked forty-third among all army posts. A spectacular example occurred on June 13, 1878, when a drunken Sgt. Moses Marshall, Twenty-fifth Infantry, stormed into the barracks, cursing an unidentified man for having insulted his wife. Late that afternoon, Marshall and Cpl. Richard Robinson exchanged "pretty rough words." Half an hour later, Marshall reentered the barracks and shot Robinson through the head. As startled enlisted men came in to investigate the noise, they asked Marshall what had happened. "Oh, nothing, only I have killed Corporal Robinson," replied Marshall coolly, who followed with a series of diatribes against anyone who dared to impugn his family's reputation. A jury found Robinson guilty of "a cool, wilful [sic], and deliberate murder."[13]

Desertion posed an even more serious threat to military order and efficiency. In 1871, Congress had reduced the pay of enlisted men to prewar levels, ranging from thirteen dollars per month for a private to twenty-two dollars for first sergeants. Small reenlistment bonuses only partially redressed the balance. Annual desertion rates promptly increased from 9 to nearly 33 percent. The resulting outcry convinced Congress to add longevity supplements of one dollar per month in each of the soldier's third, fourth, and fifth years of enlistment. The army retained the bonus until the individual's honorable discharge to deter desertion or misconduct. Even after these inducements, however, soldiers continued to leave the army in droves.[14]

Constant fatigue details, fear of punishment, the loss of a valued comrade, the "demoralizing influences" of alcohol, and alliances "with an element of loose population" all contributed to the problem. Many resented the labor details that consumed so much of their time and energies; as an officer investigating one case explained, the deserter insisted that "he had enlisted to be a soldier and not a slave." Cpl. Thomas Gatewood, Tenth Cavalry, deserted rather than face charges stemming from his having lost his horse. A cook departed after a twenty-pound bag of rice for which he was responsible disappeared. George McNeil, described as a "good" soldier but "a boy with no worldly knowledge," left because of the influence of another deserter "to whom McNeil had become greatly attached." Pvt. James Brown was "given to running after women that fill the numerous towns about this post"; deserter David Anderson, "full of syphilis, deviltry and rascality," bolted to the little settlement of Chihuahua, "where there lives a woman by the name of Maggie Weber." Pvt. James E. Martin "was very much in love with a Mexican girl at Presidio del Norte and it is supposed he went there." "Good" soldier Charles Fillmore was last seen with a flask of whiskey; George Crossin was "a drinking man" who "complained of too much work."[15]

Desertion rates at Fort Davis, with its largely black garrison of the 1870s, had traditionally been only about one-third that of the national average. But rates rose dramatically in 1881, when several companies of the all-white First Infantry Regiment were transferred to Fort Davis. Desertion rates promptly tripled. The following year, nearly a fifth of the entire garrison deserted. Not only did white troops desert more frequently than their black counterparts, but the tensions produced by the mixed-race garrison apparently convinced an unusually high number of blacks to leave their units as well.[16]

With national desertion rates alarmingly high, the army conducted a more thorough investigation in 1883. Of the 325 desertions in the Lone Star State that year, 145 had occurred during the first six months of a soldier's enlistment, and 200 had come less than ten days after payday. Without positive identification procedures, repeat offenders could join the army, receive free transportation to the frontier, get paid, then melt into the countryside. Army apologists blamed the recruits themselves and called for tougher punishment, seeing the latter as an effective means of instilling discipline and command respect. But others found such iron-fisted rules distasteful, reasoning that more humane treatment would reduce desertion. Explained Capt. Robert G. Smither, "I do not like to punish men, if I can help it, and if I do, I feel like going for them." In an effort to gain the trust of his command, Lt. John Bigelow furnished a half-dozen new balls for their baseball games. Judge Advocate General David G. Swaim concluded that "severity of punishment is no deterrent."[17]

Some linked desertion to the vagaries in the army's justice system. Virtually every action in a soldier's day risked breaking one of the articles of war. As had been the case before 1861, company sergeants handled petty transgressions informally; officers who intervened too frequently in such matters risked alienating their noncommissioned personnel. Garrison courts-martial dealt with minor infractions ranging from insubordination to petty theft. Of those formally accused of breaking regulations, violation of Article 62 ("conduct prejudicial to good order and military discipline") proved the most common offense. In a typical case, a garrison court-martial levied a five-dollar fine upon the Tenth Cavalry's Horace Brown for having failed to wash the hospital dispensary floor and responding "God damn you, go to hell," when ordered to do so. Found guilty on another Article 62 charge, Sgt. Thomas Allsup, a splendid combat veteran, was reduced to the ranks.[18]

Changing the cavalry guard at Fort Davis, 1888. Courtesy Fort Davis National Historic Site.

Punishment for more serious crimes could be draconian. Congress had abolished flogging in 1861, but prisoners could still be tied up and spread-eagled or forced to lug about heavy logs or a ball and chain. Some officers, including Lt. Charles J. Crane, seemed reluctant to hand down such sentences. But when faced with a near mutiny while accompanying his men en route from Fort Davis to Fort Sill, Crane ordered the drunken ringleader bucked and gagged. "My method of quieting the man was the best under the circumstances, as was proven at the time and on the spot," explained Crane, "but I would not advise it as something to be practiced lightly and without feeling very sure."[19]

Many hoped that improvements in the ration, which had remained largely unchanged since before the Civil War, would boost morale. A revised edition of the *Manual for Army Cooking* had been published in 1883, but a cost-conscious Congress continued to block efforts to provide for permanent cooks. "The duties are trying and laborious," explained one enlisted man seeking to escape kitchen duties at Fort Davis, "and close confinement over hot ovens is affecting my health." Many companies supplemented their diets by selling unwanted foodstuffs to local civilians or contributing their own pay to purchase vegetables. Fortunately for the garrison at Fort Davis, melons and fruits could be purchased from Limpia valley growers, lemons and oranges from Mexico, and grapes from El Paso. The post garden also flourished, producing large quantities of cabbage, sweet potatoes, beets, carrots, cucumbers, onions, squash, and tomatoes during the 1880s.[20]

When properly collected and spent, post and company funds also supplemented regular army issues. A list of equipment purchased in October and November 1885 serves as an instructive example. During this two-month period, the post fund provided 200 pounds of salt, 4 pounds of hops, five cans of lard, 1,225 pounds of potatoes, one can of mineral oil, 2 pounds of candles, and thirty-eight library books. This was in addition to the materials already on hand: twenty-four bake pans, a dough trough, a strainer and tin kettle, a sieve, fifteen benches, a clock, a composing stick, fourteen boxes of crayons, six slate pencil boxes, thirty-four library files, two maps, a printing press, six hoes, a plow, a rake, two watering pots, a dust brush, an organ, and two sets of checkers, chess pieces, and dominoes. Still, the system depended upon local conditions and the bargaining abilities of soldier-traders. Attempting to make available a balanced diet, the army tried to ensure that the subsistence department made available canned goods, tobacco, butter, dried fruits, and crackers to the troops at cost. More refined palates usually found hams, oysters, syrup, and jelly on post shelves.[21]

Others hoped that better and more diversified recreational outlets might help address problems of desertion and morale. Critics had long charged that profit-minded sutlers detracted from military efficiency. Commanding the Department of Texas, E. O. C. Ord had asserted "that *Posttrader's Establishments* are, with rare exceptions, simply dramshops, where the cheapest and most deleterious liquors are generally sold." During the mid-1880s, a system of nonprofit canteens gained momentum, and Col. Elwell Otis oversaw the December 18, 1887 opening of such an outlet in an unoccupied barrack at Fort Davis. In addition to selling "beer, tobacco, cigars, pipes, playing cards, oysters, sardines, and sundry other articles" to enlisted personnel, the canteen maintained billiard tables, chess, checkers, backgammon, dominoes, and playing cards for its patrons (civilians were not allowed). As part of new army doctrine, sales of hard liquor were forbidden. The canteen also extended limited credit (from three dollars per month to privates to five dollars per month for sergeants) to the soldiers. Its long hours (9 A.M. to 10 P.M., with an hour off for lunch and dinner), low prices, and congenial atmosphere soon lured business away from longtime sutlers Davis and Abbott.[22]

Abbott protested the new situation to Sen. Richard Coke (D-Texas), reasoning that since the canteen paid no taxes or rent, its employees received government salary, and its supplies were shipped by government transportation, it enjoyed an unfair advantage over sutlers who paid a head tax to the post fund. Furthermore, Abbott charged that the canteen allowed gambling and remained open on Sundays in flagrant violation of state law. "Its establishment is contrary to the spirit of American institutions," insisted the sutler, now a confirmed believer in unfettered free enterprise once his own monopoly had been ended. But Abbott's protests fell upon deaf ears, and in May 1890 his appointment was rescinded, a process that was occurring nationwide: the army's post traders, eighty-five strong as late as 1889, had been reduced to eleven by 1891. The Fort Davis canteen expanded to fill the void, adding two ice cream freezers and cheese, candies, pickles, jellies, toilet paper, envelopes, cherries, cookies, cigarettes, gum, and canned lobsters to its stock. Of course, the absence of hard liquor led some soldiers to patronize other unregulated civilian merchants off base.[23]

Phasing out the sutlers was only one segment of a general reform effort spearheaded by Secretary of War Redfield Proctor (1889–91). By making military life more palatable to the common soldier, Proctor reasoned, fewer men would desert. "Every captain should be to his company as a father, and should treat it as his family, as his children," explained the secretary. To allow enlisted soldiers more off-duty time, in 1889 Proctor abolished the traditional Sunday morning dress parade. Building upon the efforts of his predecessors, the secretary also sought to make punishment more equitable, establishing summary courts to assure quicker trials for minor infractions and prescribing uniform punishment codes for more serious crimes. A further change allowed enlisted men to purchase their discharge after only a year of military service. Secretary Proctor's comprehensive approach also featured an increase in the vegetable ration. The program seemed to work, and desertion fell from 11 percent in 1888–89 to 7.5 percent in 1890–91.[24]

Even as army officials struggled to improve morale and reduce desertion, modernizing facilities proved a constant challenge at a frontier post such as Davis. An 1887 inspection revealed that the accumulated filth underneath the floors of the enlisted men's barracks had reached epidemic proportions. The kitchens, bake houses, and privies also required immediate attention. The criticism sparked a frenzy of repair work on the enlisted men's barracks. Simultaneous efforts to improve the post's appearance were also evident. By 1888, four cottonwood trees graced the area in front of officers' row. Madeira vines sheltered the front porches, and Bermuda grass covered their front yards. To prevent livestock from nearby ranches from destroying everything in their wake, a "rustic fence" was subsequently erected in front of officers' row. That year, monies also became available to construct two bathhouses, complete with hot and cold running water.[25]

Still, the struggle often seemed futile. Fort Davis had traditionally been considered one of the army's healthiest positions. Its moderate climate, shel-

Members of the Fifth Infantry Regiment assemble on the Fort Davis parade ground, 1889. Officers' houses are in the background. Courtesy Fort Davis National Historic Site.

tering canyon walls, and spectacular locale made it a favorite among military personnel who enjoyed the serene isolation of the Trans-Pecos. Studies in 1884 and 1885 that revealed high sickness rates at Davis thus shocked many officials. Conditions continued to deteriorate in 1886, when the daily non-effective rate of the Davis garrison (78 per 1,000 troops) was the second highest in the nation. Furthermore, its annual hospital admission rate (2,276 per 1,000) surpassed all other Great Plains region posts. Abnormally high rates of typhoid, dysentery, malarial fevers, diarrhea, and venereal diseases accounted for the disastrous findings. "This is new and somewhat of a disappointment," acknowledged the department commander, Brigadier General Stanley, "as Fort Davis, with its temperate climate, has long been reckoned as a good sanitarium for Texas." Obviously, such a facility should not be built at an unhealthy site.[26]

Post officials linked the health problems to the local water supply. Popular belief attributed the water's bad taste and foul odor to the tadpoles that infested the distributing tank. New filters, piping, and a steam condenser were added, bringing the total amount spent on the water system for Fort Davis by early 1888 to more than ten thousand dollars. Fed up with the "thin pea soup emulsion which has been passed round to the people of this Post as distilled water," Surgeon John Lauderdale tackled the problem that summer, and five day's tinkering with the filter produced water that was "delicious, soft, and free from any odor or taste of machinery oil." But the tadpoles soon returned, rendering all efforts to improve the filtering system futile.[27]

Flooding from the surrounding hills, exacerbated by the habitual over-grazing of adjacent lands, further magnified the problems. Despite the earlier efforts by post commanders McLaughlen and Grierson, drainage ditches were too shallow to divert waters from the deluge of August 1888. A vitriolic Lauderdale faulted the post commander, Col. Melville A. Cochran, "who does not seem to know as much about looking after the interests of a Post as Barnum's fat boy," for not having anticipated the crisis. Two years later, floods broke an earthen embankment and inundated the officers' quarters. Repairing the existing drainage system seemed a huge undertaking; by November 1890, the new post commander, Lt. Col. William H. Kellogg, concluded that such action "would not be advisable unless this is quite certain to be a permanent station."[28]

Conditions such as these put everyone on edge, and during the latter 1880s the petty rivalries so common to the frontier army again reached crisis proportions at Fort Davis. Lt. Col. David R. Clendenin, Third Cavalry, received stern orders to avoid meddling in the affairs of others. The acerbic post surgeon, Lauderdale, shunned any social encounters with Lt. Joseph M. Partello, charging his "selfish pig" of a rival with having diverted materials purchased by the medical department to the quartermaster's office. But the surgeon reserved his choicest criticisms for the rotund Colonel Cochran. "*That heavyweight* next door has been tramping up and down his porch for the last half hour making a fearful racket," wrote Lauderdale. "I suppose he is trying to reduce his weight by exercise." Of Cochran's efforts to walk off a few pounds, the surgeon confided: "If he should consult me I would say start for Marfa and if that does not do it right on towards San Antonio."[29]

The opening of a new decade found Fort Davis in poor shape at a time when the army was hoping to reduce expenses by consolidating its scattered frontier forts. In 1890, the noneffective rate of its garrison was still thirteenth highest in the nation. The post school had fallen out of favor; even after War Department mandates that all soldiers in their first year of enlistment attend, only sixteen of the eighty-one-man garrison were present as of April 30, 1890. Pvt. John Wood and Cpl. Julian Longorio had made the last recorded scout against Indians on Fort Davis records in February 1888, riding seventy miles from the subpost at Nevill's Springs down the Rio Grande. With the Indian military presence defeated, the twenty-odd miles to the railroad depot at Marfa seemed just long enough to threaten the continued existence of Fort Davis.[30]

Department commander Stanley had already concluded that Fort Davis should be abandoned. "If further experience shows the water to be unwholesome," he had warned as early as 1886, "measures must be taken to vacate the post." The following year he reported that Davis was "out of place," "inconvenient," and "expensive." In April 1888, when the five companies of the Eighth Cavalry then stationed at Fort Davis were slated for routine change of station to Dakota, Stanley again seized the opportunity to reiterate his concerns about the Limpia post. But with available quarters for the troops at a premium, department officials responded in no uncertain terms: "Davis must be maintained." Undeterred, Stanley renewed his offensive the following year, pointing out that Fort Davis was one of only two military posts in Texas still under lease. Once again, however, a higher authority—this time in the person of John M. Schofield, commanding general of the army—intervened on behalf of the post on the Limpia. Schofield urged that rather than abandon Fort Davis, new shelter should be erected there for six additional cannon.[31]

A careless office clerk nearly undid the commanding general's wishes. With the War Department pushing aggressively to consolidate its western posts in order to reduce expenses, on March 20, 1890, General Schofield dutifully listed sixteen forts that might be abandoned if accommodations for their garrisons were found elsewhere. Fort Davis was not among the sixteen; instead, it fell into a different list, marked number two. But the clerk mistakenly concluded that the "abandonment" of posts on the second list "has been recommended but not fully determined upon." Wanting nothing of the sort, Schofield explained that a "clerical error" had made it appear that he wanted to eliminate Davis, when in fact he had not. The transfer of four additional companies to Fort Davis that spring, coupled with Schofield's suggestion that its quarters be used to help alleviate overcrowding in Arizona, seemed a further indication of the general's desire to maintain the Davis Mountains post.[32]

But Secretary of War Proctor continued to press the case for base closures. During a spring tour in 1891, he met Brigadier General Stanley in San Antonio, where they discussed "many important matters relative to the defence of the Rio Grande." Proctor also visited Eagle Pass, Fort Clark, and Del Rio—but not Fort Davis. Upon his return to Washington, the secretary reported his findings to Representative Lanham, whose West Texas congressional district would be most affected by possible changes. Proctor believed a larger post at El Paso advisable. Although Fort Hancock seemed "neither necessary nor desirable," the new quarters there guaranteed the army's continued presence. On Fort Davis, however, the secretary delivered a different message: Schofield had withdrawn his support. According to Proctor,

Schofield and Stanley had both concluded that it was too far from the railroad to be efficient. Warned the secretary, "The troops will probably be withdrawn from there before the first of July."[33]

News of Proctor's decision had reached Fort Davis by April 1. Long fearing such a move, local residents and merchants had petitioned Pres. Grover Cleveland for a larger garrison in 1885 and lobbied Representative Lanham on their post's behalf in 1889 and 1890. Venerable old Daniel Murphy now offered up a final plea to Secretary of State James G. Blaine. Murphy reasoned that it would be foolish for the military to leave what was destined to become "the richest mineral belt on the Continent south of us to the Pacific." This would leave the entire Big Bend region open "to the most unlaw abiding people of bought [both] countryes and we are liable at any time to be plased in a disagreeable pocession [position]." But the Texas congressional delegation's failure to intervene killed any possibility of reversing the verdict. Sen. John Reagan (D-Texas) threw his weight behind Fort Elliott; Lanham lobbied hard to protect Fort Bliss, Fort Elliott, and the post at Del Rio, personally taking his case to Schofield "several times." Davis, however, had no such champion, despite the county having supported Lanham by a 347–5 count in the 1888 election. Closing Fort Davis thus seemed economically sensible and politically feasible.[34]

Stanley and Proctor had agreed to evacuate Fort Davis by June 30, 1891, the end of the fiscal year. The Third Cavalry troop then at Davis, along with the post library, was trundled off to Fort Hancock. Four companies of the Twenty-third Infantry received orders to move to Forts McIntosh and Bliss. Fifth Infantry, Company F, was transferred to Fort Sam Houston while post quartermaster Lt. Charles B. Hardin oversaw details of the evacuation. Quartermaster stores, uniforms, nonperishable foodstuffs, and chapel furniture were shipped to San Antonio. On June 19, Lieutenant Hardin auctioned off condemned government property at a public sale even as departing soldiers and their families tried to hawk their own excess belongings at bargain-basement prices. Civilians snapped up the goods in an auction that netted the government nearly three thousand dollars; as for the soldiers, one veteran of such a process complained that selling "anything of value in this poor country at its real worth is almost impossible."[35]

The garrison had departed by July 3; Lieutenant Hardin and Pvt. William Boyer remained behind making final arrangements and hiring a custodian for the abandoned public buildings. Ex-soldier Charles Mulhern cogently reported the impact of the military's departure. "Plenty of houses in Davis now and no one to live in them," he wrote. "The Bottom is out of Ft. Davis." As Mulhern suspected, an economic depression followed the withdrawal of the military garrison. Although most civilians remained, the captive market offered by the army was gone. The John James family, owners of the former military reservation, rented out the old buildings as residences and tourist cottages for several years. But the structures inevitably fell into disrepair as looting and weather took their toll.[36]

In the end, the army's broader efforts to consolidate frontier garrisons had spelled doom for the post on the Limpia. The Indians had been driven out of the Trans-Pecos, and high sickness rates at Davis had silenced any speculation that it might become a permanent garrison or military health center. Secretary of War Proctor proudly reported that twenty-eight forts had been abandoned between June 1, 1889, and November 3, 1891. In explaining the evacuation of Fort Davis, Stanley noted, somewhat wistfully: "Fort Davis had outlived its usefulness as a military station, and yet it is to be regretted that it was discontinued, owing to its salubrious climate and its usefulness as a government sanitary hospital, to which enfeebled soldiers could be sent."[37]

EPILOGUE

The military frontier at Fort Davis had come to an end. For thirty-two of the past thirty-seven years, the post's garrison had protected non-Indians across much of the Trans-Pecos region of Texas. The army had driven the Indians who had once occupied the area south into Mexico, where scattered remnants were gradually assimilated into the general population, or west into New Mexico, where they now eked out a meager existence on a federal reservation. And, as was the case across much of the American West, the army had also engaged in activities that subsequent generations would later call "nation building." Soldiers had explored the region, built most of the structures that composed the fort itself, strung telegraph wire, and laid out and improved roads. Their presence had also provided enough physical security—or at least the appearance of security—against Indian attacks to allow ranchers to take advantage of the area's rich pastoral opportunities. Further, the garrison generated a demand for services that attracted an array of entrepreneurs and job seekers to the Davis Mountains.

The soldiers, and the civilians who had followed them, represented a diverse cross section of nineteenth-century American society. The West Point graduates who dominated the officer corps often came from middle- to upper-class backgrounds; noncommissioned personnel, on the other hand, typically came from the ranks of immigrants and blacks, whose opportunities had been much more limited. Civilians drawn to the post on the Limpia included larger-than-expected numbers of European and Mexican immigrants. Rather than the monolithic society often depicted by casual portraits of the nineteenth-century American frontier, the resulting community was multiracial and multiethnic. Although racial and ethnic boundaries were evident, they were hardly rigid, somewhat tempered by shared demands for limited resources.

The frontier community's dependence upon the federal government seems ironic in light of the myths that frequently cloud popular understanding of America's past. The West, our stereotypes sometimes suggest, was built by rugged individualists seeking opportunities free of the established practices and structures that had limited them back east. The entrepreneurs who came to Fort Davis to make their fortunes, whether from Mexico, Europe, or the United States, certainly braved great dangers and sought to capitalize on the chance to begin anew. But they did so knowing that federal dollars would flow into the Fort Davis economy, providing the capital and profits necessary for them to have a fighting chance of recognizing their dreams. Moreover, they did so in the shadow of the U.S. Army, that oft-maligned but highly useful institution of federal interest, security, and empire.

Fortunately, Fort Davis did not die with the army's departure. The population, which had grown to some 800 civilians by the late 1880s, fell to 554 by 1920, but then began to stabilize—and then to slowly rebound—as cattle, automobiles, tourism, and a concerted effort by local boosters once again attracted interest in the Davis Mountains region. A brief dalliance with the movie industry in the late 1920s and early 1930s proved a bust, but the New Deal brought a more permanent and profitable suitor in the form of an old friend: the government. The state built a "Scenic Loop" highway through the beautiful surrounding mountains, and the federal Civilian Conservation Corps erected Indian Lodge at the Davis Mountains State Park. The McDonald Observatory, constructed under the aegis of the Lone Star State's largest public institution of higher learning and dedicated in 1939, kindled additional interest in the region. The crowning glory came in 1961, when Congress passed legislation authorizing creation of the Fort Davis National Historic Site, thus paving the way for the restoration and reconstruction of the abandoned military post.

The federal government's return marked the completion of the circle begun in 1854 with the arrival of the Eighth Infantry Regiment. Modern Fort Davis remains a crossroads, albeit of a somewhat different kind than was the case during the nineteenth century. Located between the region's major thoroughfares—Interstate Highway 10 to the north and U.S. Highway 90 to the south—the community no longer serves virtually every east-west traveler through the Trans-Pecos. But as the "highest town in Texas," it remains an oasis for those lucky enough to know its charms. Tourists, hunters, campers,

and those seeking an escape from the blazing Texas heat mingle with permanent residents, who continue to hold jobs in agriculture, service industries,
and local, state, and federal government agencies in far larger numbers than
is typical in the Lone Star State. And although blacks have largely left the area,
its one thousand inhabitants are roughly equally divided between whites and
Hispanics, a fitting reminder of the region's multicultural history.[1]

APPENDIX 1

The Garrison at Fort Davis — Assigned Strength

Year	Regiments	Officers	Enlisted men	Aggregate
1854	8 Inf	23	235	258
1855	8 Inf	14	250	264
1856	8 Inf	19	419	438
1857	8 Inf	16	305	331
1858	8 Inf	11	238	249
1859	8 Inf	8	122	130
1860	8 Inf	11	127	138
1867	9 Cav	11	267	278
1868	9 Cav; 41 Inf	14	384	398
1869	9 Cav; 41 Inf	18	277	295
1870	9 Cav; 24 Inf; 25 Inf	23	404	427
1871	9 Cav; 24 Inf; 25 Inf	11	168	179
1872	9 Cav; 25 Inf	13	226	239
1873	9 Cav; 25 Inf	17	262	279
1874	9 Cav; 25 Inf	17	216	233
1875	10 Cav; 25 Inf	23	226	249
1876	10 Cav; 25 Inf	24	274	298
1877	10 Cav; 25 Inf	16	209	225
1878	10 Cav; 25 Inf	24	306	330
1879	10 Cav; 25 Inf	20	338	358
1880	10 Cav; 24 Inf	24	382	406
1881	10 Cav; 1 Inf	41	542	583
1882	10 Cav; 16 Inf	35	611	646
1883	10 Cav; 16 Inf	39	600	639
1884	10 Cav; 16 Inf	30	476	506
1885	3 Cav	17	190	207
1886	3 Cav; 16 Inf	18	249	267
1887	3 Cav; 16 Inf	22	292	314
1888	5 Inf	8	101	109
1889	5 Inf	8	95	103
1890	5 Inf; 23 Inf	19	271	290

SOURCE: Greene, *Historic Resource Study*, 20–21, 39.

APPENDIX 2

Ethnic Composition of Civilians at Fort Davis

Year	Number	White (%)	Spanish-surnamed (%)	Black (%)	Mixed (%)
1860 Wild Rose Pass	49	61	39	n.d.	n.d.
Las Limpias	116	17	83	n.d.	n.d.
1870	247	19	68	6	6
1880	509	21	68	4	7
1890	800 (est.)	n.d.	n.d.	n.d.	n.d.
1900	699	23	66	9	2
1910	675	25	67	1	6

SOURCE: Manuscript Returns, U.S. Census, 1860, Presidio County; Wright, "Residential Segregation," 301.

NOTE: n.d. = no data available.

NOTES

ABBREVIATIONS

ACP Branch	Appointment, Commission, and Personal Branch Files
AGO	Adjutant General's Office
CAH	Center for American History
DT	Department of Texas
FODA	Fort Davis National Historic Site
GPLu	Benjamin Grierson Papers, Texas Tech University, Lubbock (photocopy at Fort Davis National Historic Site)
GPNew	Benjamin Grierson Papers, Newberry Library, Chicago (microfilm copy at Fort Davis National Historic Site)
GPSpr	Benjamin Grierson Papers, Illinois State Historical Library, Springfield (microfilm copy at Fort Davis National Historic Site)
HQA	Headquarters of the Army
LC	Library of Congress
LR	Letters Received
LS	Letters Sent
NARA	National Archives and Records Administration
OR	*War of the Rebellion: A Compilation of the Official Records of the Union and Confederate Armies* (unless otherwise noted, all references are to series 1)
RLR	Register of Letters Received
SW, AR	Secretary of War, Annual Reports
TSL	Texas State Library

PREFACE

1. Froebel, *Seven Years' Travel*, 460; Taylor and McDanield, *The Coming Empire*, 381; Myer to My Dear James, Feb. 14, 1855, in Crimmins, "General Albert J. Myer," 57; Report of Stanley, Sept. 30, SW, AR, 1884, 125.

2. Sherman to Sheridan, Apr. 2, 1883, 26:553, roll 9, LS, HQA (microfilm M 857), NARA.

3. For Turner, see Billington, *America's Frontier Heritage*, 25. For a concise summary of the recent "frontier" debate, see Rischer, "Career of Francis Jennings," 517–29, especially note 8. Thanks to my colleague, David Blanke, for calling the Rischer essay to my attention.

4. Nobles, *American Frontiers*, xii–xiv.

CHAPTER ONE

1. Anderson, *Indian Southwest*, 7–28; Hickerson, *Jumanos*, 123–30.
2. Hackett, *Picardo's Treatise*, 1:137–38; Hickerson, *Jumanos*, 129–30.
3. Hickerson, *Jumanos*, 131–32; Bolton, *Spanish Exploration in the South-West*, 331–43.
4. Hutcheson, *Trans-Pecos*, 5–6; Biesaart et al., *Prehistoric Archeological Sites in Texas*, 151; Kirkland and Newcomb, *Rock Art of Texas Indians*, 127–34; Thompson, "Observations at a Trans-Pecos Rock Art Site," 1–23; Stoddard et al., *Borderlands Sourcebook*, 70–73.
5. Anderson, *Indian Southwest*, 17–34; Hickerson, *Jumanos*, xxvii, 215–18, 226–27; *Spanish Explorers in the Southern United States*, 103–104; Chipman, "In Search of Cabeza de Vaca's Route across Texas," 127–48.
6. Anderson, *Indian Southwest*, 24–29; Castañeda, *Our Catholic Heritage*, 1:157; Applegate and Hanselka, *La Junta de los Rios*, 51–53.
7. Sonnichsen, *Mescalero Apaches*, 22–23, 31; Opler, "Mescalero Apache," 10:419–39; Moorhead, *Apache Frontier*, 6, 200–203; *Spanish Explorers in the Southern United States*, 362.
8. Opler, "Mescalero Apache," 432–33.
9. Ibid., 427; John, *Storms Brewed in Other Men's Worlds*, 265–66; Carlson, *Plains Indians*, 38–39; Newcomb, *Indians of Texas*, 108, 155–57. For a revisionist study of Comanche society, see Betty, *Comanche Society*.
10. Bolton, *Spanish Exploration*, 2:172–90; Applegate and Hanselka, *La Junta de los Rios*, 13–14; Castañeda, *Our Catholic Heritage*, 1:170–73, 181–87.
11. "La Junta de los Rios"; "Nuestra Señora de Guadalupe Mission," both in Handbook of Texas Online; Castañeda, *Our Catholic Heritage*, 3:199–203; Applegate and Hanselka, *La Junta de los Rios*, 20–22, 54–55; Griffen, *Indian Assimilation*, 10–18, 97; Anderson, *Indian Southwest*, 94; Tyler, *Big Bend*, 34–36.
12. Bannon, *Spanish Borderlands*, 172–86; Faulk and Brinkerhoff, *Lancers for the King*, 53–55; Gerald, *Spanish Presidios of the Late Eighteenth Century*, 37–39; Thomas, *Teodoro de Croix*, 26, 38–43, 92–94; Moorhead, *Apache Frontier*, 37–41, 88–90, 120, 203–206, 245–48, 252–69; Griffen, *Indian Assimilation*, 107–109; Simmons, *Border Comanches*, 35–36.
13. Bannon, *Spanish Borderlands*, 229–38; Griffen, *Indian Assimilation*, 18.
14. Weber, *Mexican Frontier*, 108–17, 280; Moorhead, *Apache Frontier*, 286–90; Castañeda, *Our Catholic Heritage*, 5:114–15; Thompson, *Marfa and Presidio County*, 1:36–37, 65; Sonnichsen, *Mescalero Apaches*, 54–55.
15. Applegate and Hanselka, *La Junta de los Rios*, 23–24, 56; Thompson, *Marfa and Presidio County*, 1:33–34, 39–40, 49; Gregg, *Commerce on the Prairies*, 334n–35n.
16. Tyler, *Big Bend*, 51–52; Applegate and Hanselka, *La Junta de los Rios*, 30–32; Bancroft, *North American States*, 598–99; Smith, "Mexican and Anglo-Saxon Traffic," 98–100, 104; Weber, *Mexican Frontier*, 105.

17.   Bancroft, *North Mexican States*, 2:600–601; Smith, *Borderlander*, 149–71; Smith, "Mexican and Anglo-Saxon Traffic," 102–14; Weber, *Mexican Frontier*, 87.

18.   Weber, *Mexican Frontier*, 273–82.

19.   Tyler, *Big Bend*, 53, 67; Miles, "Old Fort Leaton," 84–90; Corning, *Baronial Forts of the Big Bend*, 25–28; Applegate and Hanselka, *La Junta de los Rios*, 24, 56–57; Thompson, *Marfa and Presidio County*, 1:67, 73.

20.   Hughes Report, 6; Hays to Marcy, Dec. 13, 1848, 65; both in S.E.D. 32, 31st Cong., 1st sess., serial 558; Tyler, *Big Bend*, 53–57; Greer, *Colonel Jack Hays*, 216–26; Goetzmann, *Army Exploration*, 9–10, 209, 214–17, 225–30; "Journal of Henry Chase Whiting," 77, 331; Report of Smith, May 25, 1849, S.E.D. 64, 31st Cong., 1st sess., serial 562, 4–7; Neighbours, *Robert S. Neighbors*, 67, 300n.

21.   Utley, *Fort Davis National Historic Site*, 4; Hunter to wife, June 2, 1849, in Stephens, *Texan in the Gold Rush*, 13–15; Greene, *Historic Resource Study*, 9; Goetzmann, *Army Exploration*, 227–32; Tyler, *Big Bend*, 62–63, 75–85; Austerman, *Sharps Rifles*, 9–10; Report of French, Dec. 26, 1849, SW, AR, 1850, 309.

22.   Austerman, *Sharps Rifles*, 20–23; Schick, "Wagons to Chihuahua," 76–77, 87; Utley, *Frontiersmen in Blue*, 87–88; Garland to Thomas, June 5, 1854, 35; Report of Garland, Jan. 31, 1855, 56; Report of French, Nov. 2, 1851, 231–32; all in SW, AR.

23.   J. K. F. Mansfield, *Mansfield on the Condition of Western Forts*, 28–29; Conrad to Smith, Apr. 30, SW, AR, 1851, 117–18. The army eventually established posts at each of the locations suggested by Mansfield.

24.   McHenry, *Webster's American Military Biographies*, 400; Utley, *Frontiersmen in Blue*, 61, 71–74; Frazer, *Forts of the West*, 139–63; Sherman, *Memoirs*, 90–95, 99–103; Crimmins, "Freeman's Report," 211–16.

25.   Report of Jesup, Nov. 20, SW, AR, 1852, 69–70; Smith to Cooper, May 6, 1854, S 358, roll 505, LR, AGO, 1822–60, RG 94 (microfilm M 567), NARA; Wilhelm, *History of the Eighth U.S. Infantry*, 47–48.

CHAPTER TWO

1.   Greene, *Historic Resource Study*, 11; Fort Davis, Oct. 1854, roll 297, Returns from United States Military Posts, RG 94 (microfilm M 617), NARA; Smith to Cooper, Oct. 9, 30, 1854, FODA (microfilm 567-506); Report of Cooper, Nov. 21, SW, AR, 1854, 58–59.

2.   Polk, Annual Message, Dec. 5, 1848, in Richardson, *Messages and Papers*, 4:629.

3.   Wooster, "Military Strategy in the Southwest," 6; Prucha, *Great Father*, 1:315–18.

4.   Reports of Conrad, Nov. 30, 1850, 5; Nov. 29, 1851, 112–13; Dec. 4, 1852, 5; all in SW, AR.

5.   Prucha, *Great Father*, 1:362–66; H.E.D. 76, 35th Cong., 1st sess., serial 963; A. C. Hyde to Bryan, Nov. 19, 1857, Guy M. Bryan Papers, CAH; Gammel, *Laws of Texas*, 4:258–59. The Tigua Indians, a small group of Pueblans who

left New Mexico with the Spaniards during the revolt of 1680, were officially recognized by the state of Texas in 1967. They occupy twenty-six acres of land at Ysleta del Sur Pueblo, near El Paso; http://www.tsha.utexas.edu/handbook/online/articles/view/TT/bmt45.html (accessed September 2, 2003).

6. Polk, Annual Message, Dec. 5, 1848, in Richardson, *Messages and Papers*, 4:631.

7. Utley, *Frontiersmen in Blue*, 2–12; *Congressional Globe*, 33d Cong., 2d sess., Appendix, 337–41; *Congressional Globe*, 31st Cong., 2d sess., 378–79; *Congressional Globe*, 35th Cong., 1st sess., 674.

8. Weigley, *History of the United States Army*, 138.

9. Cunliffe, *Soldiers & Civilians*, 135–37.

10. Utley, *Frontiersmen in Blue*, 48–51.

11. Ibid., 51–53.

12. See Wooster, "Military Strategy in the American West."

13. Ball, *Army Regulars*, 17–20; Utley, "Frontier and the American Military Tradition," 5; Utley, *Frontiersmen in Blue*, 57; Coffman, *Old Army*, 77–78; Morrison, *"Best School in the World,"* 97–101; Smith, "West Point and the Indian Wars," 32–43.

14. Utley, *Frontier Regulars*, 57; Moten, *Delafield Commission*, 186–90.

15. Utley, *Frontiersmen in Blue*, 16; *Congressional Globe*, 32d Cong., 1st sess., 515; Report of Conrad, Dec. 4, SW, AR, 1852, 4; Conrad to Hitchcock, Twiggs, Smith, and Sumner, May 5, 1852, LS, SW, vol. 33, RG 107 (microfilm M 6), NARA; Scott to Conrad, Nov. 22, SW, AR, 1852, 35; Report of Davis, Dec. 1, SW, AR, 1853, 5–6, 23; Dec. 4, 1854, 5; Dec. 1, 1856, 5–6; Davis to Sandridge, Jan. 29, 1856, vol. 34, LS, SW (microfilm M 6); Goetzmann, *Army Exploration*, 262–304.

16. Thian, *Military Geography*, 8, 98; Smith, *U.S. Army and the Texas Frontier Economy*, 18–38; Crimmins, "Mansfield's Report," 354–55; Mansfield to Thomas, Sept. 27, 1860, FODA (microfilm 567/625); Dye to Jesup, July 4, 1859, FODA (microfilm 906/8820); H.E.D. 22, 36th Cong., 1st sess., serial 1047, 7; Risch, *Quartermaster Support*, 311–12.

17. Connelly, "Camel Experiment," 442–55; Davis to Mason, Feb. 24, 1857, S.E.D. 62, 34th Cong., 3d sess., serial 881, 1; Journal of Beale, July 16–18, 1857, H.E.D. 124, 35th Cong., 1st sess., serial 959, 25–26; Lesley, *Uncle Sam's Camels*, 64.

18. Report of Hartz, 1859, 425; Diary of Echols, 1860, 35–44; both in SW, AR; Greene, *Historic Resource Study*, 23–24.

19. Connelly, "Camel Experiment," 457–62.

20. Heitman, *Historical Register*, 1:594–95; Utley, *Frontiersmen in Blue*, 20; *Congressional Globe*, Jan. 29, 1855, 440; Olmsted, *Journey through Texas*, 182–83.

21. *Telegraph and Texas Register*, Aug. 7, Sept. 7, 1850; *Texas State Gazette*, Oct. 27, 1847, Apr. 14, 1855; Montes to Steele, Sept. 18, 1875, box 2Q 400, Transcripts from the Adjutant General's Office, 1870–76, Texas Adjutant General's Office Papers, CAH; Runnels to Reagan, Oct. 30, 1858, John R. Reagan Papers, CAH;

Crawford to Wood, Jan. 19, 1850, LS, SW, vol. 30 (microfilm M 6); Crosby to Magoffin, Dec. 21, 1852, James Magoffin Papers, CAH; Utley, *Lone Star Justice*, 87–104; Report of Hardee, Sept. 14, SW, AR, 1850, 59; Myer to "My Dear James," Feb. 14, 1855, in Crimmins, "General Albert J. Myer," 52.

22. Report of Smith, Mar. 14, SW, AR, 1855, 52; Report of Simonson, Jan. 16, 23, 1855, RLR, DT, 487, NARA.

23. Fillmore, Annual Message, Dec. 2, 1850, in Richardson, *Messages and Papers*, 5:87; Tate, *Frontier Army*.

24. Report of Davis, Dec. 1, 1853, 7–13; Report of Scott, Nov. 16, 116–23; Report of Davis, Dec. 4, 1854, 5–6; all in SW, AR; Utley, *Frontiersmen in Blue*,16.

25. Heitman, *Historical Register*, 2:596.

26. Peters to Sister, Dec. 20, 1854, DeWitt C. Peters Papers, Bancroft Library; Utley, *Frontiersmen in Blue*, 33–34; Coffman, *Old Army*, 66–69, 80, 103; Letter of Bomford, July 2, 1855, 118, RLR, DT, RG 393, NARA.

27. Van Dorn to Withers, Dec. 28, SW, AR, 1858, 357; Ball, *Army Regulars*, 13–23; Myres, "Romance and Reality," 409–27; Myres, *Westering Women*, 36; Lane, *I Married a Soldier*, 22, 53–54.

28. Ball, *Army Regulars*, 13–23; Myer to James, Feb. 14, 1855, in Clary, "Myer's Letters," 42; Hunter, "Negro Trooper," 220–21.

29. Utley, *Frontiersmen in Blue*, 31; *U.S. Statutes at Large* 2 (1802): 133; "Army Register, 1853," H.E.D. 59, 33d Cong., 1st sess., serial 721, 64–65. For conversions into 2004 dollars, see Robert C. Sahr, http://oregonstate.edu/dept/pol_sci/fac/sahr/htm (accessed February 19, 2005).

30. Edward to Father, June 24, 1856, Oct. 9, 1859, Edward L. Hartz Collection, LC.

31. Report of Coolidge, S.E.D. 96, 34th Cong., 1st sess., serial 827, 625–29; Report of Floyd, Dec. 5, SW, AR, 1857, 12; *U.S. Statutes at Large* 10 (1854): 575–76.

32. Utley, *Frontiersmen in Blue*, 31; Report of Kelton, Oct. 1, SW, AR, 1891, 61; Bandel, *Frontier Life in the Army*, 105; Coffman, *Old Army*, 153–55. The private's minimum pay of $132 per year was slightly less than the wage of a farmhand, who by 1860 could expect to earn (on a national average) $163.20 with board. A cotton-mill worker might net $201; iron- and steel-mill hands averaged $346 in 1859; Lebergott, *Manpower in Economic Growth*, 539, 541.

33. Frazer, *Forts and Supplies*, 98; Lebergott, *Manpower in Economic Growth*, 541; Persons Hired at Fort Davis, Reports of Persons and Articles Hired, Entry 238, boxes 60–61, RG 92, NARA; Ball, *Army Regulars*, 57–59.

34. Utley, *Frontiersmen in Blue*, 36n69; "Table showing cost of rations, Texas forts, 1853," Martin L. Crimmins Papers, CAH; Report of Gibbons, Oct. 30, 1856, 258; Report of Taylor, Oct. 25, 1858, 801; both in SW, AR; Wooster, *Soldiers, Sutlers, and Settlers*, 116–17; Zenas R. Bliss Reminiscences, 1:171, CAH; Bandel, *Frontier Life in the Army*, 105.

35. Risch, *Quartermaster Support*, 7–8, 14, 16, 42–44, 302–303; Steffen, *Horse Soldier*, 2:6–15; U.S. Quartermaster's Department, *Uniforms of the United States Army*, 28–34.

36. Utley, *Frontiersmen in Blue*, 24–27; Steffen, *Horse Soldier*, 2:17; Crimmins, "Mansfield's Report," 210, 352–53, 355–56.

CHAPTER THREE

1. Billings, *Report on Barracks and Hospitals*, 227–28; Utley, *Fort Davis*, 6–7; Crimmins, "Mansfield's Report," 356; Heitman, *Historical Register*, 1:872; Bliss Reminiscences, 1:119–20.
2. Report of the Chief Engineer, Nov. 29, SW, AR, 1854, 109; Myer to James, Mar. 17 to Apr. 4, 1855, in Clary, "Myer's Letters," 53, 57–58, Utley, *Fort Davis*, 7–8; Crimmins, "Mansfield's Report," 352–58; Bliss Reminiscences, 1:119–20, 173–74; Greene, *Historic Resource Study*, 55; Bennett, *Forts and Forays*, 79.
3. Johnston to Cooper, May 6, 1856; Buell to Lee, July 12, 1856; both in roll 1, LS, DT, 1856–58 (microfilm M 1165); Crimmins, "Mansfield's Report," 351–52; SW, AR, 1856, 243; Lee to DT, Aug. 30, 1856, RLR, DT, 278; Greene, *Historic Resource Study*, 53–56; Buell to Lee, Sept. 30, 1856, roll 1, LS, DT, 1856–58 (microfilm M 1165).
4. Greene, *Historic Resource Study*, 56–60; Lee to Department of Texas, Oct. 24, 1856, RLR, DT, 278; McDowell to Lee, Jan. 2, 31, 1857, roll 1, LS, DT, 1856–58 (microfilm M 1165); Statement of Jones, June 4, 1857, FODA (microfilm 906/8820); Smith, *U.S. Army and the Texas Frontier Economy*, 87, 91; Twiggs to Thomas, July 25, 1857; Withers to Commanding Officer, Aug. 17, 1857; both in roll 1, LS, DT, 1856–58 (microfilm M 1165); Dye to Jesup, July 4, 1859, FODA (microfilm 906/8820).
5. Seawell to DT, Dec. 20, 22, 1854, Oct. 6, 1855, 486, 195; Lee to DT, Apr. 21, 1855, 265; June 11, 14, 1855, 268; July 5, 1855, 269; Dec. 27, 1856, 279, all in RLR, DT; Buell to Lee, Sept. 30, 1856; Buell to Seawell, Dec. 8, 1856; McDowell to Seawell, Feb. 28, May 12, 1857; Withers to Seawell, June 30, Aug. 22, 1857; Twiggs to Thomas, Oct. 4, 1857, all in roll 1, LS, DT, 1856–58 (microfilm M 1165). See also Thomas, *Fort Davis and the Texas Frontier*.
6. Edward to Father, Feb. 27, 1858, Hartz Collection; Larson, *Sergeant Larson*, 219–24; Bliss Reminiscences, 1:177–78; Wooster, *Fort Davis*, 137–38.
7. Thompson, "The Officers, Fort Davis, Texas," in Officers File, FODA; Utley, *Frontiersmen in Blue*, 33–34; Coffman, *Old Army*, 80; Proceedings of a Board of Examination, Dec. 26, 1855, S 837, roll 528; Enclosure with Lee to Cooper, Oct. 25, 1855, L 284, roll 520; both in LR, AGO, 1822–60 (microfilm M 567).
8. Slave Schedules, Manuscript Returns, U.S. Census, 1860, Presidio County; Wooster, *Soldiers, Sutlers, and Settlers*, 73–75; Rickey, *Forty Miles a Day*, 111–12; Peters to Mrs. Stoutenborough, June 12, 1860, Peters Papers; Edward to Father, June 24, 1856, Hartz Collection; Court Martial of Walter Scott, Samuel Thompson, HH 698, box 235, Court-Martial Case Files, RG 153, NARA.
9. Griswold, "Anglo Women and Domestic Ideology," 15–33; Jameson, "Women

as Workers, Women as Civilizers," 1–9; Riley, *Female Frontier,* 195–201; Myres, "Romance and Reality," 409–27.

10. Lesley, *Uncle Sam's Camels,* 48, 57; Walker to Davis, Mar. 24, 1855, S 486/177; Seawell to Cooper, June 13, 1855; both in roll 527, LR, AGO, 1822–60 (microfilm M 567); Peters to Mrs. Stoutenborough, June 12, 1860, Peters Papers.

11. Manuscript Returns, U.S. Census, 1860, Presidio County.

12. Report of Coolidge, S.E.D. 96, 34th Cong., 1st sess., serial 827, 625–26; Utley, *Frontiersmen in Blue,* 41; Report of Scott, Nov. 13, SW, AR, 1858, 762; Bliss Reminiscences, 1:3; Edward to Father, Nov. 1, Dec. 5, 1855, Hartz Collection; Thomas to Smith, Sept. 21, 1855, roll 5, LS, HQA (microfilm M 857).

13. Report of Scott, Nov. 20, SW, AR, 1857, 48; Coffman, *Old Army,* 197; Courts Martial of Robert Carson, II 104, box 260; Gottard Sanders, HH 914, box 249; John Malia, HH 953, box 251; William Gould, HH 888, box 247; William Morris, HH 698, box 235; Peter Fay, HH 747, box 238; Peter Fay, II 9, box 255; and Peter Gilhooty, II 211, box 260; all in Court-Martial Case Files; Thompson, *Texas & New Mexico on the Eve of the Civil War,* 103.

14. Edward to Father, Apr. 6, 1856, Feb. 27, 1858, Hartz Collection; Courts Martial of John Laughlin, Jacob Hetler, Lewis D. Brooks, Smith Sanderson, and John Toole, HH 652, box 232, Court-Martial Case Files; Brooks to Friend, attached to HH 652, Court-Martial Case Files.

15. Edward to Father, Apr. 6, June 24, 1856, Hartz Collection; Peters to Mrs. Stoutenborough, June 12, 1860, Peters Papers; Wooster, *Soldiers, Sutlers, and Settlers,* 83–102.

16. Wooster, *Soldiers, Sutlers, and Settlers,* 83–91; Utley, *Frontiersmen in Blue,* 38, 42–48; Coffman, *Old Army,* 164–65, 171; Crimmins, "Mansfield's Report," 354–57; Thompson, *Mansfield & Johnston Inspections,* 101–106; Bliss Reminiscences, 1:171, 180, 323–28; Letter of Hart, Apr. 2, 1856, RLR, DT, 48; Diary of Echols, July 14, SW, AR, 1860, 44; Reid, *Reid's Tramp,* 122; Maury, *Recollections of a Virginian,* 88–89.

17. Wooster, *Soldiers, Sutlers, and Settlers,* 83–91; Hartz to Father, Apr. 6, 1856, Hartz Collection.

18. Crimmins, "Mansfield's Report," 353–54; Thompson, *Mansfield & Johnston Inspections,* 71.

19. Crimmins, "General Albert J. Myer," 57–58; Woodland to Cousin Emma, Aug. 16, 1859, Woodland File, FODA; Edward to Father, June 24, 1856, Hartz Collection; Edward to Jenny, Mar. 25, 1856, Hartz Collection; Bliss Reminiscences, 1:309, 330; Crimmins, "Mansfield's Report," 354; Myer to James, Sept. 26, 1855, in Clary, "Myer's Letters," 72; Peters to Mrs. Stoutenborough, June 12, 1860, Peters Papers.

20. Greene, *Historic Resource Study,* 20–21; Gammel, *Laws of Texas,* 3:464–65, 786, 969, 4:906–907, 5:1095; Bliss Reminiscences, 2:15–20; Letter of Seawell, Oct. 13, 1855, RLR, DT, 195; Persons Hired at Fort Davis, 1857, boxes

60, 61, entry 238, Reports of Persons and Articles Hired, RG 92, NARA; Smith, *U.S. Army and the Texas Frontier Economy*, 207.

To estimate the payroll, I tried to be conservative. Base salaries were $11 per month for privates; five-year veterans, noncommissioned officers, and extra-duty laborers received extra payouts. Using an average of $14 per soldier per month, I thus estimated annual payments to enlisted personnel at $38,916. I assumed that the nine officers usually on post included one lieutenant colonel, two captains, three first lieutenants, and three second lieutenants. Salaries and various endorsements to the officers were set at $15,500.

21. Delo, *Peddlers and Post Traders*, passim; Registers of Post Traders, 1:136, 166, RG 94, NARA; Vinton to Nichols, Jan. 21, 1861, LR, DT, 1860–61; Crimmins, "Mansfield's Report," 357; Reid, *Reid's Tramp*, 123; Thompson, *Mansfield & Johnston Inspections*, 106; Peters to Stoutenborough, June 12, 1860, Peters Papers; Manuscript Returns, U.S. Census, 1860, Presidio County; Hartz to Father, Jan. 1, 1858, Hartz Collection.

22. *U.S. Statutes at Large*, 2:134; Stallard, *Glittering Misery*, 59, 61; Stewart, "Army Laundresses," 421; Wooster, *Soldiers, Sutlers, and Settlers*, 64–68, 192–93; Mansfield to Thomas, Mar. 23, Oct. 31, 1860, FODA (microfilm 567/625); Crimmins, "Mansfield's Report," 352–53; Butler, *Daughters of Joy, Sisters of Misery*, 122–46; Manuscript Returns, U.S. Census, 1860, Presidio County. Several men presumed to be their husbands were listed in the barracks. I have assumed that Patrick King (thirty-two years old, born in Ireland) was married to Catherine King (thirty years old, Ireland), Sergeant Mick Powell (thirty-five, Ireland) was matched with Mary Powell (thirty-two, Ireland), and Edward O'Brien (twenty-two, Ireland) was the husband of Julia O'Brien (twenty-one, Ireland). Because Susan Brown, a mulatto (thirty-five, Louisiana), was living with a five-year-old-black child, I have not presumed that she was married to either Frederick Brown (thirty-two, Saxony) or James Brown (twenty-one, Scotland), both of whom were white.

23. Court Martial of James McDermott, Testimony of Jane McDermott, Statement of James McDermott, filed in HH 914, box 249, Court-Martial Case Files. For a slightly different view, see Bliss Reminiscences, 1:330.

24. Manuscript Returns, U.S. Census, 1860, Presidio County.

25. Ibid.

26. Bliss Reminiscences, 1:174–76, 185, 260, 311; Manuscript Returns, U.S. Census, 1860, Presidio County; Thompson, *Marfa and Presidio County*, 1:55, 66, 78–79, 94; Tyler, *Big Bend*, 122; Scobee, *Old Fort Davis*, 72–73; Depositions of Mar. 1, 1899, Claim 2744, *Diedrick Dutchove [sic] vs. U.S. and Apache Tribe of Indians*, Indian Depredations Files, RG 205, NARA. In 2004 terms, their estates would have been valued as follows: Young—$610,000; Daniel Murphy—$250,000; Patrick Murphy—$130,000; Dutchover—$128,000; Hernandez—$13,000; Anver—$12,000.

The scarcity of marriages between white males and Hispanic females at Fort Davis before the Civil War seems to stem from the short time span of the post's existence and the absence of established Mexican landowning residents there before the military's arrival. Fifty miles to the south, Milt Faver had helped to cement his dominance of the Cibolo Creek region through his marriage to Francisca Ramirez. Tyler, *Big Bend*, 121–23; Corning, *Baronial Forts of the Big Bend*, 21–32, 44–56.

27.   Smith, *U.S. Army and the Texas Frontier Economy*, 184–86, 204–206, 210–12; Report of Meigs, Oct. 19, SW, AR, 1871, 140–41; Bowden, *Spanish and Mexican Land Grants*, 196; Greene, *Historic Resource Study*, 380, 459; Raht, *Romance of Davis Mountains*, 159; James, *Frontier and Pioneer*, 19–23; Proceedings of a Board of Officers, Orders No. 55, Apr. 23, 24, 1857, S 330/1858, roll 590; Seawell to AAG, July 6, 1858; Bryan to Floyd, Dec. 14, 1857, B 691, roll 555; Jones to Cooper, July 6, 1858; Lee to AAG, July 9, 1858; Petition of Green, Feb. 19, 1859; Townsend to Twiggs, Aug. 21, 1858; Seawell to Cooper, Oct. 13, 1860; all in LR, AGO, 1822–60 (microfilm M 567); *U.S. Statutes at Large*, 12:201. The army also rejected the claims of James W. Magoffin, a prominent West Texas businessman, to the site. Wooster, *Fort Davis*, 138–39.

CHAPTER FOUR

1.   Smith to Cooper, Oct. 9, 1854; Walker to Gibbs, Oct. 6, 1854; both in FODA (microfilm 567–506); Maury, *Recollections of a Virginian*, 84–91; Regiment of Mounted Riflemen, Oct., 1854, roll 28, Returns from Regular Army Cavalry Regiments, RG 94 (microfilm M 744), NARA; Austerman, "José Policarpo Rodriguez," 52–73.

2.   Report of Smith, Mar. 14, SW, AR, 1855, 52; Report of Simonson, Mar. 12, 1855, RLR, DT; Utley, *Frontiersmen in Blue*, 30.

3.   Garland to Thomas, June 30, 1854, 36; Report of Ewell, Feb. 10, 1855, 59–61; Report of Garland, Mar. 31, 1855, 62; all in SW, AR; Utley, *Frontiersmen in Blue*, 148–52.

4.   Seawell to DT, Mar. 19, 1855, RLR, DT, 490; "Abstract of Statements of Expenditures made on account of Indian Hostilities . . . in the month of January 1860," FODA (microfilm 906/8820); Maury, *Recollections of a Virginian*, 87; Hazen to Seawell, June 22, 1858, 182H 1858, roll 580, LR, AGO, 1822–60; Bliss Reminiscences, 1:315; Austerman, "José Policarpo Rodriguez," 65–71.

5.   Myer to James, Mar. 17 to Apr. 4, 1855, in Clary, "Myer's Letters," 55; Ball, *Army Regulars*, 30–31.

6.   Crimmins, "Mansfield's Report," 356–57; Lane, *I Married a Soldier*, 74; Myer to James, Aug. 22, 1855, in Clary, "Myer's Letters," 69; Bliss Reminiscences, 1:200–214; Hartz to Father, Feb. 10, Apr. 3, 1857, Hartz Collection.

7.   Bliss Reminiscences, 2:158; 1:303; Journal of Beale, July 8, 1857, H.E.D. 124, 35th Cong., 1st sess., serial 959, 21.

8.   Lane, *I Married a Soldier*, 166; Myer to James, Aug. 13, 1855, in Clary, "Myer's

Letters," 63–65; Wheeler, *Frontier Trail*, 314–15; Dodge, *Our Wild Indians*, 521–25.

9. *San Antonio Herald*, Aug. 21, 1855; Smith, *Old Army in Texas*, 139–40; Wooster, *Lone Star Generals*, 156–58. Randal later became a brigadier general in the Confederate army.

10. Crimmins, "Mansfield's Report," 356; Dodge, *Our Wild Indians*, 548; Seawell to DT, Mar. 6, 1856, RLR, DT, 393; Edward to Father, June 24, 1856, Hartz Collection; *San Antonio Daily Herald*, June 28, 1856.

11. Buell to Seawell, July 12, 1856; Buell to Lee, Oct. 1, Dec. 3, 1856; both in roll 1, LS, DT, 1856–58 (microfilm M 1114); Edward to Father, June 24, Oct. 18, Dec. 9, 1856, Hartz Collection; Fort Davis, Jan. 1857, roll 297, Returns from United States Military Posts, RG 94 (microfilm M 617), NARA.

12. Report of Smith, June 2, SW, AR, 1855, 54; Smith to Cooper, July 14, 1855, FODA (microfilm 567/528); Fink to Assistant Adjutant General, Feb. 4, 1860, F 11/1860, roll 623; Endorsements of Seawell, Feb. 9, and Scott, Feb. 24; all in LR, AGO, 1822–60 (microfilm M 567).

13. Goetzmann, *Army Exploration*, 367–68; Edward to Father, June 13, Sept. 13, 1857, Hartz Collection; Seawell to Cooper, June 5, 1858; Endorsement of McDowell, Aug. 2, 1858; both in 315S 1858 (filed with 161T 1858), roll 592, LR, AGO, 1822–60 (microfilm M 567); Bliss Reminiscences, 2:1–4; Pope to Humphreys, June 1, July 4, 1858, box 3, Miscellaneous Letters Received, Office of Exploration and Surveys, RG 48, NARA.

14. Austerman, *Sharps Rifles*, 14; Woolford, "Burr G. Duval Diary," 496; Taylor and McDonald, *The Coming Empire*, 329; Duffen, "Overland via 'Jackass Mail,'" 48.

15. Austerman, *Sharps Rifles*, 14, 39–40; Marcy, *Prairie Traveler*, 289; Bell, "Log of the Texas-California Cattle Trail, 1854," 227; Schick, "Wagons to Chihuahua," 79; Lane, *I Married a Soldier*, 44, 74; Crimmins, "Mansfield's Report," 355.

16. Marcy, *Prairie Traveler*, 290; Scobee, *Old Fort Davis*, 6; Reid, *Reid's Tramp*, 125–29; Lane, *I Married a Soldier*, 169.

17. Pitcher to Department of Texas, Aug. 24, 1855, RLR, DT, 401; Report of Sheridan, Aug. 14, 1855, RLR, DT, 194; Woods, "Report to Hon. A. V. Brown," CAH; Seawell to Gwin, July 13, 1858, FODA (microfilm 567-506).

18. Eighth Infantry, Annual Returns, 1857, roll 91, Returns from Regular Army Infantry Regiments (microfilm M 655); Registers of Enlistments, rolls 24, 25, Registers of Enlistments in the United States Army, 1798–1914, 128, 146, 202; all in RG 94 (microfilm M 233), NARA; "Proceedings of a Board of Officers . . ." Aug. 5, 1857, roll 1, FODA (microfilm 65-85/10427); General Orders No. 14, Nov. 13, SW, AR, 1857, 56–57.

19. Eighth Infantry, Annual Returns, 1857, roll 91, Returns from Regular Army Infantry Regiments (microfilm M 655); Registers of Enlistments, rolls 24, 25, Registers of Enlistments in the United States Army, 1798–1914, 128, 146,

202; all in RG 94 (microfilm M 233), NARA; "Proceedings of a Board of Officers . . ." Aug. 5, 1857, roll 1, FODA (microfilm 65-85/10427); General Orders No. 14, Nov. 13, SW, AR, 1857, 56–57.

20. Report of Hartz, July 30, 1857, Hartz Collection; General Orders No. 14, Nov. 13, SW, AR, 1857, 56–57.

21. For the Hazen scout, see McDowell to Commanding Officer, Feb. 23, 1857, roll 1, LS, DT, 1856–58; Bliss Reminiscences, 1:182–83; Kroeker, *Great Plains Command*, vii–viii, 3–30; Hazen to Seawell, June 22, 1858, 182H 1858, roll 580, LR, AGO, 1822–60 (microfilm M 567).

22. Twiggs to Army HQ, Aug. 24, 1858, 261–62; Twiggs to Thomas, May 27, 1859, 331–32; Brackett to Wood, May 16, 366–68; all in SW, AR; Brackett to Seawell, Mar. 25, 1859, Brackett File, FODA.

23. Twiggs to Army HQ, Aug. 24, 1858, 261–62; Twiggs to Thomas, May 27, 1859, 331–32; Brackett to Wood, May 16, 366–68; all in SW, AR; Brackett to Seawell, Mar. 25, 1859, Brackett File, FODA.

24. Lee to AG, Feb. 5, SW, AR, 1859, 360; Bliss Reminiscences, 1:153, 244, 249; Woods, "Report to Brown"; Seawell to AAG, Aug. 30, 1859, 339S 1859, roll 612, LR, AGO, 1822–60 (microfilm M 567).

25. Seawell to Cooper, Feb. 10; Endorsement of Seawell, Feb. 10; Endorsement of Floyd, May 12; all in 1860, 41S 1860, roll 632, LR, AGO, 1822–60 (microfilm M 567); Heitman, *Historical Register*, 1:872; Diary of Echols, July 10, SW, AR, 1860, 44; Eighth Infantry, July 1860, roll 92, Returns from Regular Army Infantry Regiments (microfilm M 665).

26. The following account is based upon Wooster, "'The Whole Company Have Done It,'" 19–28.

27. Thompson, *Mansfield & Johnston Inspections*, 103.

28. Greene, *Historic Resource Study*, 62–63; Thompson, *Mansfield & Johnston Inspections*, 101–106; Utley, *Fort Davis*, 56; Mariager, "Camp and Travel in Texas," 188.

29. Lee to Cooper, June 13; Endorsement of Thomas, Oct. 20; both in 1860, 41S 1860, roll 632, LR, AGO, 1822–60 (microfilm M 567); Kroeker, *Great Plains Command*, 35; *San Antonio Ledger and Texan*, Feb. 25, 1861.

30. Smith, *Old Army in Texas*, 139–47.

31. Edward to Father, Apr. 3, 1857, Hartz Collection.

CHAPTER FIVE

1. Peters to Father, Aug. 16, 1856, Peters Papers; Edward to Father, Dec. 9, 1856, Feb. 10, 1857, Hartz Collection; Bliss Reminiscences, 1:191, 231; Adams, "Personal Letters of Robert E. Lee," 721–22.

2. Wooster, *Secession Conventions of the South*, 121–35; Murphy to Pease, Feb. 25, Mar. 1, 1861, E. M. Pease Papers, Austin History Center.

3. Brown, "Old Woman," 57–61; Heidler, "'Embarrassing Situation,'" 157–72;

AAG to Waite, Feb. 4, 15, 1861, roll 5, LS, HQA (microfilm M 857); Wilhelm, *History of the Eighth U.S. Infantry*, 2:63.

4. Billings, *Report on Barracks and Hospitals*, 228; Brown, "Old Woman," 60; Lee to Sister, Apr. 20, 1861, in Adams, "Lee Letters," 754–55; Edward to Father, Feb. 25, Mar.11, 1861, Hartz Collection; Peters to Sister, Mar. 13, 1861, Peters Papers.

5. Wilhelm, *History of the Eighth U.S. Infantry*, 2:25–29; Thompson, "The Officers, Fort Davis, Texas," in Officers File, FODA; Heitman, *Historical Register*, passim.

6. Bell, "Ante Bellum," 81–82; Bliss Reminiscences, 2:238–39, 3:1–3; Utley, *Fort Davis*, 56; *San Antonio Daily Ledger and Texan*, May 10, 1861; Ruhlen, "Quitman," 110–11; Crimmins, "Border Command at Fort Davis," 9, 11; General Orders 44, Mar. 8, 1861, roll 92, Returns from Regular Army Infantry Regiments (microfilm M 665); Thomas to Waite, Feb. 15, 1861; Blake to McFenin, Mar., 1861; both in FODA (microfilm 906/8820); Peters to Sister, Mar. 13, Peters Papers; Thompson, *Marfa and Presidio County*, 1:96; Murphy to Pease, Mar. 1, 1861, Pease Papers; *OR*, 1:502, 533, 593. For the Hernandez family, see Manuscript Returns, U.S. Census, 1860, 1870, Presidio County.

7. Wilhelm, *History of the Eighth U.S. Infantry*, 2:60, 87–90, 97–105, 272, 295, 300, 303, 329; Bliss Reminiscences, 3:8–20, 40–42, 102; Brown, "Old Woman," 60; Peters to Sister, Aug. 13, 1861, Peters Papers; Davis to Bomford, Bliss, et al., Nov. 26, 1861, vol. 135, LS, DT, RG 109, NARA; 66742 AGO 1897, Dec. 7, 1897, in 965 A.C.P. 1874, ACP Branch, RG 94, NARA.

8. Wilhelm, *History of the Eighth U.S. Infantry*, 2:97–105, 125–29; Bliss Reminiscences, 3:43; DeWitt C. Thomas Reminiscences, June 12, 1878, CAH; *Army and Navy Journal* 28 (Sept. 6, 1890), 22; Hebert to Sibley, July 31, 1862, vol. 134, LS, DT, RG 109, NARA.

9. Hall, *Confederate Army of New Mexico*, 19, 377–80; Frazier, *Blood and Treasure*, 13–15, 36–37; Thompson, *From Desert to Bayou*, 14, 16–17. "The Indians in the vicinity of Fort Davis are as thick as blackbirds," wrote the Unionist editor of the San Antonio *Tri-Weekly Alamo Express* on May 3, 1861.

10. Thompson, *From Desert to Bayou*, 2–9, 17–19.

11. Hall, *Sibley's New Mexico Campaign*, 25–28; Williams, *Texas' Last Frontier*, 15–18; McCulloch to Adams, Feb. 21, 1861; ——— to Mechling, Apr. 16, 1861, fragment; both in William C. Adams Papers, FODA; Hebert to Secretary of War, Sept. 27, 1861, vol. 129, LS, DT, RG 109, NARA; Special Orders No. 40, June 18, 1861; Regimental Orders No. 12, July 13, 1861; both in James B. Berry Papers, CAH; Invoice, July 3, 1861, Adams Papers.

12. Baylor to Adams, July 12, 1861, Adams Papers; Draper to Lane, Aug. 8, Oct. 4, 1861, John H. Draper File, FODA; Townsend, "The Mays Massacre," 29–31, 38–43; Baylor, *Into the Far, Wild Country*, 193, 210–19; Utley, *Fort Davis*, 17–18; Williams, *Texas' Last Frontier*, 24–25; *OR*, 4:25–26; 15:916; Frazier, *Blood and Treasure*, 64–65; Petition of Ella P. Murphy, Dec. 6, 1873,

Claim 588, *Ella P. Ellis vs. U.S. & Mescalero Apache*, Indian Depredations Claims, RG 123, NARA; *San Antonio Herald*, Sept. 7, 1861; Williams to Hassmer, Apr. 27, 1984, John Woodland, Civilian File, FODA.

13.   Baylor to Adams, Aug. 18, 25, 1861, Adams Papers; Williams, *Texas' Last Frontier*, 29–30; Post Returns, Sept. 1861, Adams Papers; *OR* (ser. 2), 2:24–25, 1526–29; "Richard C. Daly's Account to Harry Warren on Jan. 15, 1907, at Presidio, Texas," Fort Davis, Town and Vicinity File, FODA.

14.   "Return of Soldiers in C Co. 2nd Regt. T.M.R. who have died since 8th June 1861," Mar. 1, 1862; Adams to Gibbons, Oct. 15, 1861; Baylor to Adams, Nov. 15, 1861; James to Adams, Sept. 17, 1861; Moke and Bro. to Adams, Sept. 28, 1861; Special Orders No. 216, Dec. 4, 1861; all in Adams Papers; Draper to Lane, Oct. 4, 1861, Draper File; QM to AAG Nichols, Apr. 8, 1861, LR, DT, 1860–61, RG 109, NARA; Williams, *Texas' Last Frontier*, 33–34.

15.   Special Orders No. 87, Sept. 16, 1861; Walker to Adams, Oct. 26, 1861; both in Adams Papers; Draper to Lane, Oct. 4, Nov. 6, 1861, Draper File; Post Returns, Oct. 1861, Adams Papers; Special Orders No. 108, Oct. 7, 1861; Walker to Adams, Oct. 26, 1861; both in Adams Papers; Heartsill, *Fourteen Hundred and 91 Days*, 47.

16.   Noel, *Campaign from Santa Fe to the Mississippi*, 19; Haas, "Diary of Julius Giesecke," 231–32; Howell, "Journal of a Soldier of the Confederate States Army," Dec. 13–14, 1861, CAH; Hall, *Sibley's New Mexico Campaign*, 29–49.

17.   Hall, *Sibley's New Mexico Campaign*, 37–38; Heartsill, *Fourteen Hundred and 91 Days*, 44–50; Abstract of Ordnance Expended by Co. C, 2nd Regt. T. M. Rifles, quarter ending Dec. 31, 1861; List of provisions purchased by Ellis, Dec. 1861; List of provisions purchased by Ingram; Adams to Moke and Brothers, May 6, 1862; Statement of Patrick Murphy, May 18, 1862; Post Returns, Dec. 1861–May 1862; all in Adams Papers; Williams, *Texas' Last Frontier*, 34–35; "Daly's Account," Fort Davis, Town and Vicinity File, FODA.

18.   Hall, *Confederate Army of New Mexico*, 23–36; Hall, *Sibley's New Mexico Campaign*, 59–160, 222–24; Hebert to DeBray, May 19, 1862, vol. 134, LS, DT, RG 109, NARA; *OR*, 50, pt. 1, 940–42.

19.   *OR*, 9:567, 592, 714, 721–22; Noel, *Campaign from Santa Fe*, 51–52; Alberts, *Rebels on the Rio Grande*, 118; Hall, *Sibley's New Mexico Campaign*, 210; Sibley to Cooper, May 4, 1862, in Wilson and Thompson, *Civil War in West Texas & New Mexico*, 141.

20.   Noel, *Campaign from Santa Fe*, 53; *OR*, 9:578, 696; "Instructions for Col. DeBray," May 9, 1862, vol. 134, LS, DT, RG 109, NARA; Navarro to Navarro, May 11, 1862, Confederate Interlude File, FODA; Heartsill, *Fourteen Hundred and 91 Days*, 44; Williams, *Texas' Last Frontier*, 47–48; Frazier, *Blood and Treasure*, 290.

21.   *OR*, 9:567, 577–79, 696.

22.   Ibid., 9:566–67, 574–77, 15:579, 598–602, 708.

23. Ibid., 15:675–87; vol. 34, pt. 1, 880; Mills, *Forty Years at El Paso*, 83–84.
24. *OR*, 15:858, 894–95, 1034, 1065. Another "Fort Davis" was established dur- ing the Civil War. One of the many Civil War blockhouses constructed by Texas citizens, the position lay along the Clear Fork of the Brazos River, fif- teen miles below Camp Cooper. For a description of life at the fort, see Samuel P. Newcomb Diary, CAH.
25. Utley, *Frontier Regulars*, 12–13, 16; Dobak and Phillips, *Black Regulars*, xi–xvi, 15; Sheridan to Grant, Apr. 5, 1867, series 5, roll 24, Ulysses S. Grant Papers, LC; Richter, *Army in Texas during Reconstruction*, 12–20, 66–70; Report of Reynolds, Nov. 4, SW, AR, 1868, 705; Sheridan to Grant, Oct. 3, 1866, S.E.D. 19, 45th Cong., 2d sess., serial 1780, 7.
    Originally, there were four black infantry regiments. In 1869, however, Congress reduced the forty-five infantry regiments to twenty-five; as part of this reduction, the Thirty-eighth and Forty-first Regiments were consoli- dated to form the new Twenty-fourth Regiment, and the Thirty-ninth and Fortieth Regiments combined to create the Twenty-fifth.
26. Williams, *Texas' Last Frontier*, 61–63; Winfrey and Day, *Texas Indian Papers*, 91–92, 138–39; McChristian, "Military Protection for the U.S. Mail: A Fort Davis Case Study," May 20, 1983, FODA; Immecke et al. to Hamilton, Feb. 1, 1866, Governors Records, Archives Division, TSL; Throckmorton to Roberts and Epperson, Dec. 23, 1866, James W. Throckmorton Papers, CAH; Thomp- son, *From Desert to Bayou*, 105–106n34.
27. Sheridan to Grant, Oct. 12, 1866, ser. 5, vol. 54, Grant Papers; Richter, *Army in Texas*, 67–70; Throckmorton to Sheridan, Dec. 11, 1866, Throckmorton Papers; Sheridan to Throckmorton, Jan. 18, 1867; Everett to Rapperty, Jan. 3, 1867; both in Transcript of Records, 1838–69, Texas Adjutant General's Of- fice Papers, CAH; Alberts, *Brandy Station to Manila Bay*, 180–85; E. Carpen- ter to Grant, May 19, 1866, Louis H. Carpenter Papers, Historical Society of Pennsylvania Collection; Sheridan to Rawlins, Mar. 30, 1867, roll 11, Edwin Stanton Papers, LC; Charles Kenner, *Buffalo Soldiers and Officers*, 11, 13, 41– 43, 316n9.
    Sections of the Twenty-fourth Infantry helped garrison the post from 1869 through 1872 and again in 1880. The Twenty-fifth was stationed there from 1870 to 1880. Among the cavalry, the Ninth was present between 1867 and 1875; elements of the Tenth remained at Fort Davis from 1875 to 1885.
28. Kenner, *Buffalo Soldiers and Officers*, 73–82; Hunter to AG, Nov. 26, 1866, 4143 A.C.P. 1873, ACP Branch; Griffin to Hartsuff, Apr. 19, 1867, 4:280; Taylor to Hatch, July 5, 1867, 373; both in roll 1, LS, DT, 1865–70 (microfilm M 1165); "List of Indian Engagements participated in, actively by Colonel E.M. Heyl . . . ," 4143 A.C.P. 1873, ACP Branch; Heitman, *Historical Register*, 2:527. Despite this criticism, Heyl was promoted to captain effective July 31, 1867, and transferred to the Fourth Cavalry Regiment three years later. In

that post, he participated in nine Indian fights and won three official citations for gallantry. Ironically, he later came to Fort Davis as a visiting inspector.

29. Alberts, *Brandy Station to Manila Bay*, 179; Merritt to Moore, July 1, 1867, FODA (microfilm 66-783); Greene, *Historic Resource Study*, 34; SW, AR, 1868, 764–65; Commanding Officer to Carleton, Jan. 28, 1871, FODA (photocopies of LS); Frazer, *Forts of the West*, 144, 147, 152, 158, 162; Williams, *Texas' Last Frontier*, 82.

CHAPTER SIX

1. U.S. Manuscript Census, 1870, 1880, Presidio County, Texas.

2. Dobak and Phillips, *Black Regulars*, 70, 75; Ord to Sherman, Nov. 1, 1875, roll 21, William T. Sherman Papers, LC; McConnell, *Five Years a Cavalryman*, 212–13.

3. Post Medical Returns, Nov. 1872, Fort Davis, CAH, 289; Andrews to AAG, Nov. 21; Andrews to AAG, Nov. 21; both in roll 1, FODA (microfilm 66-783); Report of Holt, Dec. 18, 1872, roll 9, FODA (microfilm 66-783).

4. Augur to Sheridan, Aug. 5, 1873, 3250 AGO 1873, roll 121, LR, AGO, 1871–80 (microfilm M 666).

5. Crane, *Experiences of a Colonel of Infantry*, 59; Custer, *Tenting on the Plains*, 3:677–78; Robert Smither to Editor, *Indianapolis News*, Aug. 31, 1880, box 10, GPNew.

6. Kinevan, *Frontier Cavalryman*, 132–33; Thybony, *Fort Davis*, 8; Thompson, "Negro Soldiers on the Frontier," 226, 232; Knapp to Mead, Jan. 12, 1867, O. M. Knapp Papers, CAH; Mullins to AG, Jan. 1, 1877, 5035 A.C.P. 1874, ACP Branch.

7. Richter, *Army in Texas during Reconstruction*, 117; Carierc to Murphy, Feb. 5, 1869, roll 2, LS, DT, 1865–70, 7:189; Merritt to Carierc, Mar. 1, 1869, D 74; Merritt to Morse, May 8, 1869, D142; both in roll 17, LR, DT, 1865–70 (microfilm M 1193); Statement of Judges of Election, Nov. 5–8, 1872, box 2-12/571, Election Returns, Presidio County, Secretary of State, TSL, Archives Division; Gammel, *Laws of Texas*, 6:206–207; Newcomb to Newcomb, June 7, 1871, James P. Newcomb Papers, CAH.

8. Newcomb to Newcomb, Nov. 12, 1872, Newcomb Papers; Gammel, *Laws of Texas*, 6:988–89.

9. Utley, *Lone Star Justice*, 140–49, 209–12; Williams, *Texas' Last Frontier*, 251–60; Thrapp, *Encyclopedia of Frontier Biography*, 1:473; Madison, *Big Bend Country of Texas*, 42; "To His Excellency O. M. Roberts"; Dean to Roberts, May 21, 1880; Frazer to Roberts, May 24, June 3, 1880; Caruthers to Jones, June 17, 1880; Nevill to Jones, Aug. 8, 26, Sept. 5, 17, 28, Oct. 23, Nov. 17, 1880; Nevill to King, May 30, 1882; all in Texas Adjutant General's Office Papers.

10. Manuscript Returns, U.S. Census, 1870, Presidio County; Wright, "Resi-

dential Segregation," 301; El Paso County Tax Rolls, 1871, TSL; Presidio County Tax Rolls, 1879, TSL; Register of Contracts, Entry 1242, Fort Davis, 1876, RG 92, NARA, 232, 253, 262; Coffman, *Old Army*, 346–47; Greene, *Historic Resource Study*, 39. Enlisted men received a base pay of $13 per month, with additional bonuses for longevity and extra-duty work. Noncommissioned personnel made between 25 and 50 percent more. As a rough estimate, I have used an average of $15 per month per enlisted man. Officers received pay ranging from $125 per month for a second lieutenant of infantry to $291 for a colonel. I have used $190 per month as an average.

11. Finkham to Miller, Nov. 4, 1871; Finkham to Shafter, Nov. 4; both in roll 1, FODA (microfilm 65-855); Miller to Shafter, Nov. 6, 1871, roll 8; Shafter to Miller, Nov. 6, 1871, roll 1; Shafter to Wood, Jan. 4, 1871 [1872], roll 1; all in FODA (microfilm 66-783).

12. Extract of Strong, n.d., SW, AR, 1868, 865; Merritt to Potter, Sept. 2, 1868, FODA (photocopies of LS); Report of J. G. Lee, June 30, SW, AR, 1868, 866, 871; Special Orders No. 4, Jan. 15, 1868, FODA (microfilm 65-855/10427); Greene, *Historic Resource Study*, 93–94.

13. Merritt to Potter, Sept. 2, 1868; Patterson to General, Dec. 19, 1868; both in roll 1, FODA (microfilm 66-783); Letter to Potter, roll 2, RLR, DT, 1865–70, 4:329 (microfilm M 1193); Greene, *Historic Resource Survey*, 95–96; Post Medical Returns, Fort Davis, CAH, 105, 113, 117; Wulff to Hatch, Nov. 6, 1869, roll 6, FODA (microfilm 66-783).

14. Report of Reynolds, Sept. 30, SW, AR, 1870, 41; Report of Sherman, Nov. 20, SW, AR, 1869, 31; Humfreville to Loud, May 1, 1870, roll 1, FODA (microfilm 65-855/10427); Greene, *Historic Resource Study*, 96–97, 115–16, 132–34; Post Medical Returns, Fort Davis, CAH, 9.

15. Post Medical Returns, Fort Davis, CAH, 9–13, 177, 197; Billings, *Report on Barracks and Hospitals*, 229; Greene, *Historic Resource Study*, 141, 145, 222–25.

16. Greene, *Historic Resource Study*, 165–71, 181–92, 200–212, 225, 240–41; Billings, *Report on Barracks and Hospitals*, 229; Weisel to Geddes, Oct. 28, 1870, Post Medical Returns, Fort Davis, CAH, 190.

17. Greene, *Historic Resource Study*, 225–29; Post Medical Returns, Fort Davis, CAH, 105, 127, 129, 135; DeGraw to QM, Mar. 14, 1874, Post Medical Returns, Fort Davis, CAH; "Annual Estimate Hospital Fort Davis, Texas," FODA (microfilm 906-8820); Billings, *Report on the Hygiene*, 199.

18. Report of Lawson, Nov. 10, SW, AR, 1855, 179; Myer, undated letter (1855?), Albert J. Myer Papers, LC (microfilm copy, FODA); Foard to Dye, Nov. 15, 1855, B 581, roll 534, LR, AGO, 1822–60; General Orders No. 22, Dec. 30, 1869, roll 6, FODA (microfilm 66-783); Clary, "Role of the Army Surgeon," 54–55.

19. Clary, "Role of the Army Surgeon," 53–55, 62–64; Conway, "Shriver's Inspection-General Report," 559–83; Weisel to Markley, Feb. 18, 1869, Post Medical Returns, Fort Davis, CAH, 109–10, 121, 133, 137, 151, 246; Weisel

to Post Adjutant, Aug. 5, 1869, roll 6, FODA (microfilm 66-783); Greene, *Historic Resource Study*, 225; Billings, *Report on Barracks and Hospitals*, 228–30; Ashburn, *History of the Medical Department*, 113; Boggs, "History of Fort Concho," 79; "Register of the Sick and Wounded at Post Hospital, Fort Davis, Texas," roll 1, FODA (microfilm 85).

20.   Hood to Post Adjutant, Mar. 1, 1871, roll 1, FODA (microfilm 65-855); Post Medical Returns, Fort Davis, CAH, 14; Andrews to AG, Nov. 3, 1872, box 15, Monthly Inspection Reports, Fort Davis, Texas, Records, RG 393, NARA; Clary, "Role of the Army Surgeon," 62, 65–66.

21.   Smith, *U.S. Army and the Texas Frontier Economy*, 21–22, 40–45; Proceedings of a Board of Survey Convened at Fort Davis on May 20, 1872, and Nov. 22, 1872, H. B. Quimby Papers, CAH; Andrews to AAG, Jan. 4, 1875, roll 1, FODA (microfilm 66-783).

22.   Quartermaster to Ekin, May 27, 1871, FODA (microfilm 906/8820); Shafter to Wood, July 24, 1871, roll 1, FODA (microfilm 66-783).

23.   Billings, *Report on Barracks and Hospitals*, 228–30; Williams, "Post and Hospital Gardens," 1–3; Greene, *Historic Resource Study*, 301–302; Inspection Reports of Bliss, May 31, July 31, 1873, roll 6, FODA (microfilm 66-783).

24.   Delo, *Peddlers and Post Traders*, 142–49; Post Medical Returns, Fort Davis, CAH, 15; Belknap to Commanding Officer, Nov. 9, 1874; Belknap to S. Chaney, Nov. 9, 1874; both in roll 69, LS, SW (microfilm M 6); Post Adjutant to S. Chaney, Dec. 23, 1874; Post Adjutant to A. W. Chaney, Nov. 27, 30, Dec. 1, 1874, Jan. 7, 1875; Andrews to Belknap, Mar. 19, June 8, 1875; all in roll 1, FODA (microfilm 66-783); Davis to Inspector General, July 27, 1875, 4914 A.C.P. 1875, box 340, ACP Branch; Andrews to AAG, June 2, 1877, roll 1; Orders No. 104, July 1, 1877, roll 4; both in FODA (microfilm 66-783); Applicants for Post Trader, vol. 2, Registers of Post Traders, RG 94, NARA; Applicants for Post Trader, Registers of Post Traders, 3:7, RG 94, NARA; Andrews to AG, Mar. 20, 1876, roll 1, FODA (microfilm 66-783); Circular, May 27, 1876, in 2496 A.C.P. 1876, box 376, ACP Branch; Post Adjutant to Davis, Oct. 4, 1876, roll 1, FODA (microfilm 66-783); Deed Records, Sept. 14, 1877, 1:15–16, Jeff Davis County Courthouse, Fort Davis; Greene, *Historic Resource Study*, 216; Wilhelmi to Post Trader, July 30, 1881, roll 1, FODA (microfilm 65-855); James Ivey, sketch of post sutler's complex, Land Acquisitions File, FODA.

25.   Coffman, *Old Army*, 358; Kramer to W. J. Palmer, Apr. 9, 1867, in Storey, "Army Officer in Texas," 250; Grierson to Alice, Aug. 31, 1879, roll 1, GP-New; Circular Letter, Jan. 17, 1873, Quimby Papers; Andrews to AAG, Oct. 4, 1875, roll 1, FODA (microfilm 66-783); Mullins to AG, Mar. 5, 1877, 5035 A.C.P. 1874, ACP Branch; Crane, *Experiences of a Colonel of Infantry*, 68–69; Buchanan, "Functions of the Fort Davis Military Bands."

26.   *Army and Navy Journal*, Mar. 22, July 19, 1884, July 12, 1890; Order of Nov. 26, 1873, Post Medical Returns, Fort Davis, CAH; Mullins to AG, Sept. 1, 1878,

5035 A.C.P. 1874, ACP Branch; Finley Diary, Feb. 3, 1884, Officers File, FODA; Leckie and Leckie, *Unlikely Warriors*, 283; Bluthardt, "Baseball on the Military Frontier," 20–21; Thompson, "Negro Soldiers," 219; John V. Lauderdale Letterbooks, Nov. 23, 1888, FODA.

27. Greene, *Historic Resource Study*, 156, 159; Post Adjutant to Post Council, Nov. 3, 1872, roll 1, FODA (microfilm 66-783); Report of McCrary, Nov. 19, SW, AR, 1877, vii–viii; "Bi-monthly Report of Schools at Fort Davis Dec. 31, 1881," roll 6, FODA (microfilm 66-783).

28. Risch, *Quartermaster Support*, 489–90; Stover, *Up from Handymen*, 49–50; Budd, *Serving Two Masters*, 67; General Orders No. 36, June 5, 1875; General Orders No. 5, Jan. 18, 1876; both in roll 4, FODA (microfilm 66-783); Mullins to AG, May 2, 1876, FODA (microfilm 905/8821); Mullins to AG, Mar. 21, 1877; Mullins to Davis, Apr. 7, 1877; both in 5035 A.C.P. 1874, ACP Branch; Orders No. 76, May 24, 1879; Orders No. 43, Mar. 21, 1879; both in roll 4, FODA (microfilm 66-783); Yard to Quartermaster, July 4, 1880, roll 1, FODA (microfilm 65-855); Report of McCook, Nov. 5, SW, AR, 1880, 296; "Report of Schools in Operation at Fort Davis, Texas," Fort Davis, Texas, Records, RG 393, NARA.

29. Bi-monthly Inspection Report, Aug. 31, 1876, roll 6, FODA (microfilm 66-783); Orders No. 102, June 29, 1877; Orders No. 37, Mar. 25, 1878; Orders No. 43, Mar. 21, 1879; Orders No. 76, May 24, 1879; Orders No. 92, June 30, 1878; Circular, Sept. 29, 1878; Orders No. 173, Dec. 1, 1878; all in roll 4, FODA (microfilm 66-783); Mullins to Post Adjutant, Dec. 7, 1878, roll 1, FODA (microfilm 65-855); Vincent to Commanding Officer, Dec. 21, 1878, roll 8, FODA (microfilm 66-783); Greene, *Historic Resource Study*, 157–58; "Report of Schools in Operation at Fort Davis, Texas," Fort Davis, Texas, Records, RG 393, NARA; Mullins to AG, Nov. 1, Dec. 1, 1875, Aug. 31, 1876, Mar. 21, 1877, Sept. 1, 1878, Feb. 1, 1879, 5035 A.C.P. 1874, ACP Branch; Mullins to Davis, Apr. 7, 1877, 5035 A.C.P. 1874, ACP Branch.

30. Manuscript Returns, U.S. Census, 1870, 1880, Presidio County; Bill dated May 1, 1885; Merrill and Sister to Clendenin, Oct. 5, 1886; both in roll 9, FODA (microfilm 66-783); Greene, *Historic Resource Study*, 245–46; Annual Inspection of Public Buildings, Mar. 31, 1883, Mar. 31, 1884, Mar. 31, 1885, FODA (microfilm 63-172).

31. Billings, *Report on the Hygiene*, 200; Andrews to Banning, Feb. 25, 1876, H.R. 354, 44th Cong., 1st sess., serial 1709, 64; Wood, "Army Laundresses," 26–34.

32. Sheire, *Fort Davis National Historic Site*, 12–21; Manuscript Returns, U.S. Census, 1870, 1880, Presidio County; Post Medical Returns, Aug., 1879, April 11, 1881, Dec. 9, 1881, Jan. 31, 1883, Fort Davis, CAH; J. T. Morrison to Post Adjutant, Jan. 31, 1884, roll 8, FODA (microfilm 66-783); General Orders 103, June 29, 1877, roll 4, FODA (microfilm 66-783); Cooper to AAG, July 30, 1873, roll 9, FODA (microfilm 66-783); Greene, *Historic Re-*

source Study, 247; Registers of Enlistments, roll 40, 76:135; roll 43, 82:106 (microfilm M 233). Fifteen married personnel can be identified on the 1870 and 1880 censuses.

33. Smither to Grierson, June 3, 1883, roll 2, GPSpr; Peelle to Shafter, Sept. 12, 1881; Shafter to Peelle, Sept. 21, 1881; both in roll 8, FODA (microfilm 66-783); *Galveston Weekly News*, Feb. 16, 1882; Registers of Enlistments, roll 41, 79:24 (microfilm M 233); *San Antonio Daily Express*, Feb. 12, 25, Apr. 5, 9, 1882.

34. McChristian, *Garrison Tangles*, 28; Alice to Grierson, Oct. 4, 1883, GPLu; Manuscript Returns, U.S. Census, 1870, 1880, Presidio County; *Army and Navy Journal*, Sept. 17, 1887, July 6, 1889, Aug. 2, 1890, Feb. 7, 1891; Mattie Belle Anderson Reminiscences, CAH; Lauderdale Letterbooks, June 9, 18, 19, Sept. 12, Oct. 26, 27, Nov. 29, Dec. 14, 1888, Apr. 15, 16, 1889, FODA; Robert to Mother, July 6, 1888, roll 2, GPSpr; Memo of J. A. Bennett, Mar. 11, 1891, FODA (microfilm 85-2).

35. Leighton Finley Diary, vol. 4, Officers File, FODA; Williams to Wooster, Feb. 23, 1989, FODA; Thompson, *Marfa and Presidio County*, 1:79, 108; "Diary of Mrs. Alex. R. Shepherd Containing Remembrances of First Trip into Mexico in 1880," FODA; Deposition of Feb. 28, 1899, claim 3889, *Daniel Murphy vs. U.S. & Apache Indians*, Indian Depredations Files; *Army and Navy Journal*, Jan. 2, 1886.

36. Lauderdale Letterbooks, Sept. 26, 1888, Feb. 17, 1890, FODA; Nolan to Grierson, Dec. 14, 1880, roll 1, GPSpr; Post Medical Returns, Feb. 14, 1881, Fort Davis, CAH; Sis to Mother, July 16, 1890; Thompson to Gram and Mother [October], Nov. 3, 1890; both in Thompson Files, FODA.

37. Case of Andrew Geddes, QQ 1387, box 1927, Court-Martial Files, NARA; Heitman, *Historical Register*, 1:451, 760; Kinevan, *Frontier Cavalryman*, 168–70. Stallard, *Glittering Misery*, 117–21, changes Orleman's name to "Orleans." Geddes was eventually dismissed from the army on another charge in December 1880; Orleman, his health broken, had retired thirteen months earlier.

38. For various studies of the case, see especially McClung, "Second Lieutenant Henry O. Flipper," 20–31; Crane, *Experiences of a Colonel of Infantry*, 55; Harris, *Negro Frontiersman*, 2–3, 15–16, 19–21; Johnson, *Flipper's Dismissal*, 8–11, 16–17, 82; Carlson, *"Pecos Bill,"* 122–27; and Robinson, *Court-Martial of Lt. Henry Flipper*.

39. Johnson, *Flipper's Dismissal*, 18–19, 32–36, 40, 44, 69–73; Dinges, "Court-Martial of Lt. Henry O. Flipper," 59.

40. Johnson, *Flipper's Dismissal*, 40, 44; Harris, *Memoirs of Flipper*, 40–41; Dinges, "Court-Martial of Lt. Henry O. Flipper," 59–60; Carlson, *"Pecos Bill,"* 122–27; "To whom it concerns," Nov. 1, 1880, roll 1, GPNew. In 1976, a review board posthumously awarded Flipper an honorable discharge. Paul H. Carlson, Shafter's biographer, concludes that the colonel was indeed a racist but had not initiated a conspiracy to frame Flipper.

CHAPTER SEVEN

1. Utley, *Frontier Regulars*, 15–16, 61–69; Sherman to Schofield, July 27, 1870, box 8, John M. Schofield Papers, LC; Sherman to Ord, Oct. 28, 1870, William T. Sherman Letters, Missouri Historical Society; Sherman to Augur, Mar. 18, 1871, roll 45, Sherman Papers; Sargent to Schofield, Feb. 6, 1874, box 8, Schofield Papers.

2. Lessoff, *Nation and Its City*, 164–98. The notion of a "multipurpose" army is best explored in Tate, *Frontier Army*.

3. Chappell, *Search for the Well-Dressed Soldier*, 1–20, 32–37; McConnell, *Five Years a Cavalryman*, 230–31; Report of Meigs, Oct. 11, SW, AR, 1870, 148–49; General Orders No. 45, July 1, 1875, roll 4; Bliss to AAG, Aug. 28, 1876, roll 1; both in FODA (microfilm 66-783); Report of Holabird, Oct. 9, SW, AR, 1884, 323; Report of Holabird, Oct. 5, SW, AR, 1888, 307; Report of J. F. Rodgers, Aug. 28, SW, AR, 1890, 774.

4. Report of Meigs, Oct. 11, SW, AR, 1870, 148–49; Utley, *Frontier Regulars*, 69–73; Endorsement of July 14, 1871, roll 8, FODA (microfilm 66-783); Summary of Ordnance . . . ending March 1872, FODA (microfilm 816-8091); Sherman to Belknap, July 12, 1870, roll 39, LS, AGO (microfilm M 565); Jamieson, *Crossing the Deadly Ground*, 45–47.

5. Wooster, *Soldiers, Sutlers, and Settlers*, 48; Special Orders No. 130, Sept. 2, 1875; Andrews to Carpenter, Oct. 8, 1875; Woodward to Carpenter, Mar. 4, 1869; all in Carpenter Papers; Andrews to AG, Nov. 17, 1875, roll 1, FODA (microfilm 66-783); Crane, *Experiences of a Colonel of Infantry*, 105, 111–13; Raht, *Romance of Davis Mountains*, 218; Report of Ord, Oct. 1, SW, AR, 1880, 111; Woodward to Benjamin Grierson, Dec. 29, 1879, roll 2, GPNew.

6. Billings, *Report on Barracks and Hospitals*, 230; Ellis, "Greely's Report," 69, 85–86; Sutton, "Glimpses of Fort Concho," 122–34.

7. Schick, "Wagons to Chihuahua," 72–75. Santleben, *Texas Pioneer*, 167–68, 202–203; Taylor and McDonald, *The Coming Empire*, 357–64.

8. Shafter to McDonald, Dec. 8, 1870; Shafter to Wood, Jan. 4, 1871; both in roll 1, FODA (microfilm 66-783); Wooster, "Army and the Politics of Expansion," 151–67; Belknap to Secretary of State, Feb. 3, 1871, roll 61; Feb. 23, 1872, roll 63; both in LS, SW (microfilm M 6); Brown to Shafter, Nov. 20, 1871, roll 8; Shafter to Merritt, Feb. 17, 1872, roll 1; both in FODA (microfilm 66-783); Augur to Shafter, Feb. 2, 1872, roll 1, William Shafter Papers, Manuscripts Division, Stanford University Library; Brown to Commanding Officer, June 27, 1872, roll 1, FODA (microfilm 65-855); Shafter to AAG, July 23, 1872, roll 1, FODA (microfilm 66-783); Patterson to Post Adjutant, July 27, 1872, roll 1, FODA (microfilm 65-855).

9. Williams to Smith, July 14, 1875, W 1142; Crosby to Secretary of Interior, Sept. 11, 1875, W 1435; both in roll 374, Letters Received by the Office of Indian Affairs, 1824–80: Kickapoo Agency, 1872–76, RG 75 (microfilm M

234), NARA; Cowen to Secretary of Treasury, Sept. 9, 1875; Cowen to SW, Sept. 9, 1875; both in roll 17, Indian Division Letters Sent, 1849–1903, RG 48 (microfilm M 606), NARA; Bristow to Delano, Sept. 23, 1875, BA-1:395–96, Letters Sent to the Interior Department, RG 56, NARA; Endorsement of Andrews, Oct. 27, 1875, FODA (photocopies of LS); Andrews to Caldwell, Sept. 19, 1875; Andrews to AG, Nov. 17, 1875; both in roll 1, FODA (microfilm 66-783); Belknap to Secretary of Interior, Jan. 22, 1876, roll 72, LS, SW (microfilm M 6).

10. Bliss to Shafter, Nov. 24, 1876; Andrews to Commanding Officer, Dec. 10, 11, 1876; both in roll 1, FODA (microfilm 66-783); Nankivell, *History of the Twenty-fifth Regiment*, 27.

11. Nankivell, *History of the Twenty-fifth Regiment*, 27, 28; Andrews to AAG, Dec. 29, 1876, Feb. 14, 1878, roll 1; Sheridan to Ord, Jan. 25, 1877, roll 8; Kelley to Andrews, Feb. 11, 1877, roll 8; all in FODA (microfilm 66-783).

12. McChristian, "Military Protection," 4–6, 10–12, 14; Shafter to Taylor, undated [probably Jan. 4, 1872]; Andrews to AAG, Aug. 25, 1872; Andrews to AAG, July 21, Nov. 21, 1877; all in roll 1, FODA (microfilm 66-783).

13. SW, AR, 1860, 102; SW, AR, 1868, 766; Cusack to Merritt, Sept. 15, 1868; Merritt to Morse, Sept. 15, 1868; Classified Return of wounds and injuries; all in 6663 PRD 1894, box 532, Principal Record Division File, RG 94, NARA; Fort Davis, Sept. 1868, roll 297, Returns from United States Military Posts (microfilm M 617); *San Antonio Daily Herald*, Sept. 22, 29, 1868; Thompson, "Negro Soldiers," 219; Heitman, *Historical Register*, 1:347.

14. Heitman, *Historical Register*, 1:376; Fort Davis, January 1870, roll 297, Returns from United States Military Posts (microfilm M 617); Adjutant General's Office, *Chronological List of Actions, &c., with Indians*, 44.

15. Civilians File, José Maria Bill, FODA; "Tabular Statement of Expeditions and Scouts," box 14, Fort Davis, Texas, Records, RG 393, NARA; Woodward to Grierson, Mar. 11, 1880, roll 1, GPSpr; Orders No. 42, Mar. 26, 1880, roll 4, FODA (microfilm 66-783); Reed to Wilson, Apr. 7, 1880, roll 4, FODA (microfilm 85-3); Orders No. 65, May 9, 1880, roll 4, FODA (microfilm 66-783); Mills to Commanding Officer, May 13, 1880, roll 4, FODA (microfilm 85-3); Commanding Officer to Fort Bliss, Feb. 3, 1882, roll 1, FODA (microfilm 65-855); Dunlay, *Wolves for the Blue Soldiers*, 230n8.

16. See Wooster, *The Military and United States Indian Policy*.

17. Alice to Baldwin, Mar. 31, 1877, box 9, Frank Dwight Baldwin Papers, Huntington Library; Upton to Greene, Oct. 3, 1879, box 2, F. V. Greene Papers, New York Public Library; Hatch to Wood, Aug. 24, 1870; Rucker to Starr, Mar. 7, 1871; both in roll 1, FODA (microfilm 66-783). For less critical assessments of army tactics and policy, see Jamieson, *Crossing the Deadly Ground*, 22–53; and Birtle, *U.S. Army Counterinsurgency*, 55–98.

18. McChristian, "Incidents Involving Hostile Indians," Sept. 9, 1975; Burgess to Merritt, Aug. 5, 1869, roll 6, FODA (microfilm 66-783); Report of Reynolds,

Oct. 21, SW, AR, 1869, 144; French to Carleton, Jan. 28, 1871, roll 1, FODA (microfilm 66-783); Post Medical Returns, June, 1869, Fort Davis, CAH; Report of Commissioners, Dec. 10, 1872, H.E.D. 39, 42d Cong., 3d sess., serial 1565, 2–3.

19.   Carlson, *"Pecos Bill,"* 55–63; Shafter to Wood, June 5, July 18, 1871, Feb. 1, 1872, FODA (photocopies of LS); "Tabular Statement of Expeditions and Scouts against Indians in Fort Davis, Texas," third quarter, 1871, roll 1, FODA (microfilm 66-783).

20.   Shafter to Wood, Feb. 1, 1872, FODA (photocopies of LS); Shafter to Wood, Feb. 5, 1872; Shafter to Augur, Feb. 12, 1872; both in roll 1, FODA (microfilm 66-783); General Orders No. 5, Apr. 3, 1872, "The Regular Army in Texas," Martin L. Crimmins Collection, CAH.

21.   McChristian, "Military Protection"; Shafter to AAG, Mar. 1, 1872, roll 1, FODA (microfilm 66-783); Utley, *Fort Davis*, 56–60; Carlson, *"Pecos Bill,"* 62–63; "Tabular Statement of Expeditions and Scouts against Indians," Fort Davis, Texas, Records, RG 393, NARA.

22.   Murphy to AAG, Oct. 23, 1871; first endorsement, Oct. 25; second endorsement, Nov. 3; all in roll 1, FODA (microfilm 65-855); Andrews to AG, Nov. 17, 1875, roll 1, FODA (microfilm 66-783); *Lizzie Crosson vs. U.S. and the Apache Indians*, Indian Depredation No. 6322, Crosson Ranch Collection, Archives of the Big Bend; McChristian, "Military Protection," 9–10; Andrews to CO, Ft. Quitman, Sept. 5, 1875, FODA (photocopies of LS); Bi-monthly inspection report, Mar. 6, 1876, Mar. 3, 1877, roll 6, FODA (microfilm 66-783); Andrews to Crosson, Dec. 19, 1876, Crosson Ranch Collection; Mullins to AG, Apr. 2, 1877, 5035 A.C.P. 1874, ACP Branch; Sheffly, "Letters and Reminiscences of Gen. Theodore A. Baldwin," 24.

23.   Keesey to Cardis, June 8, 1876, box 2Q 400, Transcripts from the Adjutant General's Office, 1870–76, Texas Adjutant General's Office Papers, CAH; McChristian, "Incidents Involving Hostile Indians"; Tabular Statement of Expeditions and Scouts, Fort Davis; Baldwin to Andrews, Dec. 25, 1877, Report of Persons Killed or Captured by Indians; both in box 14, Part V, Entry 16, RG 393, NARA; Fort Davis, Aug. 1877, roll 297, Returns from U.S. Military Posts (microfilm M 617); "Report of persons killed or capt. by Indians . . . during the 1st quarter, 1878," roll 6, FODA (microfilm 66-783); McCrary to Commanding Officer, Apr. 22, 1878, roll 76, LS, SW (microfilm M 6); Hernandez to Commanding Officer, District of Pecos, Apr. 21, 1878, roll 1; Grierson to Commanding Officer, May 1, 1878, roll 8; Andrews to AG, May 2, 1878, roll 1; endorsement of June 14, 1878; all in FODA (microfilm 66-783).

24.   Lebo to Post Adjutant, Apr. 27, 1878; Russell to Andrews, Mar. 13, 1878; Read to Post Adjutant, July 17; all in roll 1, FODA (microfilm 65-855); Heitman, *Historical Register*, 1:819; Russell to Andrews, July 21, 1878, roll 8; Carpenter to Post Adjutant, July 24, 1878, roll 8; Wilson to Carpenter, July 28, 1878, roll 8; Andrews to Russell, July 25, 1878, roll 1; Andrews to Norvell,

July 28, 1878, roll 1; all in FODA (microfilm 66-783); "Tabular Statement of Expeditions and Scouts against Indians," SW, AR, 1879, 102–106; French to AG, Aug. 20, 1878, FODA (photocopies of LS); Carpenter to Post Adjutant, Oct. 8, 1878, roll 1, FODA (microfilm 65-855); Post Adjutant to Commanding Officer Co. H, June 20, 1878, roll 1, FODA (microfilm 66-783).

25.   "Tabular Statement," SW, AR, 1879, 102–106; Carpenter to AG, Nov. 27, 1878, roll 1; Orders No. 131, Sept. 2, 1878, roll 4; Carpenter to AG, Dec. 1, 1878, roll 1; all in FODA (microfilm 66-783); materials attached in Crisman to Levy, May 9, 1969, Stagecoaching File, Travel and Transportation Section, FODA.

26.   Report of Ord, Oct. 1, SW, AR, 1879, 113; Russell to Carpenter, Dec. 22, 1878, roll 1, FODA (microfilm 65-855).

27.   "Tabular Statement," 1879, 102–106; "Tabular Statement," 1880, 137–39; both in SW, AR; Smith, *Old Army*, 162; Courtney to Post Adjutant, Aug. 3, Oct. 7, 1879, roll 5, Records of the District of the Pecos, RG 393 (microfilm M 1361), NARA.

28.   Depositions of Mar. 1, 1899, claim 2744, *Deiderick Dutchove [sic] vs. U.S. & Apache Tribe of Indians;* Deposition of Aug. 11, 1891, claim 3889, *Daniel Murphy vs. US & Apache Indians;* both in Indian Depredations Files; Thompson, *Marfa and Presidio County*, 1:156–57; Ayres to Crosson, Aug. 28, 1888, box 1, Crosson Ranch Collection. Lizzie Crosson finally won a $2,590 judgment in 1902. See Weed to Crosson, Mar. 8, 1902, box 1, Crosson Ranch Collection.

29.   Read to Post Adjutant, Sept. 25, 1879, roll 5, Records of the District of the Pecos; Utley, *Indian Frontier*, 67; Godfrey to Dudley, Apr. 22, 1878, FODA (microfilm 905/8821); Report of Van Valzah, Aug. 28, SW, AR, 1879, 15–16; Eve Ball, *Indeh*, xiii, 11, 14–15, 41; Utley, *Frontier Regulars*, 368–69.

30.   Briggs to Post Adjutant, Jan. 28, 1880, FODA (microfilm 85-3); Grierson to AAG, Oct. 1, SW, AR, 1880, 154; Leckie and Leckie, *Unlikely Warriors*, 258–59.

31.   Grierson to AAG, Oct. 1, SW, AR, 1880, 154–55.

32.   Ibid., 155–58; Grierson to Alice, Apr. 20, 1880, GPNew.

33.   Williams, *Texas' Last Frontier*, 239–40; Delaport to Commanding Officer, May 16, 1880, FODA (microfilm 85-3); Munson to McLaughlin, May 16, 1880; McLaughlin to AAG, May 17, 1880; Carpenter to AAG, June 13, 1880; Post Adjutant to Baker, June 24, 1880; all in roll 1, FODA (microfilm 65-855); Vincent to Commanding Officer, June 14, 1880, roll 6, FODA (microfilm 66-783); "Tabular Statement," SW, AR, 1880, 136–39; Grierson to AAG, Sept. 20, SW, AR, 1880, 158; Dinges, "Victorio Campaign," 87. Gillett, *Six Years with the Texas Rangers*, 285–86, reports that five or six regulars were also killed at Eagle Springs.

34.   Grierson to AAG, Sept. 20, SW, AR, 1880, 159; Smithers to Nolan, July 7, 1880, Nicholas Nolan Papers, U.S. Army History Research Collection, Carlisle Barracks; McChristian, "Grierson's Fight at Tinaja," 50; Grierson to

Alice, July 20, 1880, roll 1, GPNew; Dinges, "Victorio Campaign," 89; Grierson, "Journal," FODA.

35. McChristian, "Grierson's Fight at Tinaja," 45, 50–54, 59–62; Grierson to AAG, Sept. 20, SW, AR, 1880, 159–61; Grierson to Alice, Aug. 2, 1880, roll 1, GPNew; Grierson, "Journal," FODA.

36. McChristian, "Grierson's Fight at Tinaja," 45, 50–54, 59–62; Grierson to AAG, Sept. 20, SW, AR, 1880, 159–61; Grierson to Alice, Aug. 2, 1880, roll 1, GPNew; Grierson, "Journal," FODA.

37. McChristian, "Grierson's Fight at Tinaja," 45, 50–54, 59–62; Grierson to AAG, Sept. 20, SW, AR, 1880, 159–61; Grierson to Alice, Aug. 2, 1880, roll 1, GPNew; Grierson, "Journal," FODA.

38. Ibid.; Baylor to Jones, Aug. 26, 1880, Papers from Texas Adjutant General's Office; Glass, *History of the Tenth Cavalry*, 22–23; *Roster of Non-commissioned Officers of the Tenth Cavalry*, 28; Tenth Cavalry, Aug. 1880, roll 96, Returns from Regular Army Cavalry Regiments (microfilm M 744); Registers of Enlistments, roll 40, Registers of Enlistments in the United States Army, 1798–1914 (microfilm M 233).

39. Grierson to AAG, Sept. 20, SW, AR, 1880, 161; Grierson, "Journal."

40. Grierson to AAG, Sept. 20, SW, AR, 1880, 161; Grierson, "Journal"; Baylor to Jones, Aug. 26, 1880, Papers from Texas Adjutant General's Office, CAH; McChristian, "Incidents Involving Hostile Indians"; Grierson to AAG, Sept. 20, SW, AR, 1880, 162; Dinges, "Victorio Campaign," 90–91.

41. Peck to Commanding Officer, Aug. 22, 1880, roll 8, FODA (microfilm 66-783); Report of Ord, Oct. 1, SW, AR, 1880, 116–21; materials compiled by Robert Utley, accompanying Crisman to Levy, May 9, 1969, Travel and Transportation File, FODA. For good secondary accounts of the subpost system, see McChristian, "Grierson's Fight at Tinaja," 49, and Temple, "Grierson's Administration of the District of the Pecos," 85–96; Report of Ord, Oct. 1, SW, AR, 1880, 116–21; Guffee, "Camp Peña Colorado," 20–21.

42. Muster Roll, Co. G, Tenth Cavalry, June–Aug. 1880, Tenth Cavalry; Muster Roll, Co. A, Tenth Cavalry, June–Aug. 1880, Tenth Cavalry; both in Units File, FODA; Grierson, "Journal," 7, 14, 17, 20, 25, 27, 30, 1880, FODA; Robert to Mama, July 26, 1880, roll 1, GPNew.

43. Dinges, "Victorio Campaign," 93; Thompson, "Negro Soldiers," 224; Nolan to Grierson, Sept. 12, 1880, Nolan Papers; Nolan to AAG, Sept. 16, 1880, Nolan Papers; McChristian, "Incidents Involving Hostile Indians"; Gillett, *Six Years with the Texas Rangers*, 286–88; Baylor to Jones, Oct. 28, 1880; Nevill to Jones, Oct. 27, Dec. 20, 1880, Feb. 9, 1881; both in Papers from Texas Adjutant General's Office, CAH; Whitall to Post Adjutant, Jan. 21, 1881, FODA (microfilm 85-3).

44. Goldblatt, "Scout to Quitman Canyon," 155–58; Nevill to Jones, Feb. 6, 1881, Papers from Texas Adjutant General's Office; Baylor, *Into the Far, Wild Country*, 304–19.

45. Smith, *Old Army in Texas*, 18–37; Fort Davis, July 1867–Jan. 1871, roll 297, Returns from United States Military Posts (microfilm M 617); "Tabular Statement of Expeditions and Scouts," Fort Davis, Texas, Part V, entry 16, box 14, RG 393, NARA.

46. Smith, *Old Army in Texas*, 18–37; Fort Davis, July 1867–Jan. 1871, roll 297, Returns from United States Military Posts (microfilm M 617); "Tabular Statement of Expeditions and Scouts," Fort Davis, Texas, Part V, entry 16, box 14, RG 393, NARA.

47. Grierson to AAG, Sept. 20, SW, AR, 1880, 163; General Orders No. 1, Feb. 7, 1881, roll 5, Records of the District of the Pecos (microfilm M 1381).

CHAPTER EIGHT

1. Dinges, "Benjamin H. Grierson"; Leckie and Leckie, *Unlikely Warriors*, 269, 294; Williams, "Empire Building," 61.

2. Grierson to Alice, May 31, 1878, roll 1, June 25, 27, 30, July 8, 1882, roll 2, GPSpr; Temple, "Grierson's Administration," 88; Grierson to Alice, May 29, 1878, roll 1, GPNew.

3. Williams, "Empire Building," 59–60, 69; Maxon to Grierson, Aug. 18, 1882, roll 2, GPNew; Vincent to Commanding Officer, Jan. 16, 1883, roll 7, LS, DT, 1870–98 (microfilm M 1114), 20:39.

4. Smith to Commanding Officer, June 10, 18, 1885, 24:341, 406–407; Ruggles to Commanding Officer, June 17, 1885, 24:366; both in roll 8, LS, DT, 1870–98 (microfilm M 1114); HQ, Dept. of Texas, Dec. 15, 1885, roll 9, FODA (microfilm 66-783); Ruggles to Commanding Officer, May 7, 1886, roll 8, LS, DT, 1870–98 (microfilm M 1114), 25:115.

5. Reed, *History of the Texas Railroads*, 197–98, 360–61, 365; Ruhlen, "Fort Hancock," 19–22; Young to Childs, Feb. 12, 1886, S. B. M. Young Papers, U.S. Army Military History Institute, Carlisle Barracks; Sheridan to Augur, Mar. 1, 1874; Augur to Sheridan, Mar. 12; both in H.E.D. 282, 43d Cong., 1st sess., serial 1615, 44; Sheridan to Sherman, Mar. 19, H.E.D. 282, 43d Cong., 1st sess., serial 1615, 45; Endorsement of Augur, Aug. 24, 1881, H.E.D. 20, 47th Cong., 1st sess., serial 2027, 6; Report of Augur, Sept. 27, SW, AR, 1881, 129; Sherman to Augur, Feb. 1, 1882, Christopher Augur Papers, Illinois State Historical Library; Sherman to Lincoln, Mar. 18, 1882, roll 47; Sherman to Sheridan, Oct. 3, 1882; Sherman to Augur, Mar. 26, 1882; all in Sherman Papers, LC; Sherman, "Estimates for Buildings at Military Posts," Oct. 16, SW, AR, 1882, 11; Sherman to Sheridan, Mar. 7, Apr. 2, 1883, roll 9, LS, HQA (microfilm M 857), 26:545, 553; Report of Stanley, Sept. 30, SW, AR, 1884, 125.

6. *Congressional Globe*, Jan. 11, 1873, 506; Report of the Committee on Military Affairs, Jan. 11, 1873, H.R. 26, 42d Cong., 3d sess., serial 1576, 1; Holabird and Morrow to Augur, Dec. 15, 1873, H.E.D. 282, 43d Cong., 1st sess., serial

1615, 42; Report of Holabird, Gentry, and Morrow; Belknap to House, May 20, 1874; both in H.E.D. 282, 43d Cong., 1st sess., serial 1615, 12–13; Report of Belknap, n.d., SW, AR, 1874, viii. The asking price seemed more reasonable when considering that the owner of Fort Quitman originally demanded $100,000.

7. Report of Meigs, n.d., SW, AR, 1880, 329–30; S.R. 40, 46th Cong., 2d sess., serial 1893, 1; Report of Upson, Jan. 14, 1880, H.R. 88, 46th Cong., 2d sess., serial 1934, 1–6; Ord to AG, Nov. 11, 1880, H.E.D. 20, 47th Cong., 1st sess., serial 2027, 11; Lincoln to Speaker of the House, Jan. 20, 1882, H.E.D. 20, 47th Cong., 1st sess., serial 2027, 1; Sherman to Augur, Dec. 9, 1882, Augur Papers; Report of Ingalls, Oct. 9, SW, AR, 1882, 265; Report of J. M. Moore, Sept. 11, SW, AR, 1882, 452; Mills to AG, Nov. 24, 1882; Sherman to Secretary of War, Dec. 29, 1882; both in FODA (microfilm 905-8821); James to Augur, Jan. 24, 1883; Grierson to AG, Jan. 30, Mar. 16, 1883; both in roll 2, FODA (microfilm 65-855).

8. Murphy to Grierson, Feb. 26, 1883; Thompson survey, May 22, 1883; Grierson to AG, Mar. 16, 1883; Brenner to Grierson, Mar. 15, 1883; Keesey to Grierson, Mar. 15, 1883; Shields to Grierson, Mar. 15, 1883; undated memo filed after Shields to Grierson, Mar. 15, 1883; Grierson to AG, Mar. 16, 1883; Sheridan to AG, Apr. 18, 1883; all in roll 2, FODA (microfilm 65-855); Williams, "Empire Building," 62; AG to Sheridan, Apr. 27, 1883, roll 2, FODA (microfilm 905-8821); Warranty Deed, Presidio Co., May 24, 1883, Land Acquisitions File, FODA; Drum, "Case of Proposed Purchase of Additional Land at Fort Davis, Texas," Nov. 6, 1883; Drum to Commanding General, Division of the Missouri, Nov. 19, 1883; both in FODA (microfilm 905-8821); Report of Holabird, Oct. 6, SW, AR, 1883, 409; Vincent to Commanding Officer, Nov. 9, 1883, roll 9, LS, DT, 1870–98 (microfilm M 1114), 21:55; Holabird to AG, June 17, 1884; Endorsement of Sheridan, July 9, 1884; both in Land Acquisitions File, FODA; Statement B, attached to Report of Chandler, Sept. 10, SW, AR, 1886, 443.

9. Greene, *Historic Resource Study*, 118–24, 138–39, 146–47, 172–73; Charles to Mother, Aug. 4, 1882, GPLu; Augur to Sherman, Aug. 16, 1882, roll 6, LS, DT, 1870–98 (microfilm M 1114), 18:535; Alice to Grierson, Oct. 2, 1883, GPLu; Charlie to Grierson, Oct. 7, 1883, GPLu.

10. Greene, *Historic Resource Study*, 106–109, 131, 232–33; Statement A, Report of Construction and Repairs, SW, AR, 1883, 419; Report of Chandler, Appendix A, SW, AR, 1884, 432; Statement A, Report of Construction and Repairs, SW, AR, 1885, 475; Report of Ingalls, Sept. 26, SW, AR, 1882, 18; "Estimate for One Barracks . . . ," 1884, FODA (microfilm 65-855); Williams, "Empire Building," 64.

11. Report of Weisel, Circular No. 4, 229; Weisel to W. Webster, Feb. 28, 1870; Entries for Jan. 1875, and June 30, 1878; DeGraw to D. Wilson, June 30, 1876; all in Post Medical Returns, Fort Davis, CAH; Grierson, "Journal,"

July 19, 1880, FODA; clipping from the El Paso *Times* (probably 1954), in scrapbook, David A. Simmons Papers, CAH; Report of Perry, Sept. 11, SW, AR, 1883, 557; "Office Brief as to Water Supply"; "Plan of the Reservation and Post of Fort Davis, Texas, showing the Water Supply System," traced from Colonel W. H. Owens; both in Fort Davis Water System File, FODA.

12. Dinges, "Colonel Grierson Invests," 6–11; Leckie and Leckie, *Unlikely Warriors*, 280; Memoirs of William George Wedemeyer, Dec. 16, 1884, 2:262 (typescript), FODA; Williams, "Empire Building," 67; Brenner to Grierson, Sept. 28, 1882, roll 2, GPSpr.

13. Post Adj. to Rooney, Jan. 27, 1882; Viele to Post Adjutant, Aug. 2, 1882; both in roll 1, FODA (microfilm 65-855); Vincent to Commanding Officer, Sept. 23, 1882, roll 2, FODA (microfilm 66-783); Table XVIII, SW, AR, 1891, 667; Report of Stanley, Sept. 30, SW, AR, 1884, 124; Guffee, "Camp Peña Colorado," 13–16, 20, 21, 33; Williams, "Empire Building," 63; Grierson to AG, June 25, 1883; Woodward to Commanding Officer, Viejo Pass, Dec. 10, 1883; both in roll 1, FODA (microfilm 65-855); Endorsement of Lee, Feb. 19, 1884, roll 8, FODA (microfilm 66-783).

14. Memorandum of October 18, 1883, GPLu; Proceedings of Stockholders, Fort Davis & Marfa RR Co., Jan. 12, 1885, roll 1, GPNew; Ayers to Grierson, Oct. 29, 1883; Jonathan to Grierson, Nov. 1, 1883; both in GPLu.

15. Proceedings of Stockholders, Fort Davis & Marfa RR Co., Jan. 12, 1885, roll 1, GPNew; Grierson to Pierce, Jan. 29, 1884; Grierson to Charles, Feb. 11, 1885; Ayers to Grierson, Jan. 20, Feb. 3, 24, Mar. 16, 27, Apr. 14, Oct. 17, 1885; all in GPLu.

16. Hale, "Prospecting and Mining," 92–94, 117, 127, 149–51, 154, 171; Taylor and McDanield, *The Coming Empire*, 375; Woodward to Grierson, Dec. 29, 1879, roll 2; Strout to US Commandt, Mar. 12, 1883; both in GPNew; Woolford, "Burr G. Duval Diary," 488; Burr G. Duval, "Journal of a Prospecting Trip to West Texas in 1879," 1, 48, 56, 66–67, 69, 71, CAH; Unsigned report of AAG, Dec. 10, 1886, box 17, Fort Davis, Texas, Records, RG 393, NARA; Tyler, *Big Bend*, 135–45; *Galveston Weekly News*, Apr. 8, 1880.

17. *Presidio Mining Company vs. Alice Bullis*, Aug. 1887, Supreme Court of Texas, No. 5909, in 2220 A.C.P. 1879, box 570, ACP Branch; Shafter to Baldwin, Dec. 25, 1889, box 6, Baldwin Papers.

18. Grace Paulding Memoirs, 10, William and Grace Paulding Papers, U.S. Army History Research Collection, Carlisle Barracks; Young to Brackett, Feb. 4, 7, 1886, Young Papers; Merton to Church, Sept. 13, 1890, box 2, William C. Church Papers, LC.

19. Thompson, "The Officers, Fort Davis, Texas," Officers File, FODA; Wedemeyer Memoirs, 2:99, 247, 255, 272, FODA; Mills, *My Story*, 186; Williams, "Empire Building," 65–66.

20. Wedemeyer Memoirs, 2:254, 262; Woodward to Grierson, July 27, 1880, roll 2, GPNew; Leckie and Leckie, *Unlikely Warriors*, 280; Mills to Grierson,

Oct. 1, 1882, roll 2, GPSpr; McChristian, *Garrison Tangles*, 23, 26; Smither to Post Adjutant, July 21, 1884, roll 2, GPNew; Smither to Grierson, Mar. 4, 1883, roll 2, GPSpr; Vincent to Commanding Officer, Aug. 23, 1884, roll 7, LS, DT, 1870–98 (microfilm M 1114); Grierson to Alice, Nov. 15, 1878, roll 1, GPNew; Grierson, "Journal," FODA; Robert to Mama, July 26, 1880, FODA; Douglas McChristian, "Notes from Archives," in Units, Company C File, FODA.

21. Wedemeyer Memoirs, 2:128, 253, FODA; McChristian, *Garrison Tangles*, 26, 27, 52–53n; Vincent to Commanding Officer, Dec. 22, 1884 roll 7, LS, DT, 1870–98 (microfilm M 1114), 23:76; Fuller to Alice, Dec. 11, 1884, GPLu.

22. Mills, *My Story*, 186; Post Adjutant to Landon, Mar. 21, 1877, roll 1; Circular No. 1, Feb. 3, 1876, Circulars, Dec. 3, 7, 19, 1879, roll 4; both in FODA (microfilm 66-783); Nenninger, *Leavenworth Schools and the Old Army*, 16; Carpenter to AAG, Sept. 1, 1878, roll 1, FODA (microfilm 66-783); Mc-Christian, *Garrison Tangles*, 30–35; Testimony of Sherman, Nov. 23, 1877, House Misc. Doc. 64, 45th Cong., 2d sess., serial 1820, 49. See also McChristian, *Army of Marksmen*.

23. Vincent to Commanding Officer, Feb. 13, 1884, 22:62–63; Dec. 23, 1884, 23:80; both in roll 7, LS, DT, 1870–98 (microfilm M 1114); Vincent to Commanding Officer, Sept. 6, 1884, roll 9, FODA (microfilm 66-783).

24. Lizzie to Twohig, Dec. 18, 1881, box 1, Crosson Ranch Collection; Grierson to Harry, Nov. 10, 1882, GPLu; Alice to Grierson, Sept. 23, 28, 1883, roll 2, GPSpr. For a superb family biography, see Leckie and Leckie, *Unlikely Warriors*.

25. *Army and Navy Journal*, Mar. 22, 1884; Leckie and Leckie, *Unlikely Warriors*, 126, 165, 276, 284, 293; Robert to Mother, May 10, 1885, GPLu; Robert to Mother, May 26, June 10, GPSpr.

26. Leckie and Leckie, *Unlikely Warriors*, 280; George to Harry, Nov. 14, 30, 1884; Fairalds to Harry, Nov. 15, 30, 1884; both in Benjamin Grierson Letters and Documents, FODA.

27. "Diary of Mrs. Alex. B. Shepherd Containing Remembrances of First Trip into Mexico in 1880," FODA; Mariager, "Camp and Travel in Texas," 188; Boyd, *Cavalry Life*, 253; Robert to Momma, July 19, 1880, roll 1, GPNew; printed invitation, Sept. 10, 1880, roll 2, GPNew; Augur to Sherman, Aug. 16, 1882, roll 6, 18:535–36; Vincent to Commanding Officer, Mar. 20, 1883, roll 7, 20:195; Jan. 24, 1885, roll 8, 24:56; all in LS, DT, 1870–98 (microfilm M 1114); *Army and Navy Journal*, Oct. 14, 1882, Mar. 17, 1883.

28. *Army and Navy Journal*, Jan. 19, 1884; McChristian, *Garrison Tangles*, 21.

29. Dinges, "Benjamin H. Grierson," 168–73; Wedemeyer Memoirs, Mar. 10, 1885; Grierson to Charles, Feb. 21, 1885, GPLu; Grierson to Alice, Apr. 13, 1885, roll 2, GPSpr; McChristian, *Garrison Tangles*, 27.

30. Stanley to Schofield, Nov. 26, 1884, box 15; Schofield memorandum, Sept. 28, 1891, box 55; both in Schofield Papers; Stanley to AG, Dec. 19, 1884, roll 7,

LS, DT, 1870–98 (microfilm M 1114), 23:74–75; McChristian, *Garrison Tangles*, 5; Grierson to Charles, Feb. 21, 1885, GPLu; Leckie and Leckie, *Unlikely Warriors*, 284.

31. McChristian, *Garrison Tangles*, 39; Grierson to Alice, Apr. 6, 1885, roll 2, GPSpr; Robert to Mother, Apr. 14, 26, 1885, GPLu; "An Account of a 10th Cavalry March . . . ," Helen Grierson Fuller Davis, Civilians File, FODA. For costs associated with the move, see Table D, SW, AR, 1885, 531–35.

32. Robert to Mother, May 26, Oct. 16, 1885, roll 2, GPSpr; Hepburn to Grierson, Mar. 6, 1886; Stanley to Grierson, Mar. 10, 1886; both in GPLu.

CHAPTER NINE

1. *San Antonio Daily Express*, Aug. 11, 1881.

2. Manuscript Returns, U.S. Census, 1880, Presidio County; Wright, "Residential Segregation," 301; Register of Contracts, Entry 1242, Fort Davis, 1883, RG 92, NARA, 164, 165, 179, 219–21. For the methodology used to estimate military salaries, see chapter 6, note 10.

3. Holt, "Texas Had Hot County Elections," 11; Keesey to Newcomb, Apr. 3, 1879, Newcomb Papers; Bush, *Gringo Doctor*, 49; *Army and Navy Journal*, June 5, Dec. 25, 1886, Feb. 5, 1887, Feb. 22, 1889; Thompson, *Marfa and Presidio County*, 1:137, 143, 183, 198–99, 202, 205, 252, 259, 270, 278; Anderson Reminiscences, CAH; Deed Records, Presidio County, 1:76–77; "The First Baptist Church of Fort Davis, Texas: A Preliminary History" (typescript), FODA; Lauderdale Letterbooks, July 19, 1889, Apr. 28, 1890, FODA; Barber, *Faith West of the Pecos*, 4; unknown to Gram and Mother, Nov. 3, 1890, Thompson File, FODA; clipping attached to Abbott to SW, Mar. 2, 1888, 1303 A.C.P. 1888, box 1139, ACP Branch; typescript memo, Sept. 1975, Enlisted Men File, FODA; Keesey to Grand Army of the Republic, Feb. 18, 1890, box 4, Baldwin Papers; *Presidio County News*, May 31, 1884 (reprint). The *Apache Rocket*, purported to be the county's first newspaper, had briefly appeared in 1882.

4. Manuscript Returns, U.S. Census, 1880, Presidio County; Bush, *Gringo Doctor*, 33; *Presidio County News*, May 31, 1884 (reprint); Wright, "Property Ownership," 66–70; Register of Contracts, entry 1245, RG 92, NARA, 1:192, 274, 314, 318, 321, 345.

5. Manuscript Returns, U.S. Census, 1870, 1880, Presidio County; Jeff Davis County Tax Rolls, 1887; "Fort Davis Administrative History," 2–3, www.nps.gov/foda/adhi (accessed April 21, 2003); Bush, *Gringo Doctor*, 36–37; Lauderdale Letterbooks, May 22, Aug. 1, 1888; unsigned report, Dec. 10, 1886, box 17, Fort Davis, Texas, Records, RG 393, NARA; Wright, "Residential Segregation," 299.

6. Ledger 7, W. Keesey Collection, Archives of the Big Bend; Dinges, "San Angelo Riot," 35–45; Christian, *Black Soldiers*; Marriage Records, Fort Davis,

1874–80, Presidio County; Manuscript Returns, U.S. Census, 1870, 1880, Presidio County; Election Returns, Presidio County, boxes 2–12, Secretary of State Papers, TSL, 559, 571, 582, 638, 648; Wright, "Residential Segregation," 300, 302–303, 305, 309. For a different perspective on the intermarriages, see González, *Refusing the Favor.*

7.   Anderson Reminiscences; McChristian, *Garrison Tangles,* 7–8, 28; Nevill to Jones, Sept. 5, 1880, Texas Adjutant General's Office Papers; Post Medical Returns, July 1, 1879, July 31, 1882, Fort Davis, CAH; Manuscript Returns, U.S. Census, 1870, 1880, Presidio County. One of El Paso's largest barrios was called "Chihuahuita." García, *Desert Immigrants,* 6.

8.   Manuscript Returns, U.S. Census, 1870, 1880, Presidio County; Presidio County Tax Rolls, 1876, TSL; Jeff Davis County Tax Rolls, 1887, TSL; Marriage Records, Fort Davis, 1874–80, Presidio County; "Civilian Employees at Fort Davis, Texas," www.nps.gov/foda/Fort_Davis_WEB_PAGE/About_the_Fort/Civilian_Employees (accessed March 21, 2003).

9.   Manuscript Returns, U.S. Census, 1870, 1880, Presidio County; Wright, "Residential Segregation," 305.

10.   Manuscript Returns, U.S. Census, 1880, Presidio County; Jeff Davis County Tax Rolls, 1887, TSL; Bess Gray Higgins, "The Old Rock Wall . . ."; Thompson, "Private Bentley's Buzzard," Apr. 2, 1965; both in Local History File, FODA; L. T. Brown to Friend, May 21, 1965, Enlisted Men File, FODA; Jeff Davis County Deed Records, 1:505–506, Jeff Davis County Courthouse, Fort Davis; Parker to Edwards, Mar. 27, 1973, Charles Mulhern; Scobee to Mike, July 18, 1969; both in Enlisted Men File, FODA; Newspaper clipping, *Alpine Avalanche,* Apr. 1947, Simmons Papers; Scobee, *Old Fort Davis,* 73–74; George to Harry, Nov. 30, 1884, GPLu; "Case of Fort Davis," Oct. 4, 1878, 4570 A.C.P. 1878, box 530, ACP Branch.

11.   Robert to Mother, June 10, 1885, Oct. 20, 1886, roll 2, GPSpr; Leckie and Leckie, *Unlikely Warriors,* 175n27, 287, 290–93, 303–308.

12.   Hammond to Commanding Officer, Apr. 11, 1885, FODA (microfilm 85-3); Ruggles to Commanding Officer, Jan. 27, 29, 1887; Ruggles to Hammond, June 21, 1887; all in roll 8, LS, DT, 1870–98 (microfilm M 1114); Legard to SW, Jan. 4, 1887; Geegge to SW, Jan. 5, 1887; "Investigation of the Complaint against Hospital Steward Richard Dare . . ." Jan. 23, 1887; Kelton to Lanham, Feb. 15, 1887; all in FODA (microfilm 905-8821); Rumbaugh to Clendenin, Oct. 26, 1887, roll 8, LS, DT, 1870–98 (microfilm M 1114).

13.   Table XVIII, SW, AR, 1891, 667; Proceedings at Coroner's Inquest on the Body of Richard Robinson, June 16, 1878, roll 1, FODA (microfilm 65-855); entry for June, 1878, Post Medical Returns, Fort Davis, CAH, 222. Marshall escaped from civil authorities, was recaptured by the army, and discharged. Twenty-fifth Infantry, Oct. 1878–May 1879, roll 255, Returns from Regular Army Infantry Regiments (microfilm M 665).

14.   Coffman, *Old Army,* 346–47, 371–72.

15.   Report of Howard, Sept. 15, SW, AR, 1880, 149–50; Report of Drum, Oct. 15, SW, AR, 1884, 218; Orders No. 90, Apr. 23, 1883, roll 4, FODA (microfilm 66-783). For individual cases, see "Separate Special Report in the Case of Pvt. James Brown," May 29, 1884, roll 6; M. F. Eggleston to Post Adj., June 19, 1884, roll 8; both in FODA (microfilm 66-783); Separate Special Reports (Reports of Individual Deserters) 1883–90, box 15, Fort Davis, Texas, Records, RG 393, NARA.

16.   Ifera, "Crime and Punishment at Fort Davis," tables; Mullins to Adjutant General, Aug. 31, 1876, 5035 A.C.P. 1874, ACP Branch; Coffman, *Old Army*, 371n95; Report of Proctor, Nov. 23, SW, AR, 1889, 9.

17.   Report of Sherman, Nov. 6, 1882, 6; Report of Lincoln, Nov. 15, 1883, 6; Report of Drum, Oct. 1883, 50–52; Report of Augur, Sept. 21, 1883, 147; Report of Sacket, Oct. 17, 1884, 84–87; Report of Schofield, Oct. 22, 1889, 64; all in SW, AR; Smither to Grierson, Oct. 21, 1882, roll 2, GPSpr; Smither to AG, Dec. 20, 1884; Sheridan endorsement of Feb. 7, 1885; both in 6246 A.G.O. 1884, roll 317, LR, AGO, 1881–89 (microfilm M 689); *Army and Navy Journal*, Mar. 28, 1891, 534; McChristian, *Garrison Tangles*, 26, 33; Extract of Report of Claus, SW, AR, 1883, 399; Report of Swaim, Oct. 1, SW, AR, 1883, 388.

18.   Kinevan, *Frontier Cavalryman*, 73–84; Coffman, *Old Army*, 375; Ifera, "Crime and Punishment at Fort Davis," 56, 61–63; Orders No. 122, Aug. 15, 1878, roll 4, FODA (microfilm 66-783); Orders No. 13, Jan. 24, 1884, Thomas H. Allsup File, FODA.

19.   Ifera, "Crime and Punishment at Fort Davis," 53–54, 85; Post Medical Returns, Jan. 1869, Fort Davis, CAH, 105; Crane, *Experiences of a Colonel of Infantry*, 120. In the latter punishment, a gagged soldier was made to sit, knees up and arms outstretched, with a stick passed under his knees and over his elbows and wrists.

20.   Coffman, *Old Army*, 340–42; Forsyth, *Story of the Soldier*, 96; Report of Schofield, Nov. 20, SW, AR, 1868, iv; Turrill to Post Adj., May 31, 1874, Post Medical Returns, Fort Davis, CAH; McConnell, *Five Years a Cavalryman*, 210; Smith to AAG, Nov. 3, 1880, FODA (microfilm 905/8821); Report of Macfeely, Oct. 8, SW, AR, 1883, 590; Wedemeyer Memoirs, 2:298; Report of Stanley, Aug. 27, 1887, 137; Report of Baird, Nov. 7, 1887, 110; both in SW, AR; Kentner to Post Treasurer, Mar. 31, 1889, roll 9, FODA (microfilm 66-783); *Army and Navy Journal*, Sept. 26, 1885; Ruggles to Commanding Officer, Mar. 26, 1886, roll 8, LS, DT, 1870–98 (microfilm M 1114); Williams, "The Post and the Hospital Gardens"; unsigned report, Dec. 10, 1886, box 17, Fort Davis, Texas, Records, RG 393, NARA; Order No. 27, Apr. 27, 1890, box 4, Baldwin Papers.

21.   "Account Current Post Fund," Oct.–Nov. 1885, roll 6, FODA (microfilm 66-783); Report of Eaton, Oct. 5, SW, AR, 1872, 293; "Abstracts of Provisions," Quimby Papers, CAH and FODA; Andrews to AAG, Jan. 4, 1875, roll 1,

FODA (microfilm 66-783); Small to Comm. Gen., Aug. 26, 1881, FODA (microfilm 906/8820).

22. Rickey, *Forty Miles a Day*, 202; Ord endorsement of Jan. 17, 1877, to report of Chaplain Mullins, roll 8, FODA (microfilm 66-783); Otis to Adjutant General, Nov. 11, 1887, roll 1, FODA (microfilm 65-855); Register of Post Traders, 4:5, RG 94, NARA; Otis to AG, Feb. 4, 1888; Abbott to SW, Jan. 12, 1888; both in 179 A.C.P. 1888, box 1135, ACP Branch; Coffman, *Old Army*, 360.

23. Abbott to SW, Jan. 12, 1888, 279 A.C.P. 1888, box 1135, ACP Branch; clipping with Abbott to SW, Mar. 2, 1888, box 1139, ACP Branch; *Congressional Record*, 51st Cong., 1st sess., vol. 21, pt. 3, 2818; Otis to AG, Feb. 4, 1888; AG to Abbott, Mar. 2, 1888; both in 279 A.C.P. 1888, box 1135, ACP Branch; Drum to Division of the Missouri, Feb. 5, 1889, roll 9, FODA (microfilm 66-783); Register of Post Traders, RG 94, NARA, 4:5; Report of Proctor, Nov. 3, SW, AR, 1891, 17; Brooks to Tynes, Jan. 29, 1890, General Correspondence, box 2, #1017, Records of the Office of Secretary of War, RG 107, NARA; Normoyle to Post Adjutant, Aug. 13, 1890, roll 9, FODA (microfilm 66-783); "List of fixtures and furniture . . . May 10, 1891"; "List and valuation of stock . . . May 10, 1891"; both in FODA (microfilm 905/8821); Criminal Docket #30, Criminal Docket Book 1, Jeff Davis County Courthouse, Fort Davis.

24. Bowie, "Redfield Proctor," 186–90; Proctor to J. Wheeler, Feb. 20, 1891, box 3, Redfield Proctor Papers, Proctor Free Library; Report of Schofield, Oct. 25, 1888, 66–67; Report of Proctor, Nov. 23, 1889, 8; Report of Proctor, Nov. 15, 1890, 9; Report of Proctor, Nov. 3, 1891, 3–4, 11; Report of Kelton, Oct. 1, 1891, 63; all in SW, AR; Graham, "Duty, Life, and Law," 275–77.

25. Post Medical Returns, May 31, 1884, Apr. 1889, Fort Davis, CAH; "Extracts of inspection report . . . January, 1887, by Lieut. Col. E. M. Heyl," roll 9, FODA (microfilm 66-783). See also Martin to Commanding Officer, Aug. 5, 1889, roll 9, LS, DT, 1870–98 (microfilm M 1114); Statement A, Report of Construction and Repairs, SW, AR, 1887, 425; Lauderdale Letterbooks, May 22, June 11, 30, 1888, Apr. 30, 1889; McGonnigle to AAG, Aug. 13, 1888, Annual Report of Brig. Genl. D. S. Stanley . . . 1888, in Rosters of Troops, RG 393, NARA.

26. *Army and Navy Journal*, Oct. 14, 1882; Vollum to AG, Aug. 31, 1886, FODA (microfilm 906/8820); Report of Moore, SW, AR, 1887, 622–24, 644–45; Report of Stanley, Sept. 4, SW, AR, 1886, 126.

27. Vollum to Surgeon General, Apr. 22, 1886, FODA (microfilm 905/8821); "Office Brief as to Water Supply," Fort Davis, Water System File, FODA; Report of Sawtelle, Sept. 20, SW, AR, 1889, 491; Lauderdale Letterbooks, June 23, 28, Aug. 4, 1888.

28. Lauderdale Letterbooks, July 21, Aug. 22, 1888; *Army and Navy Journal*, June 20, 1885; Skinner to Post Adjutant, Aug. 31, 1890; Normoyle, endorse-

ments of Sept. 2, Nov. 4, 1890; both in Medicine File, FODA; Baldwin, *Major General Frank D. Baldwin*, 35.

29. Kimbrough to Clendenin, Oct. 26, 1887, roll 8, LS, DT, 1870–98 (microfilm M 1114); Sis to Mother, July 19, 1890; Sis to Gram and Mother, Nov. 3, 1890; both in James K. Thompson Files, FODA; Lauderdale Letterbooks, May 22, Aug. 16, 18, 22, Sept. 6, 10, 1888, Nov. 3, 13, 1889.

30. Report of Schools in Operation at Fort Davis, box 17, Fort Davis, Texas, Records, RG 393, NARA; Report of Drum, Oct. 9, SW, AR, 1886, 80; White, "ABC's for the American Enlisted Man," 479–96; Report of Breckinridge, Oct. 1, 1890, 110; Report of Moore, Aug. 8, 1890, 933, 979; both in SW, AR; Smith to Commanding Officer, Nov. 28, 1887, roll 8, LS, DT, 1870–98, (microfilm M 1114); Quarterly Tabular Reports of Expeditions and Scouts, 1871–88, box 17, Fort Davis, Texas, Records, RG 393, NARA.

31. Report of Stanley, Sept. 4, 1886, 126; Report of Stanley, Aug. 27, 1887, 136; both in SW, AR; Stanley to AG, Nov. 18, 1887, roll 8; Smith to Commanding Officer, Apr. 21, 1888, roll 8; May 5, 1888, roll 9; all in LS, DT, 1870–98 (microfilm M 1114); Blunt to Williams, Apr. 23, 1888, roll 11, LS, HQA (microfilm M 857); Stanley to AAG, Apr. 24, 1888, roll 9, LS, DT, 1870–98 (microfilm M 1114); Report of Stanley, Sept. 13, SW, AR, 1888, 141; "Dept. of Texas" (1885), File "S," box 14, Schofield Papers; Schofield to SW, Sept. 27, 1889, roll 11, LS, HQA (microfilm M 857).

32. Two letters from Schofield to the Secretary of War, March 20, 1890, have been found. That in box 55, Schofield Papers, lists thirteen posts suitable to be abandoned. A typewritten note in box 3 (1890), file 2425, General Correspondence, Secretary of War, RG 107, NARA, lists twenty-four posts, sixteen marked number one and eight marked number two. Davis appears in the latter group. The note in Schofield's personal papers was undoubtedly a draft.

    Chief Clerk, Apr. 2, 1890, General Correspondence, Secretary of War, RG 107, NARA; Schofield to AG, Apr. 29, 1890, box 55, Schofield Papers; Mott to Baldwin, May 22, 1890, box 3, Baldwin Papers; Schofield to McCook, Dec. 9, 1890, box 55, Schofield Papers; Schofield to Commander, Department of Texas, Dec. 1, 1890, roll 12, LS, HQA (microfilm M 857).

33. Proctor to McCook, Nov. 21, 1890, box 2, Proctor Papers; *San Antonio Daily Express*, Mar. 27, 1891; *Army and Navy Journal*, Apr. 4, 1891; Proctor to Sayres, Apr. 25, 1891; Proctor to Lanham, Apr. 27, 1891; both in box 3, Proctor Papers; Stanley to AG, July 30, 1891, roll 9, LS, DT, 1870–98 (microfilm M 1114).

34. Petition to President, Sept. 17, 1885, FODA (microfilm 905-8821); Endicott to Davis, Oct. 7, 1885, roll 95, LS, SW (microfilm M 6); Patterson to Grierson, Mar. 26, 1889; Thompson to Lanham, Feb. 4, 1890; both in box 4, Thompson Collection; Gilliss to James, Apr. 1, 1891, roll 2, FODA (microfilm 65-855); Murphy to Blaine, May 15, 1891, FODA (microfilm 66-876/7833); *San Antonio Daily Express*, Apr. 12, May 1, 17, 1891; Schofield to Reagan, Jan. 13, 1890; Schofield to Lanham, Jan. 10, 25, 1890; both in roll

11, LS, HQA (microfilm M 857); Schofield to Lanham, Mar. 18, June 2, 1890, roll 12, LS, HQA (microfilm M 857); Schofield to SW, Mar. 3, 1890, box 55, Schofield Papers; Proctor to Woods, Mar. 9, 1891, box 3, Proctor Papers; *Congressional Record*, 20:1628; Schofield to Quartermaster General, Aug. 12, 1890, box 55; Stanley to Schofield, Dec. 5, 1890, box 42; both in Schofield Papers; Proctor to Reed, Mar. 3, 1891, box 3, Proctor Papers; Election Returns, Jeff Davis County, 1888, box 2-12/631, Secretary of State Papers, Texas State Archives.

35. Stanley to AG, July 30, 1891, roll 9, LS, DT, 1870–98 (microfilm M 1114); Martin to Commanding Officer, June 1, 1891, roll 9, FODA (microfilm 66-783); Devon to Commanding Officer, June 18, 20, 1891, roll 9, LS, DT, 1870–98 (microfilm M 1114); Hardin to Quartermaster, July 13, 1891, Book of Letters Sent by C. B. Hardin, FODA; Phelps, "From Texas to Dakota," 1–3; Alice to Baldwin, Dec. 19, 1890, Baldwin Papers.

36. Fifth Infantry, July, 1891, roll 60, Returns from Regular Army Infantry Regiments (microfilm M 665); Devon to Commanding Officer, June 30, 1891, roll 9, LS, DT, 1870–98 (microfilm M 1114); Hardin to Quartermaster, July 6, 1891, Book of Letters Sent by C. B. Hardin, FODA; Mulhern to Maxon, June 30, Aug. 31, 1891; Maxon to Mulhern, Dec. 28, 1891; both in Mason M. Maxon Papers, FODA; Ed Bartholomew, Oral Interview, June 16, 1983, Archives of the Big Bend; Scobee, *Old Fort Davis*, 89.

37. Report of Proctor, 16; Report of Stanley, 156; both Nov. 3, SW, AR, 1891.

EPILOGUE

1. 2000 Census Bureau data are available at "American FactFinder," http://factfinder.census.gov/servlet/BasicFactsServlet (accessed September 30, 2003).

BIBLIOGRAPHY

PRIMARY SOURCES
Archival Materials

Archives of the Big Bend. Sul Ross State University, Alpine, Tex. Bartholomew, Ed, Oral Interview. Crosson Ranch Collection. Epsy, Pansy Evans, Oral Collection. Keesey, W., Collection. Thomas, S. A., Papers.

Austin History Center. Austin Public Library, Austin, Tex. Pease, E. M., Papers.

Bancroft Library. Berkeley, Calif. Ord, Edward O. C., Papers. Peters, DeWitt C., Papers.

Center for American History. Austin, Tex. Anderson, Mattie Belle, Reminiscences. Andrews, Emily K., Diary. Berry, James B., Papers. Bliss, Zenas R., Reminiscences. Bryan, Guy M., Papers. Crimmins, Martin L., Collection. Duval, Burr G., "Journal of a Prospecting Trip to West Texas in 1879." Eberstadt Collection. Haley, J. Evatts, "Interview with Jeff D. Milton." Howell, W. Randolph, "Journal of a Soldier of the Confederate States Army." Knapp, O. M., Papers. Magoffin, James, Papers. Newcomb, James P., Papers. Newcomb, Samuel P., Diary. Post Medical Returns, Fort Davis (microfilm). Quimby, H. B., Papers. Reagan, John R., Papers. Simmons, David A., Papers. Smithers, W. D., Collection. Texas Adjutant General's Office Papers. Thomas, Dewitt C., Reminiscences. Throckmorton, James W., Papers. Woods, I. C., "Report to Hon. A. V. Brown, Postmaster General . . ." Wright, H. C. "Reminiscences of H. C. Wright of Austin."

Fort Davis National Historic Site. Fort Davis, Tex. Adams, William C., Papers. Allsup, Thomas H., File, "The First Baptist Church of Fort Davis, Texas: A Preliminary History." Brackett File. Campaigns and Battles File. Canteens File. Civilians File. Civil War Documents File. "Company F, Second Regiment Texas Mounted Rifles, The Walter P. Lane Rangers at Fort Lancaster, Texas." Confederate Interlude File. Consolidated Correspondence File, Selected Documents Relating to Fort Davis, RG 92, National Archives (microfilm). Consolidated File Unarranged, Fort Davis, Texas, 1855–90, RG 92, National Archives (microfilm). Correspondence, 1867–1917 (microfilm). Diary of Mrs. Alex R. Shepherd Containing Remembrances of First Trip into Mexico in 1880. Draper, John H., File. First Fort Davis File. Fort Davis Letters and Documents File. Fort Davis, Local History File. Fort Davis, National Historic Site File. Fort Davis, Texas Reservation File (microfilm). Fort Davis, Town and Vicinity File. Fort Davis, Water System File. Forts (other than Davis) File. Gardens File. Geldard, Gordon W., "The Lost Patrol," 1982. Granger, T. T., Oral Interview. Grierson, Benjamin H., Letters and Documents, Edward Ayer Collection, MS 343A (microfilm). Grierson, Benjamin

H., Papers (microfilm of collection at Illinois State Historical Library). Grierson, Benjamin H., Papers (photocopies of collection at Texas Tech University). Grierson, Robert K., "Journal Kept on the Victorio Campaign in 1880." Land Acquisitions File. Lauderdale, John V., Letterbooks (microfilm). Laundresses File. Medicine File. Miscellaneous Papers, Miscellaneous Circulars, 1890–91 (microfilm). Myer, Albert James, Papers (microfilm). "Notes on Driving Tour and Interview with Mrs. Pansy Epsy," May 7, 1986. Officers File. Post Records, Registered Letters Received, 1876–91 (microfilm). Post Trader File. Quimby, H. B., Papers. Selected Documents Relating to Fort Davis, Texas, RG 77, National Archives (microfilm). Selected Documents, 1867–91 (microfilm). Servants File. Thompson Files. Travel and Transportation File. Wedemeyer, William George, Memoirs. 870 ACP 1890, Lt. William E. Shipp (microfilm).

Historical Society of Pennsylvania Collection. Philadelphia, Penn. Carpenter, Louis H., Papers.

Huntington Library. San Marino, Calif. Baldwin, Frank Dwight, Collection. Overland Mail Collection. Schuyler, Walter S., Papers.

Illinois State Historical Library. Springfield, Ill. Augur, Christopher C., Papers.

Jeff Davis County Courthouse. Fort Davis, Tex. Criminal Docket Book. Deed Records.

Library of Congress. Manuscript Division, Washington, D.C. Church, William C., Papers. Grant, Ulysses S., Papers. Gregg, David M., Collection. Hartz, Edward L., Collection. Schofield, John M., Papers. Sheridan, Philip H., Papers. Sherman, William T., Papers. Stanton, Edwin, Papers.

Library of Congress. Map Division, Washington, D.C. "Map of Texas and Part of New Mexico Compiled in the Bureau of Topograph'l Engrs Chiefly for Military Purposes," 1857. "Military Map of Western Texas," 1884. Warren, G. K., "Map of the Military Dep't of Texas," 1859. Young, J. H., "Map of the State of Texas from the Latest Authorities," 1853.

Missouri Historical Society. St. Louis, Mo. Sherman, William T., Letters.

National Archives. Manuscript Division. Washington, D.C.

RG 48. Records of the Office of the Secretary of the Interior: Indian Division, Letters Sent, 1849–1903, Microfilm M 606. Office of Exploration and Surveys, Miscellaneous Letters Received.

RG 56. Office of the Secretary of the Treasury: Letters Sent to the Interior Department, vol. BA-1.

RG 75. Records of the Bureau of Indian Affairs: Letters Received by the Office of Indian Affairs, 1824–80, Microfilm M 234.

RG 77. Records of the Office of the Chief of Engineers: "Journal Showing the Route Taken by the Government Train Accompanying the 15th RGT. U.S. Infantry from Austin, Tex. to Ft. Craig, N.M., and Returning to San Antonio, July–December, 1869. Prepared under Direction of Brvt. Lt. Col. Thos. B. Hunt A.Q.M. U.S.A."

RG 92. Records of the Office of the Quartermaster General: Register of Contracts, 1871–76, Entry 1242. Register of Contracts, 1881–90, Entry 1245. Reports of Persons and Articles Hired, Entry 238.

RG 94. Records of the Adjutant General's Office: Appointment, Commission, and Personal Branch Files. Letters Received by the Office of the Adjutant General (Main Series) 1822–60, Microfilm M 567. Letters Received by the Office of the Adjutant General, 1871–80, Microfilm M 666. Letters Received by the Office of the Adjutant General (Main Series), 1881–89, Microfilm M 689. Letters Sent by the Office of the Adjutant General (Main Series), 1800–1890, Microfilm M 565. The Negro in the Military Service of the United States, 1639–1886, Microfilm M 858. Organizational Returns, Tenth Cavalry. Principal Record Division File. Register of Post Traders. Registers of Enlistments in the United States Army 1798–1914, Microfilm M 233. Registers of Letters Received, Adjutant General's Office, 1812–89, Microfilm M 711. Registers of the Records of the Proceedings of the U.S. Army General Courts-Martial, 1809–90, Microfilm M 1105. Returns from Regular Army Infantry Regiments, June 1821–December 1916, Microfilm M 665. Returns from Regular Army Cavalry Regiments, 1833–1916, Microfilm M 744. Returns from United States Military Posts, Microfilm M 617.

RG 107. Records of the Office of the Secretary of War: Letters Received by the Secretary of War, 1890–1916. Letters Sent Relating to Military Affairs, 1800–1889, Microfilm M 6.

RG 108. Records of the Headquarters of the Army: Letters Sent by the Headquarters of the Army (Main Series), 1828–1903, Microfilm M 857.

RG 109. Confederate Records: General Orders, Department of Texas, 1861–62. Records of the Department of Texas and the Trans-Mississippi Department.

RG 112. Records of the Office of the Surgeon General: Selected Documents Relating to Fort Davis, Texas.

RG 153. Records of the Judge Advocate General's Office: Court-Martial Files.

RG 156. Records of the Office of the Chief of Engineers: Summary of Ordnance Stores in Hands of Troops.

RG 205. Records of the Court of Claims Section (Justice): Indian Depredations Files.

RG 393. Records of U.S. Continental Commands, 1821–1920: Fort Davis, Texas, Records. Charges and Specifications of Garrison Courts Martial. Daily Instructions of Commanding Officer and Record of Post Events, 1889–91. Letters Sent by the Department of Texas, the District of Texas, and the Fifth Military District 1856–58 and 1865–70, Microfilm M 1165. Letters Sent, Department of Texas, 1870–98, Microfilm 1114. Miscellaneous Records. Monthly Inspection Reports of the Post. Monthly Reports of Prisoners in Arrest and Confinement. Quarterly Tabular Reports of Expeditions and Scouts, 1871–88. Register of Baptisms, Marriages and Deaths. Registers of Letters Received, 1851–57. Registers of Letters Received and Letters Received of the Department of Texas, the District of Texas, and the Fifth Military District, 1865–70, Microfilm M 1193. Reports of Individual Deserters. Reports of Non-Commissioned Officers. Reports of Persons Killed or Captured by Indians. Reports of Post Schools. Rosters of Troops. Semimonthly Reports Held and Released; Headquarters Records of the District of the Pecos, 1878–81, Microfilm M 1381. Subdistrict of the Pecos, Letters Received, 1870.

Newberry Library. Chicago, Ill. Grierson, Benjamin, Papers.

New York Public Library. New York, New York. Greene, F. V., Papers.

Presidio County Courthouse, Marfa, Tex. Deed Records. Marriage Records.

Proctor Free Library. Proctor, Vt. Proctor, Redfield, Papers.

Stanford University Library, Manuscripts Division. Stanford, Calif. Shafter, William, Papers.

Texas State Library, Archives Division. Austin, Tex. Adjutant General's Military Papers. Election Registers. Election Returns. Governors Records. Hanna, Ebenezer, "Journal of Ebenezer Hanna, February 10 to March 27, 1862." Manuscript Returns, Seventh, Eighth, Ninth, Tenth U.S. Censuses, Bexar, Presidio, Jeff Davis Counties. Maxey, Samuel Bell, Papers. Register of Elected and Appointed State and County Officials. Tax Rolls, El Paso, Jeff Davis, and Presidio Counties.

Texas State Library, Archives Division, Map Collection. Austin, Tex. "Best Route for the Movement of Troops from San Antonio to El Paso, Texas," no. 1004K. "Description of the Best Military Route from Fort Davis to Fort Hudson," no. 1004 B. "Plan of Fort Davis, Texas," 1883, no. 1675.

U.S. Army Military History Institute. Carlisle Barracks, Penn. Nolan, Nicholas, Papers, 1878–80. Order of Indian Wars Collection. Paulding, William and Grace, Papers. Tenth Cavalry Regiment Collection. Young, S. B. M., Papers.

U.S. Military Academy Archives. West Point, New York. Barnitz, Bertha Rice, Collection. Official Registers of the Officers and Cadets of the U.S. Military Academy, West Point, New York.

Congressional Documents

Secretary of War, Annual Reports.

1850 H.E.D. 1, 31st Cong., 2d sess., vol. 1, serial 595.

1851 S.E.D. 1, 32d Cong., 1st sess., vol. 1, serial 611.

1852 S.E.D. 1, 32d Cong., 2d sess., vol. 2, serial 659.

1853 S.E.D. 1, 33d Cong., 1st sess., vol. 2, serial 691.

1854 S.E.D. 1, 33d Cong., 2d sess., vol. 2, serial 747.

1855 S.E.D. 1, 34th Cong., 1st sess., vol. 2, serial 811.

1856 S.E.D. 5, 34th Cong., 3d sess., vol. 2, serial 867.

1857 S.E.D. 11, 35th Cong., 1st sess., vol. 3, serial 920.

1858 S.E.D. 1, 35th Cong., 2d sess., vols. 2, 3, serial 975, 976.

1859 S.E.D. 2, 36th Cong., 1st sess., vols. 2, 3, serial 1024.

1860 S.E.D. 1, 36th Cong., 2d sess., vol. 2, serial 1079.

1861 S.E.D. 1, 37th Cong., 2d sess., vol. 2, serial 1118.

1866 H.E.D. 1, 39th Cong., 2d sess., vol. 3, serial 1285.

1867 H.E.D. 1, 40th Cong., 2d sess., vol. 2, serial 1324.

1868 H.E.D. 1, 40th Cong., 3d sess., vol. 3, serial 1367.

1869 H.E.D. 1, pt. 2, 41st Cong., 2d sess., vol. 2, serial 1413.

1870 H.E.D. 1, pt. 2, 41st Cong., 3d sess., vol. 2, serial 1446.

1871 H.E.D. 1, pt. 2, 42d Cong., 2d sess., vol. 2, serial 1503.

1872 H.E.D. 1, pt. 2, 42d Cong., 3d sess., vol. 2, serial 1558.

1873 H.E.D. 1, pt. 2, 43d Cong., 1st sess., vol. 2, serial 1597.

1874 H.E.D. 1, pt. 2, 43d Cong., 2d sess., vol. 2, serial 1635.

1875 H.E.D. 1, pt. 2, 44th Cong., 1st sess., vol. 2, serial 1674.

1876 H.E.D. 1, pt. 2, 44th Cong., 2d sess., vol. 2, serial 1742.

1877 H.E.D. 1, pt. 2, 45th Cong., 2d sess., vol. 2, serial 1794.

1878 H.E.D. 1, pt. 2, 45th Cong., 3d sess., vol. 2, serial 1843.

1879 H.E.D. 1, pt. 2, 46th Cong., 2d sess., vol. 2, serial 1903.

1880 H.E.D. 1, pt. 2, 46th Cong., 3d sess., vol. 2, serial 1952.

1881 H.E.D. 1, pt. 2, 47th Cong., 1st sess., vol. 2, serial 2010.

1882 H.E.D. 1, pt. 2, 47th Cong., 2d sess., vol. 2, serial 2091.

1883 H.E.D. 1, pt. 2, 48th Cong., 1st sess., vol. 2, serial 2182.

1884 H.E.D. 1, pt. 2, 48th Cong., 2d sess., vol. 2, serial 2277.

1885 H.E.D. 1, pt. 2, 49th Cong., 1st sess., vol. 2, serial 2369.

1886 H.E.D. 1, pt. 2, 49th Cong., 2d sess., vol. 2, serial 2461.

1887 H.E.D. 1, pt. 2, 50th Cong., 1st sess., vol. 2, serial 2533.

1888 H.E.D. 1, pt. 2, 50th Cong., 2d sess., vol. 2, serial 2628.

1889 H.E.D. 1, pt. 2, 51st Cong., 1st sess., vol. 2, serial 2715.

1890 H.E.D. 1, pt. 2, 51st Cong., 2d sess., vol. 2, serial 2831.

1891 H.E.D. 1, pt. 2, 52d Cong., 1st sess., vol. 2, serial 2921.

S.E.D. 32, 31st Cong., 1st sess., serial 558. Operations along the Rio Grande.

S.E.D. 64, 31st Cong., 1st sess., serial 562.

H.E.D. 59, 33d Congress., 1st sess., serial 721. Army Register, 1853.

S.E.D. 7, 34th Cong., 1st sess., serial 815. War Departments Contracts.

S.E.D. 96, 34th Cong., 1st sess., serial 827. Coolidge, Richard H. "Statistical Report on the Sickness and Mortality in the Army of the United States."

H.E.D. 135, 34th Cong., 1st sess., serial 832. Emory, William H. "Report on the United States and Mexican Boundary Survey Made under the Direction of the Secretary of the Interior, 1849–1857."

S.E.D. 62, 34th Cong., 3d sess., serial 881. Purchase of Camels.

H.E.D. 23, 34th Cong., 3d sess., serial 897. Balances of Appropriations.

H.E.D. 46, 35th Cong., 1st sess., serial 955. Report on War Department Balances.

H.E.D. 124, 35th Cong., 1st sess., serial 959. Wagon Road from Fort Defiance to the Colorado River.

H.E.D. 76, 35th Cong., 1st sess., serial 963. Indians in Texas.

S.E.D. 19, 35th Cong., 2d sess., serial 981. Balances of Appropriations.

H.E.D. 27, 35th Cong., 2d sess., serial 1004. Protection of the Texas Frontier.

H.E.D. 22, 36th Cong., 1st sess., serial 1047. Quartermaster Contracts.

S.E.D. 52, 36th Cong., 1st sess., serial 1035. Sickness and Mortality in the Army.

S.E.D. 39, 36th Cong., 1st sess., serial 1038. "Resolutions of the Legislature of Texas . . . for the Protection of the Frontier."

H.E.D. 249, 41st Cong., 2d sess., serial 1425. Sales by Post Traders.

H.E.D. 39, 42d Cong., 3d sess., serial 1565. Depredations on the Frontiers of Texas.

H.R. 26, 42d Cong., 3d sess., serial 1576. Military Posts in Texas.

H.E.D. 282, 43d Cong., 1st sess., serial 1615. Military Sites in Texas.

H.R. 395, 43d Cong., 1st sess., serial 1624. Depredations on the Texas Frontier.

H.R. 343, 44th Cong., 1st sess., serial 1709. Texas Frontier Troubles.

H.R. 354, 44th Cong., 1st sess., serial 1709. Reduction of Army Officers' Pay.

H.E.D. 13, 45th Cong., 1st sess., serial 1773. Mexican Border Troubles.

S.E.D. 19, 45th Cong., 2d sess., serial 1780. Claims of Texas.

S.E.D. 47, 45th Cong., 2d sess., serial 1781. Company Cooks in the Army.

H.E.D. 79, 45th Cong., 2d sess., serial 1809. Abandonment of Military Posts.

House Misc. Doc. 64, 45th Cong., 2d sess., serial 1820. Mexican Border Troubles.

H.R. 701, 45th Cong., 2d sess., serial 1824. Texas Frontier Troubles.

S.R. 40, 46th Cong., 2d sess., serial 1893. Protection of the Rio Grande Frontier.

H.R. 88, 46th Cong., 2d sess., serial 1934. Posts on the Rio Grande Frontier.

H.E.D. 20, 47th Cong.,1st sess., serial 2027. Posts on the Rio Grande Frontier.

H.E.D. 100, 48th Cong., 1st sess., serial 2205. Star Route Investigations.

U.S. Congress. *Congressional Globe* (1854–73).

U.S. Congress. *Congressional Record* (1873–91).

U.S. Statutes at Large.

Published Primary Materials

Adjutant General's Office. *Chronological List of Actions, &c., with Indians, from January 15, 1837 to January 1891.* N.p.: Old Army Press, 1979.

Alberts, Don E., ed. *Rebels on the Rio Grande: The Civil War Journal of A. B. Peticolas.* Albuquerque: University of New Mexico Press, 1984.

Anderson, Mrs. M. B. "A School Is Started in Old Fort Davis." In *Women Tell the Story of the Southwest*, edited and compiled by Mattie Lloyd Wooten. San Antonio: Naylor, 1940.

Baldwin, Alice Blackwood. *Memoirs of the Late Major General Frank D. Baldwin.* Los Angeles: Wetzel Publishing, 1929.

Ball, Eve. *Indeh: An Apache Odyssey.* Provo, Utah: Brigham Young University Press, 1980.

Bandel, Eugene. *Frontier Life in the Army, 1854–1861.* Edited by Ralph P. Bieber. Glendale, Calif.: Arthur H. Clark, 1932.

Baylor, George Wythe. *Into the Far, Wild Country: True Tales of the Old Southwest.* Edited by Jerry D. Thompson. El Paso: Texas Western Press, 1996.

Bell, James G. "A Log of the Texas-California Cattle Trail, 1854." Edited by J. Evatts Haley. *Southwestern Historical Quarterly* 35 (January 1932): 208–37; (April 1932): 290–316.

Bell, William H. "Ante Bellum: The Old Army in Texas in '61." *Magazine of History* 3 (February 1906): 80–86.

Bennett, James A. *Forts and Forays: A Dragoon in New Mexico 1850–1856.* Edited by Clinton E. Brooks and Frank D. Reeve. Albuquerque: University of New Mexico Press, 1984.

Billings, John S. *A Report on Barracks and Hospitals, with Descriptions of Military Posts.* 1870. Circular 4, War Department Surgeon General's Office. Reprint, New York: Sol Lewis, 1974.

———. *Report on the Hygiene of the United States Army, with Descriptions of Military Posts.* Circular 8, War Department Surgeon General's Office. Washington, D.C.: Government Printing Office, 1875.

Bolton, Herbert Eugene, ed. *Spanish Exploration in the South-West 1542–1706.* 1908. Original Narratives of Early American History. Reprint, New York: Barnes and Noble, 1963.

Boyd, Mrs. Orsemus Bronson. *Cavalry Life in Tent and Field.* 1894. Reprint, Lincoln: University of Nebraska Press, 1970.

Brackett, Albert G. *History of the United States Cavalry, from the Formation of the Federal Government to the 1st of June, 1863.* 1865. Reprint, Freeport, N.Y.: Books for Libraries Press, 1970.

Bush, I. J. *Gringo Doctor.* Caldwell, Idaho: Caxton Printers, 1939.

Clary, David A., ed. "'I Am Already Quite a Texan': Albert J. Myer's Letters from Texas, 1854–1856." *Southwestern Historical Quarterly* 82 (July 1978): 25–76.

Conway, Walter C., ed. "Colonel Edmund Schriver's Inspection-General Report on Military Posts in Texas, November 1872–January 1873." *Southwestern Historical Quarterly* 67 (April 1964): 559–83.

Crane, Charles J. *Experiences of a Colonel of Infantry.* New York: Knickerbocker Press, 1923.

Crimmins, M. L., ed. "Colonel J. K. F. Mansfield's Report of the Inspection of the Department of Texas in 1856." *Southwestern Historical Quarterly* 42 (October 1938–April 1939): 122–48, 215–57, 351–87.

———, ed. "General Albert J. Myer: The Father of the Signal Corps." *West Texas Historical Association Year Book* 29 (October 1953): 47–66.

———, ed. "W. G. Freeman's Report on the Eighth Military Department." *Southwestern Historical Quarterly* 51 (July 1947): 54–58; (October 1947): 167–74; (January 1948): 252–58; (April 1948): 350–57; 52 (July 1948): 100–108; (October 1948): 227–33; (January 1949): 349–53; (April 1949): 444–47; 53 (July 1949): 71–77; (October 1949): 202–208; (January 1950): 308–19; (April 1950): 443–73; 54 (July 1950–April 1951): 122–48, 215–57, 351–87.

Custer, Elizabeth B. *Tenting on the Plains; or General Custer in Kansas and Texas.* 3 vols. 1887. Reprint, Norman: University of Oklahoma Press, 1971.

Dodge, Richard Irving. *Our Wild Indians: Thirty-three Years' Personal Experience among the Red Men of the Great West.* 1882. Reprint, New York: Archer House, 1959.

Duffen, William A., ed. "Overland via 'Jackass Mail' in 1858: The Diary of Phocion R. Way." *Arizona and the West* 2 (Spring 1960): 35–53.

Ellis, L. Tuffly, ed. "Lt. A. W. Greely's Report on the Installation of Military Telegraph Lines in Texas, 1875–1876." *Southwestern Historical Quarterly* 69 (July 1965): 66–87.

Faulk, Odie B., and Sidney B. Brinkerhoff, eds. *Lancers for the King: A Study of the Frontier Military System of Northern New Spain, with a Translation of the Royal Regulations of 1772.* Phoenix: Arizona Historical Foundation, 1965.

Flipper, Henry O. *The Colored Cadet at West Point.* New York: Homer and Lee, 1878.

Forsyth, George A. *The Story of the Soldier.* New York: D. Appleton, 1900.

Froebel, Julius. *Seven Years' Travel in Central America, Northern Mexico, and the Far West of the United States.* London: R. Bentley, 1859.

Gammel, H. P. N., comp. *The Laws of Texas 1822–1897.* 10 vols. Austin: Gammel, 1898.

Gillett, James B. *Six Years with the Texas Rangers, 1875–1881.* Edited by M. M. Quaife. 1921. Reprint, New Haven, Conn.: Yale University Press, 1963.

Goldblatt, Kenneth A. "Scout to Quitman Canyon: Report of Captain Geo. W. Baylor of the Frontier Battalion." *Texas Military History* 6 (Summer 1967): 149–59.

Gregg, Josiah. *Commerce on the Prairies; or the Journal of a Santa Fe Trader.* New York: Henry G. Langley, 1844.

Haas, Oscar, trans. "The Diary of Julius Giesecke, 1861–1862." *Texas Military History* 3 (Winter 1963): 228–42.

Hackett, Charles Wilson, ed. *Picardo's Treatise on the Limits of Louisiana and Texas: An Argumentative Historical Treatise with Reference to the Verification of the True Limits of the Provinces of Louisiana and Texas.* 4 vols. Austin: University of Texas Press, 1931–46.

Hammond, George P., and Agapito Rey, eds. *Expedition into New Mexico Made by Antonio de Espejo, 1582–1583, as Revealed in the Journal of Diego Perez de Luxan, a Member of the Party.* Quivira Society Publications, no. 1. 1929. Reprint, New York: Arno Press, 1967.

———. *The Rediscovery of New Mexico, 1580–1594: The Explorations of Chamuscado, Espejo, Castno de Sosa, Morlete, and Leyva de Bonilla and Humana.* Albuquerque: University of New Mexico Press, 1966.

Harris, Theodore D., ed. *Negro Frontiersman: The Western Memoirs of Henry O. Flipper.* El Paso: Western College Press, 1963.

Heartsill, W. W. *Fourteen Hundred and 91 Days in the Confederate Army.* Jackson, Tenn.: McCowat-Mercer Press, 1954.

Hunter, John W. "A Negro Trooper of the Ninth Cavalry." In *The Black Military*

Experience in the American West, edited by John M. Carroll, Shorter edition, 217–22. New York: Liverwright, 1973.

James, Vinton Lee. *Frontier and Pioneer: Recollections of Early Days in San Antonio and West Texas*. San Antonio: Artes Graficas, 1938.

"Journal of Henry Chase Whiting, 1849." In *Exploring Southwestern Trails, 1846– 1854*, edited by Ralph P. Bieber and Averam B. Bender. Glendale: Arthur H. Clark, 1938.

Lane, Lydia Spencer. *I Married a Soldier; or, Old Days in the Old Army*. 1893. Reprint, Albuquerque, N.M.: Horn and Wallace, 1964.

Larson, James. *Sergeant Larson, 4th Cavalry*. San Antonio: Southern Literary Institute, 1935.

Leckie, Shirley A. *The Colonel's Lady on the Western Frontier: The Correspondence of Alice Kirk Grierson*. Lincoln: University of Nebraska Press, 1989.

Lesley, Lewis Burt, ed. *Uncle Sam's Camels: The Journal of May Humphreys Stacey Supplemented by the Report of Edward Fitzgerald Beale (1857–1858)*. 1929. Reprint, Glorieta, N.M.: Rio Grande Press, 1970.

McChristian, Douglas C. *Garrison Tangles in the Friendless Tenth: The Journal of First Lieutenant John Bigelow, Jr., Fort Davis, Texas*. Bryan, Tex.: J. M. Carroll, 1985.

McConnell, H. H. *Five Years a Cavalryman; or, Sketches of Regular Army Life on the Texas Frontier, Twenty Odd Years Ago*. Jacksboro, Tex.: J. N. Rogers, 1889.

Mansfield, J. K. F. *Mansfield on the Conditions of the Western Forts, 1853–54*. Edited by Robert Frazier. Norman: University of Oklahoma Press, 1963.

Marcy, Randolph B. *The Prairie Traveler: A Handbook for Overland Expeditions. With Maps, Illustrations, and Itineraries of the Principal Routes between Mississippi and the Pacific*. 1859. Reprint, Williamstown, Mass.: Corner House Publishing, 1968.

Mariager, Dagmar. "Camp and Travel in Texas. I." *The Overland Monthly*, 2d ser., 17 (February 1891): 177–93.

Maury, Dabney Herndon. *Recollections of a Virginian in the Mexican, Indian, and Civil Wars*. New York: Charles Scribner's Sons, 1894.

Military Division of the Missouri. *Outline Descriptions of the Posts in the Military Division of the Missouri, Commanded by Lieutenant P. H. Sheridan, Accompanied by Tabular Lists of Indian Superintendencies, Agencies and Reservations, and a Summary of Certain Indian Treaties*. 1876. Reprint, Bellevue, Neb.: Old Army Press, 1969.

Mills, Anson. *My Story*. Edited by C. H. Claudy. 2d ed. Washington, D.C.: Press of Byron S. Adams, 1921.

Mills, William W. *Forty Years at El Paso*. El Paso: Privately printed, 1901.

Noel, Theophilus. *A Campaign from Santa Fe to the Mississippi: Being a History of the Old Sibley Brigade*. . . . Edited by Martin H. Hall and Edwin Adams Davis. Houston: Stagecoach Press, 1961.

Olmsted, Frederick Law. *A Journey through Texas: A Saddle-Trip on the Southwestern Frontier*. New York: Dix, Edwards, 1857.

Phelps, Capt. F. E. "From Texas to Dakota: The Eighth Cavalry's Long March." *Journal of the U.S. Cavalry Association* (April 1905).

Regulations concerning Barracks and Quarters from the Army of the United States, 1860. Washington, D.C.: George W. Bowman, 1861.

Reid, John C. *Reid's Tramp, or a Journal of Ten Months Travel through Texas, New Mexico, Arizona, Sonora, and California, Including Topography, Climate, Soil, Minerals, Metals, and Inhabitants; with a notice of the Great Inner-Oceanic Rail Road.* 1858. Reprint, Austin: Steck, 1935.

Reindorp, Reginald C., trans. "The Founding of Missions at La Junta de los Rios." *Supplementary Studies of the Texas Catholic Historical Society* 1 (April 1938).

Richardson, James D., comp. *A Compilation of the Messages and Papers of the Presidents, 1789–1908.* 10 vols. New York: Bureau of National Literature and Art, 1908.

Roster of Non-commissioned Officers of the Tenth Cavalry. 1897. Reprint, Bryan, Tex.: J. M. Carroll, 1983.

Santleben, August. *A Texas Pioneer.* New York: Neal, 1910.

Sheffly, L. F., ed. "Letters and Reminiscences of Gen. Theodore A. Baldwin: Scouting after Indians on the Plains of West Texas." *Panhandle-Plains Historical Review* 2 (1938): 7–30.

Sherman, William T. *Memoirs of General W. T. Sherman.* 2d ed. New York: Library of America, 1990.

Simmons, Marc, ed. *Border Comanches: Seven Spanish Colonial Documents, 1785–1819.* Santa Fe, N.M.: Stagecoach Press, 1967.

Spanish Explorers in the Southern United States, 1528–1543: The Narrative of Alvar Nuñez Cabeça de Vaca. Edited by Frederick W. Hodge; *The Narrative of the Expedition of Hernando de Soto by the Gentleman of Elvas.* Edited by Theodore H. Lewis; *The Narrative of the Expedition of Coronado, by Pedro de Castañeda.* Edited by Frederick W. Hodge. 1907. Reprint, Austin: Texas State Historical Association, 1990.

Stephens, Robert W., ed. *A Texan in the Gold Rush: The Letters of Robert Hunter, 1849–1851.* Bryan, Tex.: Barnum and White, 1972.

Storey, Brit Allen. "An Army Officer in Texas." *Southwestern Historical Quarterly* 72 (October 1968): 241–52.

Taylor, N. A., and H. F. McDaniel. *The Coming Empire, or Two Thousand Miles in Texas on Horseback.* New York: A. S. Barnes, 1877.

Thompson, Jerry M. Introduction and notes to *From Desert to Bayou: The Civil War Journal and Sketches of Morgan Wolfe Merrick.* El Paso: Texas Western Press, 1991.

———, ed. *Texas & New Mexico on the Eve of the Civil War: The Mansfield & Johnston Inspections, 1859–1861.* Albuquerque: University of New Mexico Press, 2001.

War of the Rebellion: A Compilation of the Official Records of the Union and Confederate Armies. 128 vols. Washington, D.C.: U.S. Government Printing Office, 1881–1901.

Wheeler, Homer W. *The Frontier Trail; or, from Cowboy to Colonel, an Authentic Nar-*

rative of Forty-three Years in the Old West as Cattleman, Indian Fighter and Army Officer. Los Angeles: Times-Mirror Press, 1923.

Whiting, William Henry Chase. "Diary of a March from El Paso to San Antonio." *Publications of the Southern History Association* 6 (September 1902): 389–99.

Wilhelm, Thomas, ed. *History of the Eighth U.S. Infantry from Its Organization in 1838.* 2d ed. 2 vols. New York: Headquarters, Eighth Infantry, 1873.

Wilson, John P., and Jerry Thompson, eds. *The Civil War in West Texas & New Mexico: The Lost Letterbook of Brigadier General Henry Hopkins Sibley.* El Paso: Texas Western Press, 2001.

Winfrey, Dorman, and James M. Day, eds. *Texas Indian Papers, 1846–1859.* Austin: Texas State Library, 1959.

———, eds. *Texas Indian Papers, 1860–1916.* Austin: Texas State Library, 1961.

Woolford, Sam, ed. "The Burr G. Duval Diary." *Southwestern Historical Quarterly* 65 (April 1962): 487–511.

Newspapers

Army and Navy Journal.
Galveston Daily News.
Galveston Weekly News.
Presidio County News (reprint).
San Antonio Daily Herald.
San Antonio Daily Express.
San Antonio Ledger and Texan.
Telegraph and Texas Register.
Texas State Gazette.
Tri-Weekly Alamo Express (San Antonio).

SECONDARY SOURCES
Books

Alberts, Don E. *Brandy Station to Manila Bay: A Biography of General Wesley Merritt.* Austin: Presidial Press, 1981.

Anderson, Gary Clayton. *The Indian Southwest, 1580–1830: Ethnogenesis and Reinvention.* Norman: University of Oklahoma Press, 1999.

Applegate, Howard G., and C. Wayne Hanselka. *La Junta de los Rios del Norte y Conchos.* El Paso: Texas Western Press, 1974.

Ashburn, P. M. *History of the Medical Department of the United States Army.* Boston: Houghton Mifflin, 1929.

Austerman, Wayne R. *Sharps Rifles and Spanish Mules: The San Antonio–El Paso Mail, 1851–1881.* College Station: Texas A&M University Press, 1985.

Ball, Durwood. *Army Regulars on the Western Frontier, 1848–1861.* Norman: University of Oklahoma Press, 2001.

Bancroft, Hubert H. *History of the North American States and Texas.* 2 vols. San Francisco: The History Company, 1884–89.

Bannon, John F. *The Spanish Borderlands Frontier, 1513–1821.* New York: Holt, Rinehart and Winston, 1970.

Barber, Natalie. *Faith West of the Pecos.* Denton, Tex.: Terrill Wheeler Printing, 1984.

Betty, Gerald. *Comanche Society before the Reservation.* College Station: Texas A&M University Press, 2002.

Biesaart, Lynne A., et al., comps. *Prehistoric Archeological Sites in Texas: A Statistical Overview.* Special Report no. 28. Austin: Office of the State Archeologist, 1985.

Billington, Ray Allen. *America's Frontier Heritage.* 1963. Reprint, Albuquerque: University of New Mexico Press, 1974.

Birtle, Andrew J. *U.S. Army Counterinsurgency and Contingency Operation Doctrine, 1860–1941.* Washington, D.C.: Center of Military History, 1998.

Bowden, J. J. *Spanish and Mexican Land Grants in the Chihuahuan Acquisition.* El Paso: Texas Western Press, 1971.

Budd, Richard M. *Serving Two Masters: The Development of Military Chaplaincy, 1860–1920.* Lincoln: University of Nebraska Press, 2002.

Butler, Anne M. *Daughters of Joy, Sisters of Misery: Prostitutes in the American West, 1865–1890.* Urbana: University of Illinois Press, 1984.

Carlson, Paul H. *"Pecos Bill": A Military Biography of William R. Shafter.* College Station: Texas A&M University Press, 1989.

———. *The Plains Indians.* College Station: Texas A&M University Press, 1998.

Casey, Clifford B. *Soldiers, Ranchers and Miners in the Big Bend.* Washington, D.C.: Division of History, Office of Archaeology and Historic Preservation, 1969.

Castañeda, Carlos E. *Our Catholic Heritage in Texas, 1519–1936.* 7 vols. Austin: Von Boeckmann-Jones, 1936–58.

Chappell, Gordon S. *The Search for the Well-Dressed Soldier, 1865–1890: Developments and Innovations in U.S. Army Uniforms on the Western Frontier.* Tucson: Arizona Historical Society, 1972.

Christian, Garna L. *Black Soldiers in Jim Crow Texas, 1899–1917.* College Station: Texas A&M University Press, 1995.

Coffman, Edward M. *The Old Army: A Portrait of the American Army in Peacetime, 1784–1898.* New York: Oxford University Press, 1986.

Corning, Leavitt, Jr. *Baronial Forts of the Big Bend: Ben Leaton, Milton Faver and Their Private Forts in Presidio County.* San Antonio: Trinity University Press, 1967.

Cunliffe, Marcus. *Soldiers & Civilians: The Martial Spirit in America, 1775–1865.* New York: Free Press, 1973.

Delo, David Michael. *Peddlers and Post Traders: The Army Sutler on the Frontier.* Salt Lake City: University of Utah Press, 1992.

Dobak, William A., and Thomas D. Phillips. *The Black Regulars, 1866–1898.* Norman: University of Oklahoma Press, 2001.

Dunlay, Thomas W. *Wolves for the Blue Soldiers: Indian Scouts and Auxiliaries with the United States Army, 1860–90*. Lincoln: University of Nebraska Press, 1982.

Frazer, Robert W. *Forts and Supplies: The Role of the Army in the Economy of the Southwest, 1846–1861*. Albuquerque: University of New Mexico Press, 1983.

———. *Forts of the West: Military Forts and Presidios and Posts Commonly Called Forts West of the Mississippi River to 1898*. Norman: University of Oklahoma Press, 1965.

Frazier, Donald S. *Blood and Treasure: Confederate Empire in the Southwest*. College Station: Texas A&M University Press, 1995.

García, Mario T. *Desert Immigrants: The Mexicans of El Paso, 1880–1920*. New Haven, Conn.: Yale University Press, 1981.

Gerald, Rex E. *Spanish Presidios of the Late Eighteenth Century in Northern New Spain*. Santa Fe: Museum of New Mexico Press, 1968.

Glass, E. L. N., ed. *The History of the Tenth Cavalry, 1866–1921*. Fort Collins, Colo.: Old Army Press, 1972.

Goetzmann, William H. *Army Exploration in the American West 1803–1863*. New Haven, Conn.: Yale University Press, 1959.

González, Deena J. *Refusing the Favor: The Spanish-Mexican Women of Santa Fe, 1820–1880*. New York: Oxford University Press, 1999.

Greene, Jerome A. *Historic Resource Study: Fort Davis National Historic Site, Texas*. Denver, Colo.: National Park Service, 1986.

Greer, James K. *Colonel Jack Hays, Texas Frontier Leader and California Land Builder*. New York: Dutton, 1952.

Griffen, William B. *Indian Assimilation in the Franciscan Area of Nueva Viscaya*. Anthropological Papers of the University of Arizona. Tucson: University of Arizona, 1979.

Hall, Martin H. *The Confederate Army of New Mexico*. Austin: Presidial Press, 1978.

———. *Sibley's New Mexico Campaign*. Austin: University of Texas Press, 1960.

Heitman, Francis B. *Historical Register and Dictionary of the United States Army*. 2 vols. Washington D.C.: Government Printing Office, 1899.

Hickerson, Nancy Parrott. *The Jumanos: Hunters and Traders of the South Plains*. Austin: University of Texas Press, 1994.

Horgan, Paul. *Great River: The Rio Grande in North American History*. 2 vols. New York: Rinehart, 1954.

Hutcheson, Barry Wade. *The Trans-Pecos: A Historical Survey and Guide to Historic Sites*. College of Agricultural Sciences, Research Report no. 3. Lubbock: Texas Tech University, 1970.

Hutton, Paul A., ed. *Soldiers West: Biographies from the Military Frontier*. Lincoln: University of Nebraska Press, 1987.

Jamieson, Perry D. *Crossing the Deadly Ground: United States Army Tactics, 1865–1899*. Tuscaloosa: University of Alabama Press, 1994.

John, Elizabeth A. H. *Storms Brewed in Other Men's Worlds: The Confrontation of*

Indians, Spanish, and French in the Southwest, 1540–1795. College Station: Texas A&M University Press, 1975.

Johnson, Barry C. *Flipper's Dismissal.* London: Privately printed, 1980.

Jones, Oakah. *Nueva Viscaya: Heartland of the Spanish Frontier.* Albuquerque: University of New Mexico Press, 1988.

Kenner, Charles. *Buffalo Soldiers and Officers of the Ninth Cavalry 1867–1898: Black & White Together.* Norman: University of Oklahoma Press, 1999.

Kinevan, Marcos E. *Frontier Cavalryman: Lieutenant John Bigelow with the Buffalo Soldiers in Texas.* El Paso: Texas Western Press, 1998.

Kirkland, Forrest, and W. W. Newcomb, Jr. *The Rock Art of Texas Indians.* Austin: University of Texas Press, 1967.

Kroeker, Marvin, E. *Great Plains Command: William B. Hazen in the Frontier West.* Norman: University of Oklahoma Press, 1978.

Lebergott, Stanley. *Manpower in Economic Growth: The American Record since 1800.* New York: McGraw-Hill, 1964.

Leckie, William H., and Shirley A. Leckie. *Unlikely Warriors: General Benjamin H. Grierson and His Family.* Norman: University of Oklahoma Press, 1978.

Leiker, James N. *Racial Borders: Black Soldiers along the Rio Grande.* College Station: Texas A&M University Press, 2002.

Lessoff, Alan. *The Nation and Its City: Politics, "Corruption," and Progress in Washington, D.C., 1861–1902.* Baltimore, Md.: Johns Hopkins University Press, 1994.

McChristian, Douglas C. *An Army of Marksmen: The Development of U.S. Army Marksmanship in the Nineteenth Century.* Ft. Collins, Colo.: Old Army Press, 1981.

McHenry, Robert, ed. *Webster's American Military Biographies.* New York: Dover Publications, 1978.

Madison, Virginia. *The Big Bend Country of Texas.* New York: October House, 1968.

Moorhead, Max L. *The Apache Frontier: Jacobo Ugarte and Spanish-Indian Relations in Northern New Spain, 1769–1791.* Norman: University of Oklahoma Press, 1968.

Morrison, James L., Jr. *"The Best School in the World": West Point, the Pre–Civil War Years, 1833–1861.* Kent, Ohio: Kent State University Press, 1986.

Moten, Matthew. *The Delafield Commission and the American Military Profession.* College Station: Texas A&M University Press, 2000.

Myres, Sandra L. *Westering Women and the Frontier Experience 1800–1915.* Histories of the American Frontier. Albuquerque: University of New Mexico Press, 1982.

Nankivell, John H., ed. and comp. *The History of the Twenty-fifth Regiment of United States Infantry, 1869–1926.* Regular Regiments Series. Fort Collins, Colo.: Old Army Press, 1972.

Neighbours, Kenneth F. *Robert S. Neighbors and the Texas Frontier, 1836–1859.* Waco, Tex.: Texian Press, 1975.

Nenninger, Timothy K. *The Leavenworth Schools and the Old Army: Education, Profes-*

sionalism, and the Officer Corps of the United States Army, 1881–1918. Westport, Conn.: Greenwood Press, 1978.

Newcomb, W. W., Jr. *The Indians of Texas from Prehistoric to Modern Times.* Austin: University of Texas Press, 1975.

Nobles, Gregory H. *American Frontiers: Cultural Encounters and Continental Conquest.* New York: Hill and Wang, 1997.

Norton, Herman A. *Struggling for Recognition: The United States Army Chaplaincy, 1791–1865.* Washington D.C.: Office of the Chief of Chaplains, 1977.

Prucha, Francis Paul. *Great Father: The United States Government and the American Indians.* 2 vols. Lincoln: University of Nebraska Press, 1984.

Raht, Carlysle Graham. *The Romance of Davis Mountains and Big Bend Country.* Odessa, Tex.: Raht, 1963.

Reed, S. G. *A History of the Texas Railroads and of Transportation Conditions under Spain and Mexico and the Republic and the State.* Houston: St. Clair Publishing, 1941.

Richter, William L. *The Army in Texas during Reconstruction, 1865–1870.* College Station: Texas A&M University Press, 1987.

Rickey, Don, Jr. *Forty Miles a Day on Beans and Hay: The Enlisted Soldier Fighting the Indian Wars.* Norman: University of Oklahoma Press, 1963.

Riley, Glenda. *The Female Frontier: A Comparative View of Women on the Prairies and the Plains.* Lawrence: University Press of Kansas, 1988.

Risch, Erna. *Quartermaster Support of the Army: A History of the Corps, 1775–1939.* Washington, D.C.: Government Printing Office, 1960.

Robinson, Charles M., III. *The Court-Martial of Lieutenant Henry Flipper.* El Paso: Texas Western Press, 1994.

Scobee, Barry. *Fort Davis, Texas 1583–1960.* El Paso: Hill Printing, 1963.

———. *Old Fort Davis.* San Antonio: Naylor, 1947.

Sheire, James. *Fort Davis National Historical Site. Furnishing Study, Enlisted Men's Barracks HB-21.* Denver, Colo.: National Park Service, 1972.

Skogen, Larry. *Indian Depredation Claims, 1796–1920.* Norman: University of Oklahoma Press, 1996.

Smith, David Paul. *Frontier Defense in the Civil War: Texas' Rangers and Rebels.* College Station: Texas A&M University Press, 1992.

Smith, Ralph. *Borderlander: The Life of James Kirker, 1793–1852.* Norman: University of Oklahoma Press, 1999.

Smith, Thomas T. *The Old Army in Texas: A Research Guide to the U.S Army in Nineteenth-Century Texas.* Austin: Texas State Historical Association, 2000.

———. *The U.S. Army and the Texas Frontier Economy.* College Station: Texas A&M University Press, 1999.

Sonnichsen, C. L. *The Mescalero Apaches.* Norman: University of Oklahoma Press, 1958.

Stallard, Patricia Y. *Glittering Misery: Dependents of the Indian Fighting Army.* Fort Collins and San Rafael, Colo.: Old Army Press and Presidio Press, 1978.

Steffen, Randy. *The Horse Soldier, 1776–1943: The United States Cavalryman: His*

Uniforms, Accoutrements, and Equipments. Vol. 2, *The Frontier, the Mexican War, the Civil War, the Indian Wars, 1851–1881.* Norman: University of Oklahoma Press, 1978.

Stoddard, Ellwyn R., et al., eds. *Borderlands Sourcebook: A Guide to the Literature on Northern Mexico and the American Southwest.* Norman: University of Oklahoma Press, 1983.

Stover, Earl F. *Up from Handymen: The United States Army Chaplaincy, 1865–1920.* Washington D.C.: Office of the Chief of Chaplains, 1977.

Tate, Michael. *The Frontier Army in the Settlement of the West.* Norman: University of Oklahoma Press, 1999.

Taylor, Quintard. *In Search of the Racial Frontier: African-Americans in the American West, 1528–1990.* New York: W. W. Norton, 1998.

Thian, Raphael P., comp. *Notes Illustrating the Military Geography of the United States, 1813–1880.* Edited by John M. Carroll. Austin: University of Texas Press, 1979.

Thomas, Alfred B. *Teodoro de Croix and the Northern Frontier of New Spain, 1776–1783.* Norman: University of Oklahoma Press, 1941.

Thomas, W. Stephen. *Fort Davis and the Texas Frontier: Paintings by Arthur T. Lee, Eighth U.S. Infantry.* College Station: Texas A&M University Press, 1976.

Thompson, Cecilia. *History of Marfa and Presidio County, Texas, 1535–1947.* 2 vols. Austin: Nortex Press, 1985.

Thrapp, Dan L. *Encyclopedia of Frontier Biography.* 3 vols. Glendale, Calif: Arthur H. Clark, 1988.

Thybony, Scott. *Fort Davis: The Men of Troop H.* Tucson, Ariz.: Southwestern Parks and Monuments Association, 1990.

Tyler, Ronnie C. *The Big Bend: A History of the Last Texas Frontier.* Washington, D.C.: National Park Service, 1975.

Uglow, Loyd M. *Standing in the Gap: Army Outposts, Picket Stations, and the Pacification of the Texas Frontier 1866–1886.* Fort Worth: Texas Christian University Press, 2001.

Utley, Robert M. *Fort Davis National Historic Site, Texas.* National Park Service Historical Handbook Series no. 38. Washington D.C.: U.S. Department of the Interior, 1965.

———. *Frontier Regulars: The United States Army and the Indian, 1866–1891.* New York: Macmillan, 1973.

———. *Frontiersmen in Blue: The United States Army and the Indian, 1848–1865.* 1967. Reprint, Lincoln: University of Nebraska Press, 1981.

———. *The Indian Frontier of the American West, 1846–1890.* Albuquerque: University of New Mexico Press, 1984.

———. *Lone Star Justice: The First Century of the Texas Rangers.* New York: Oxford University Press, 2002.

Weber, David J. *The Mexican Frontier, 1821–1846: The American Southwest under Mexico.* Albuquerque: University of New Mexico Press, 1982.

Weigley, Russell F. *History of the United States Army.* 1967. Enl. ed., Bloomington: Indiana University Press, 1984.

Williams, Clayton. *Texas' Last Frontier: Fort Stockton and the Trans-Pecos, 1861–1895.* Edited by Ernest Wallace. College Station: Texas A&M University Press, 1982.

Wooster, Ralph A. *Lone Star Generals in Gray.* Austin: Eakin Press, 2001.

———. *The Secession Conventions of the South.* Princeton, N.J.: Princeton University Press, 1962.

Wooster, Robert. *Fort Davis: Outpost on the Texas Frontier.* Austin: Texas State Historical Association, 1994.

———. *History of Fort Davis, Texas.* Southwest Cultural Resources Center Professional Papers no. 34. Santa Fe, N.M.: National Park Service, 1990.

———. *The Military and United States Indian Policy, 1865–1903.* New Haven, Conn.: Yale University Press, 1988.

———. *Soldiers, Sutlers, and Settlers: Garrison Life on the Texas Frontier.* College Station: Texas A&M University Press, 1987.

Articles and Essays

Ambrose, David C. "The Major Reasons for Army Desertions at Fort Davis, Texas, 1882–1885." *Panhandle-Plains Historical Review* 45 (1972): 38–45.

Austerman, Wayne R. "José Policarpo Rodriguez: Chicano Plainsman." *West Texas Historical Association Year Book* 59 (1983): 52–73.

Biessart, Lynne A., et al., comps. *Prehistoric Archeological Sites in Texas: A Statistical Overview.* Special Report no. 28 Austin: Office of the State Archeologist, 1985.

Bluthardt, Robert F. "Baseball on the Military Frontier." *Fort Concho Report* 19 (Spring 1987): 17–26.

Breeden, James O. "Health of Early Texas: The Military Frontier." *Southwestern Historical Quarterly* 80 (April 1977): 357–98.

Brown, Russell K. "An Old Woman with a Broomstick: General David E. Twiggs and the U.S. Surrender in Texas, 1861." *Military Affairs* 48, no. 2 (1984): 57–61.

Butler, Anne. "Military Myopia: Prostitution on the Frontier." *Prologue* 13 (Winter 1981): 233–50.

Campbell, Thomas N., and William T. Field. "Identification of Comanche Raiding Trails in Trans-Pecos Texas." *West Texas Historical Association Year Book* 44 (1968): 128–44.

Chipman, Donald E. "In Search of Cabeza de Vaca's Route across Texas: An Historiographical Survey." *Southwestern Historical Quarterly* 91 (October 1987): 127–48.

Clary, David A. "The Role of the Army Surgeon in the West: Daniel Weisel at Fort Davis, Texas, 1868–1872." *Western Historical Quarterly* 3 (January 1972): 53–66.

Clemensen, A. Berle. *Historic Furnishing Study. Enlisted Men's Barracks, HB-21, Fort Davis National Historic Site.* Denver, Colo.: National Park Service, 1978.

Connelly, Thomas L. "The American Camel Experiment: A Reappraisal." *Southwestern Historical Quarterly* 69 (April 1966): 442–62.

Crimmins, M. L. "The Border Command at Fort Davis." *West Texas Historical and Scientific Society Publications* (1926) 1: 7–15.

Daniel, James M. "The Spanish Frontier in West Texas and Northern Mexico." *Southwestern Historical Quarterly* 71 (April 1968): 481–95.

Dinges, Bruce J. "Benjamin H. Grierson." In *Soldiers West: Biographies from the Military Frontier*, edited by Paul Andrew Hutton, 175–76. Lincoln: University of Nebraska Press, 1987.

———. "Colonel Grierson Invests on the West Texas Frontier." *Fort Concho Report* 16 (Fall 1984): 2–14.

———. "Court-Martial of Lt. Henry O. Flipper." *American West* 9 (January 1972): 12–17, 59–60.

———. "The San Angelo Riot of 1881: The Army, Race Relations, and Settlement on the Texas Frontier." *Journal of the West* 41 (Summer 2002): 35–45.

———. "Victorio Campaign of 1880: Cooperation and Conflict on the United States–Mexico Border." *New Mexico Historical Review* 62 (January 1987): 81–94.

Forbes, Jack D. "Unknown Athapaskans: The Identification of the Jano, Jocomo, Jumano, Manso, Suma, and Other Indian Tribes of the Southwest." *Ethnohistory* 6 (Spring 1959): 97–159.

Frantz, Joe. "The Significance of Frontier Forts to Texas." *Southwestern Historical Quarterly* 74 (October 1970): 204–205.

Graham, Roy Eugene. "Federal Fort Architecture in Texas during the Nineteenth Century." *Southwestern Historical Quarterly* 74 (October 1970): 165–88.

Graham, Stanley S. "Duty, Life and Law in the Old Army, 1865–1900." *Military History of Texas and the Southwest* 12, no. 4 (1974): 273–81.

Griswold, Robert L. "Anglo Women and Domestic Ideology in the American West in the Nineteenth and Early Twentieth Centuries." In *Western Women: Their Land, Their Lives*, edited by Lillian Schlissel et al., 15–46. Albuquerque: University of New Mexico Press, 1988.

Heidler, Jeanne T. "'Embarrassing Situation': David E. Twiggs and the Surrender of United States Forces in Texas, 1861." *Military History of the Southwest* 21 (Fall 1991): 157–72.

Holt, R. D. "Texas Had Hot County Elections." *West Texas Historical Association Year Book* 24 (1948): 3–26.

Jameson, Elizabeth. "Women as Workers, Women as Civilizers: True Womanhood in the American West." *Frontiers: A Journal of Women Studies* 7, no. 3 (1984): 1–9.

Kelley, J. Charles, Jr. "The Historic Indian Pueblos of La Junta de los Rios." *New Mexico Historical Review* 26 (October 1952): 257–95; (January 1953): 21–51.

———. "Juan Sabeata and Diffusion in Aboriginal Texas." *American Anthropologist* 57 (October 1955): 981–95.

Lammons, Frank Bishop. "Operation Camel: An Experiment in Animal Transportation in Texas, 1857–1860." *Southwestern Historical Quarterly* 61 (July 1957): 20–50.

McChristian, Douglas C. "Apaches and Soldiers: Mail Protection in West Texas." *Periodical: Journal of the Council on America's Military Past* 13 (August 1985): 3–17.

———. "The Commissary Sergeant: His Life at Fort Davis." *Military History of Texas and the Southwest* 14, no. 1 (1978): 21–32.

———. "Company C, 3rd Cavalry." *Military Images Magazine* 4 (March–April 1983): 4–7.

———. "Grierson's Fight at Tinaja de las Palmas: An Episode in the Victorio Campaign." *Red River Valley Historical Review* 7 (Winter 1982): 45–63.

———. "Incidents Involving Hostile Indians within the Influence of Fort Davis, Texas." Typescript. Fort Davis National Historic Site, September 9, 1975.

———. "Military Protection for the U.S. Mail: A Fort Davis Case Study." Typescript. Fort Davis National Historic Site, May 20, 1988.

McClung, Donald R. "Second Lieutenant Henry O. Flipper: A Negro Officer on the West Texas Frontier." *West Texas Historical Association Year Book* 47 (1971): 20–31.

Matthews, James T. "Always in the Vanguard: Patrolling the Texas Frontier with Captain Louis Carpenter and Company H of the Tenth Cavalry." *West Texas Historical Association Year Book* 75 (1999): 110–20.

Miles, Elton. "Old Fort Leaton: A Saga of the Big Bend." In *Hunters and Healers: Folklore Tales and Topics*, edited by Wilson M. Hudson. Austin: Encino Press, 1971.

Myres, Sandra L. "Romance and Reality on the Western Frontier: Views of Army Wives." *Western Historical Quarterly* 13 (October 1982): 409–27.

Olch, Peter D. "Medicine in the Indian Fighting Army, 1866–1890." *Journal of the West* 21 (July 1982): 32–41.

Opler, Morris E. "The Apachean Culture Pattern and Its Origins." In *Handbook of North American Indians*, vol. 10, edited by Alfonzo Ortiz, 368–92. Washington, D.C.: Smithsonian Institution, 1983.

———. "Mescalero Apache." In *Handbook of North American Indians*, vol. 10, edited by Alfonzo Ortiz, 419–39. Washington, D.C.: Smithsonian Institution, 1983.

Price, Byron. "The Ninth Cavalry Mutiny at San Pedro Springs." *By Valor and Arms* 1, no. 3 (1975): 31–34.

Rayburn, John C. "General Sherman Visits the Mexican Frontier." *West Texas Historical Association Year Book* 38 (1962): 72–84.

Rischer, Kirsten. "In Retrospect: The Career of Francis Jennings." *Reviews in American History* 30 (December 2002): 517–29.

Roth, Jeffrey M. "Civil War Defense Challenges in Northwest Texas." *Military History of the West* 30 (Spring 2000): 21–44.

Ruhlen, George. "Fort Hancock: Last of the Frontier Forts." *Password* 4 (January 1959): 19–30.

———. "Quitman: The Worst Post at Which I Ever Served." *Password* 11 (Fall 1966): 107–26.

———. "Quitman's Owners: A Sidelight on Frontier Reality." *Password* 5 (April 1960): 54–64.

Rust, Thomas C. "Settlers, Soldiers, and Scoundrels: Economic Tension in a Frontier Military Town." *Military History of the West* 31 (Fall 2001): 117–38.

Scheips, Paul J. "Albert James Myer, an Army Doctor in Texas, 1854–1857." *Southwestern Historical Quarterly* 82 (July 1978): 1–24.

Schick, Robert. "Wagons to Chihuahua." *The American West* 3 (Summer 1966): 72–79.

Smith Ralph. "The Comanche Bridge between Oklahoma and Mexico, 1843–1844." *Chronicles of Oklahoma* 39 (Spring 1961): 54–69.

———. "Mexican and Anglo-Saxon Traffic in Scalps, Slaves, and Livestock, 1835–1841." *West Texas Historical Association Year Book* 36 (1960): 98–115.

———. "The Scalp Hunters in the Borderlands, 1835–1850." *Arizona and the West* 6 (Spring 1964): 5–22.

Smith, Thomas T. "West Point and the Indian Wars, 1802–1891." *Military History of the West* 24 (Spring 1994): 24–56.

Somers, Dale A. "James P. Newcomb: The Making of a Radical." *Southwestern Historical Quarterly* 72 (April 1969): 449–69.

Stewart, Miller J. "Army Laundresses: Ladies of the 'Soap Suds Row.'" *Nebraska History* 61 (Winter 1980): 421–36.

Sutton, Mary. "Glimpses of Fort Concho through the Military Telegraph." *West Texas Historical Association Year Book* 30 (1956): 26–58.

Temple, Frank M. "Colonel B. H. Grierson's Administration of the District of the Pecos." *West Texas Historical Association Year Book* 38 (October 1962): 85–96.

Thompson, Eileen. "Observations at a Trans-Pecos Rock Art Site." *Journal of Big Bend Studies* 10 (1998): 1–28.

Thompson, Erwin N. "The Negro Soldiers on the Frontier: A Fort Davis Case Study." *Journal of the West* 7 (April 1968): 217–35.

———. "Private Bentley's Buzzard." Typescript. Fort Davis National Historic Site, April 2, 1965.

Townsend, E. E. "The Mays Massacre." *West Texas Scientific and Scientific Society Publications* 5 (December 1933): 29–43.

Utley, Robert M. "The Frontier and the American Military Tradition." In *Soldiers West: Biographies from the Military Frontier,* edited by Paul Andrew Hutton, 1–10. Lincoln: University of Nebraska Press, 1987.

White, W. Bruce. "ABC's for the American Enlisted Man: The Army's Post School System, 1866–1898." *History of Education Quarterly* 8 (Winter 1968): 479–96.

Williams, Mary. "Care of the Dead: A Neglected Duty; the Military Cemeteries at Fort Davis, Texas." Typescript. Fort Davis National Historic Site, 1983.

———. "Empire Building: Colonel Benjamin H. Grierson at Fort Davis, 1882–1885." *West Texas Historical Association Year Book* 66 (1985): 58–73.

———. "The Post and the Hospital Gardens at Fort Davis, Texas 1854–1891." Typescript. Fort Davis National Historic Site.

———. "Servants at Military Posts: A Glimpse at 'Domesticity' through the Letters of Alice Kirk Grierson." *Journal of Big Bend Studies* 11 (1999): 145–58.

Wood, Cynthia A. "Army Laundresses and Civilization on the Western Frontier." *Journal of the West* 41 (Summer 2002): 26–34.

Wooster, Robert. "The Army and the Politics of Expansion: Texas and the Southwestern Borderlands, 1870–1886." *Southwestern Historical Quarterly* 93 (October 1989): 151–68.

———. "Military Strategy in the Southwest, 1848–1860." *Military History of Texas and the Southwest* 15, no. 2 (1979): 5–15.

———. "'The Whole Company Have Done It': The U.S. Army and the Fort Davis Murder of 1860." *Journal of the West* 32 (April 1993): 19–28.

Wright, Paul. "Changes in the Statutory Boundaries of Big Bend Counties, 1850–1904." *Journal of Big Bend Studies* 14 (2002): 109–40.

———. "Life on Both Sides of the Tracks in Early Alpine." *West Texas Historical Association Year Book* 73 (1997): 96–112.

———. "Property Ownership in the Early Big Bend." *West Texas Historical Association Year Book* 76 (2000): 66–90.

———. "Residential Segregation in Two Early West Texas Towns." *Southwestern Historical Quarterly* 102 (January 1999): 295–320.

Theses and Dissertations

Adams, Francis Raymond, Jr. "An Annotated Edition of the Personal Letters of Robert E. Lee, April 1855–April 1861." Ph.D. diss., University of Maryland, 1955.

Ballew, Elvis Joe. "Supply Problems of Fort Davis, Texas, 1867–1880." Master's thesis, Sul Ross State University, 1971.

Boggs, Herschel. "A History of Fort Concho." Master's thesis, University of Texas, 1940.

Bowie, Chester Winston. "Redfield Proctor: A Biography." Ph.D. diss., University of Wisconsin–Madison, 1980.

Buchanan, John Strauss. "Functions of the Fort Davis Military Bands and Musical Proclivities of the Commanding Officer, Col. B. H. Grierson, Late 19th C." Master's thesis, Sul Ross State College, 1968.

Guffee, Eddie J. "Camp Peña Colorado, Texas, 1879–1893." Master's thesis, West Texas State University, 1976.

Hale, Duane Kendall. "Prospecting and Mining on the Texas Frontier." Ph.D. diss., Oklahoma State University, 1977.

Ifera, Raymond Philip. "Crime and Punishment at Fort Davis, 1867–1891." Master's thesis, Sul Ross State College, 1974.

Kelley, J. C. "Jumano and Patarabueye: Relations at La Junta de los Rios." Ph.D. diss., Harvard University, 1947.

Wooster, Robert. "Military Strategy in the American West, 1815–1860." Master's thesis, Lamar University, 1979.

Internet Resources

"Civilian Employees at Fort Davis, Texas." http://www.nps.gov/foda/Fort_Davis_WEB_PAGE/About_the_Fort/Civilian_Employees.htm (accessed March 21, 2003).

"Fort Davis Administrative History." www.nps.gov/foda/adhi (accessed April 7, 2003).

Handbook of Texas Online. http://www.tsha.utexas.edu/handbook/online (accessed Aug. 15, 2002).

Sahr, Robert C. "Inflation Conversion Factors for Dollars 1665 to Estimated 2015." http://oregonstate.edu/dept/pol_sci/fac/sahr/sahr.htm (accessed February 19, 2005).

Welsh, Michael. "Special Place, A Sacred Trust: Preserving the Fort Davis Story." http://www.nps.gov/foda/adhi/adhi.htm (accessed March 21, 2003).

INDEX

Page numbers in italics refer to tables.